THE DAILY STUDY BIBLE

THE GOSPEL OF JOHN

THE GOSPEL OF JOHN

JOHN

(VOLUME TWO : CHAPTERS VIII to XXI)

The Rev. WILLIAM BARCLAY, D.D.

Lecturer in New Testament Language and Literature and in Hellenistic Greek in the University of Glasgow

THE SAINT ANDREW PRESS

EDINBURGH

Published by The Saint Andrew Press
121 George Street, Edinburgh 2
and printed in Scotland by
McCorquodale & Co., Ltd., Glasgow

First Edition	-	*September,* 1955
Second Edition	-	*November,* 1956
Second Impression	-	*September,* 1957
Third Impression	-	*December,* 1958
Fourth Impression	-	*May,* 1960
Fifth Impression	-	*October,* 1961

GENERAL INTRODUCTION

It may truly be said that this series of Daily Bible Studies began almost accidentally. A series which the Church of Scotland was using came to an end, and another series was immediately required. I was asked to write a volume on *Acts*, and, at the moment, had no intention beyond that. But one volume followed another, until the demand for one volume became a plan to write on the whole New Testament.

The translation which is given in each volume claims no special merit. It was included in order that the reader might be able to carry both the text of the New Testament and the comments on it wherever he went, and that he might be able to read it anywhere. While I was making the translation, the translations of Moffatt, Weymouth, and Knox were ever beside me. *The American Revised Standard Version, The Twentieth Century New Testament,* and *The New Testament in Plain English,* by Charles Kingsley Williams, have been in constant use. Since its publication, I have consistently consulted *The Authentic New Testament,* translated by Hugh J. Schonfield.

I cannot see another edition of these books going out to the public without expressing my very deep and sincere gratitude to the Church of Scotland Publications Committee for allowing me the privilege of first beginning, and then continuing, this series. And in particular I wish to express my very great gratitude to the convener, Rev. R. G. Macdonald, O.B.E., M.A., D.D., and to the committee's secretary and manager, Rev. Andrew McCosh, M.A., S.T.M., for constant encouragement and never-failing sympathy and help.

As these volumes went on, the idea of the whole series developed. The aim is to make the results of modern scholarship available to the non-technical reader in a form that it does not require a theological education to understand; and then to seek to make the teaching of the New Testament books relevant to life and work to-day. The whole aim of these books is summed up in Richard of Chichester's famous prayer; they are meant to enable men and women to know Jesus Christ more clearly, to love Him more dearly, and to follow Him more nearly. It is my prayer that they may do something to make that possible.

CONTENTS

THE GOSPEL OF JOHN

CONTENTS

THE GOSPEL OF JOHN

CONTENTS

THE GOSPEL OF JOHN

CONTENTS

JOHN

WRETCHEDNESS AND PITY

John 7: 53—8: 11

And each of them went to his own house; but Jesus went to the Mount of Olives. Early in the morning He was again in the Temple precincts, and all the people came to Him. He sat down and went on teaching them. The Scribes and Pharisees brought a woman arrested for adultery. They set her in the midst and said to Him: " Teacher, this woman was arrested as she was committing adultery—in the very act. In the law Moses enjoined us to stone women like this. What do *you* say about her? " They were testing Him when they said this, so that they might have some ground on which to accuse Him. Jesus stooped down and wrote with His finger on the ground. When they went on asking Him their question, He straightened Himself and said to them: " Let the man among you who is without sin be the first to cast a stone at her." And again He bent down and wrote with His finger on the ground. One by one those who had heard what He said went out, beginning from the eldest down to the youngest. So Jesus was left alone, and the woman was still there in the midst. Jesus straightened Himself and said to her: " Woman, where are they? Has no one condemned you? " She said: " No one, sir." Jesus said: " I am not going to pass judgment on you either. Go, and from now on, sin no more."

THE Scribes and Pharisees were out to get some charge on which they could discredit Jesus; and here in this incident they thought that they had impaled Him inescapably on the horns of a dilemma. In the time of Jesus, when a difficult legal question arose, the natural and routine thing was to take it to a Rabbi for a decision. So the Scribes and Pharisees approached Jesus as a Rabbi. They brought to Him a woman taken in adultery. In the eyes of the Jewish law adultery was a serious crime. The Rabbis said: " Every Jew must die before he will commit idolatry, murder or adultery." Adultery was one of the three gravest sins. The law was quite clear on this matter. There were certain differences in respect of the way in which the death penalty was to be carried out; but for the crime of adultery the law did lay down the penalty of death. *Leviticus* 20: 10 lays it down: " The man that committeth adultery with another man's wife, even he that committeth adultery with his neighbour's wife, the adulterer and the adulteress shall surely be put to death." There the method of death is not laid down. *Deuteronomy* 22: 13-24 lays down the penalty in the case of a girl who is already betrothed. In a case like that she and the man who seduced her are to be brought outside the city gates, " and ye shall stone them with stones until they die." The *Mishnah*, that is, the Jewish codified law, states that the penalty for adultery is strangulation, and even the method of strangulation is laid down. " The man is to be enclosed in dung up to his knees, and a soft towel set within a rough towel is to be placed around his neck (in order that no mark may be made, for the punishment is God's punishment). Then one man draws in one direction and another in the other direction, until he be dead." The *Mishnah* reiterates that death by stoning is the penalty for a girl who is betrothed and who then commits adultery. From the purely legal point of view the Scribes and Pharisees were perfectly correct. This woman was liable to the death penalty.

When the Scribes and Pharisees confronted Jesus with this decision the dilemma into which they sought to put Him was this. If Jesus gave the decision that the woman ought to be stoned to death, two things followed. First, He would lose for ever the name He had gained for love and for mercy, and never again would He be called the friend of sinners. Second, if He recommended death, He would immediately come into collision with the Roman law, for the Jews had no power to pass or carry out the death sentence on anyone. So if Jesus said this woman must die, He would lose the love and devotion of the great mass of the ordinary people, and He would become a criminal in the eyes of the Roman government. If Jesus gave the decision that the woman should be pardoned, it could immediately be said that He was teaching men to break the law of Moses, and that He was condoning and even encouraging people to commit adultery. That was the trap in which the Scribes and Pharisees sought to entrap Jesus. But Jesus turned their attack in such a way that it recoiled against themselves.

At first Jesus stooped down and wrote with his finger on the ground. What exactly is the meaning of that? Why did Jesus do that? There may be four possible reasons. (i) Jesus may quite simply have wished to gain time, and not to be rushed into a decision. In that brief moment He may have been both thinking the thing out and taking it to God. (ii) Certain manuscripts add, "As though He did not hear them." In the ordinary printing of the Authorised Version these words are in italic type, and italic type denotes that the words so printed are not in the best manuscripts, but may legitimately be supplied to amplify and clarify the sense of the passage. Jesus may well have deliberately forced these Scribes and Pharisees to repeat their charges, so that, in repeating them, they might possibly realize the sadistic cruelty which lay behind them. He may have wanted them to realize what they were saying. (iii) Seeley in *Ecce Homo* makes an interesting suggestion. "Jesus was seized with an intolerable sense of shame. He could not meet the eye of the crowd, or of the accusers, and perhaps at that moment least of all of the woman. . . . In His burning embarrassment and confusion He stooped down so as to hide His face, and began writing with His fingers upon the ground." It may well be that the leering, lustful look on the faces of the Scribes and Pharisees, the bleak cruelty in their eyes, the prurient curiosity of the crowd, the shame of the woman, all combined to twist the very heart of Jesus in agony and pity, so that He hid His eyes.

3

(iv) By far the most interesting suggestion emerges from certain of the later manuscripts. The Armenian translation of the New Testament translates this passage this way: " He Himself, bowing His head, was writing with His finger on the earth to declare their sins; and they were seeing their several sins on the stones." The suggestion is that Jesus was writing in the dust the sins of the very men who were accusing the woman. There may be something in that. The normal Greek word for *to write* is *graphein*; but here the word used is *katagraphein*, which can mean *to write down a record against someone*. (One of the meanings of *kata* is *against*). So in *Job* 13: 26 Job says: " Thou *writest* (*katagraphein*) bitter things against me." It may be that Jesus was confronting those self-confident sadists with the record of their own sins.

However that may be, the Scribes and Pharisees continued to insist on an answer—and they got it. Jesus said in effect: " All right! Stone her! But let the man that is without sin be the first man to cast a stone." It may well be that the word for *without sin* (*anamartētos*) means not only *without sin*, but even *without a sinful desire*. Jesus was saying: " Yes, you may stone her—but only if you never wanted to do the same thing yourselves." There was a silence—and then slowly the accusers drifted away.

So Jesus and the woman were left alone. As Augustine put it: " There remained a great misery (*miseria*) and a great pity (*misericordia*)." Jesus said to the woman: " Has no one condemned you? " " No one, sir," she said. Jesus said: " I am not for the moment going to pass judgment on you either. Go, and make a new start, and don't sin any more."

WRETCHEDNESS AND PITY

John 7: 53—8: 11 (*continued*)

THE great light of this passage is the light that it shows on different attitudes to people. It shows us two things about the attitude of the Scribes and the Pharisees.

4

(i) It shows us their *conception of authority*. The Scribes and the Pharisees were the legal experts of the day. To them the problems were taken for decision and they were regarded as the authorities on the law. Their whole attitude makes it clear that to them authority was something which was characteristically critical, censorious and condemnatory. That authority should be based on sympathy, that the aim of authority should be to reclaim the criminal and the sinner, never entered their heads. They conceived of their function as giving them the right to stand over others like grim invigilators, to watch for every mistake and every deviation from the law, and to descend on every breach of the law with savage and unforgiving punishment.

 They conceived of their function as giving them the right to destroy the sinner; they never dreamed that it might lay upon them the obligation to cure the sinner. There are still those who regard a position of authority as giving them the right to condemn and the duty to punish. They think of authority as entailing only punishment and condemnation. They think that such authority as they have has given them the right to be moral watch-dogs trained to tear the sinner to pieces. All true authority is founded on sympathy. When George Whitefield saw the criminal on the way to the gallows, he uttered the famous sentence: " There, but for the grace of God, go I." The first duty of authority is to try to understand why the man who made the mistake acted as he did, to try to understand the force of the temptations which drove him to sin, to try to understand the circumstances in which sin became so easy and so attractive. No man can pass any judgment on another unless he at least tries to understand what the other man has come through. The second duty of authority is to seek to reclaim the wrong-doer. Any authority which is solely concerned with punishment is a wrong authority. Any authority, which, in its exercise, drives a wrong-doer either to despair or to sullen or bitter resentment, is a failure. The function of authority is not to banish the sinner from all decent society, still less to wipe out the sinner; it is to make the sinner into a good man. The man set in authority must be like a wise physician; his one desire must be to heal.

(ii) This incident shows vividly and cruelly *the attitude of the Scribes and Pharisees to people*. These Scribes and Pharisees were not looking on this woman as a person at all; they were looking on her only as a thing, an instrument whereby they could formulate a charge against Jesus. They were using her, as a man might use a tool, for their own purposes. To them she had no name, no personality, no heart, no feelings, no emotions; she was simply a pawn in the game whereby they sought to destroy Jesus. It is always wrong to regard people as things; it is always wrong, inhuman and unchristian to regard people as cases. It was said of Beatrice Webb, afterwards Lady Passmore, the famous economist, that " she saw men as specimens walking." To her a man was not a person; he was an instance, a case, a specimen of something or other. Dr. Paul Tournier in *A Doctor's Casebook* talks of what he calls " the personalism of the Bible." He points out how fond the Bible is of names. God says to Moses: " I know thee by name " (*Exodus* 33: 17). God said to Cyrus: " I am the Lord, which call thee by name " (*Isaiah* 45: 3). There are whole pages of names in the Bible. Dr. Tournier insists that this is the proof that the Bible thinks of people first and foremost, not as fractions of the mass, or abstractions, or ideas, or cases, but as persons. " The proper name," Dr. Tournier writes, " is the symbol of the person. If I forget my patients' names, if I say to myself, ' Ah! There's that gall-bladder type or that consumptive that I saw the other day,' I am interesting myself more in their gall-bladders or in their lungs than in themselves as persons." He insists that a patient must be always a person, and never a case. It is extremely unlikely that the Scribes and the Pharisees even knew this woman's name. To them she was nothing but the case of someone who had most shamelessly committed adultery and who could now be used as an instrument and a tool to suit their purposes. The minute people become things the spirit of Christianity is dead.

God uses His authority to love men into goodness; to God no person ever becomes a thing. We must use such authority as we have always to understand and always at least to try to heal and to mend and to cure the person who had made the mistake; and we will never even begin to do that unless we remember that every man and woman is a person, and not a thing.

WRETCHEDNESS AND PITY

John 7: 53—8: II (*continued*)

STILL further, this incident tells us a great deal about Jesus and His whole attitude to the sinner.

(i) It was a first principle of Jesus that only the man who himself is without fault has the right to express judgment on the fault of others. " Judge not," said Jesus, " that ye be not judged " (*Matthew* 7: I). He said that the man who attempted to judge his brother was like a man with a plank in his own eye trying to take a speck of dust out of someone else's eye (*Matthew* 7: 3-5). One of the commonest faults in life is that so many of us demand standards from others that we never even try to fulfil ourselves; so many of us condemn faults in others which are glaringly obvious in our own lives. Many a parent punishes and rebukes a child for that which he time and again himself does; many a church member criticises another for faults of which he himself is at least as guilty. The qualification for judging is not knowledge—we all possess that; it is achievement in goodness—we none of us possess that. The very facts of the human situation mean that only God has the right to judge, for the simple reason that no man is good enough to judge any other man.

(ii) It was a first principle with Jesus that our first emotion towards anyone who has made a mistake should be pity. It has been said that the duty of the doctor is " sometimes to heal, often to afford relief and always to bring consolation." When a person who is suffering from some disease is brought to a physician or a surgeon, the man of medical skill does not regard the patient with loathing even if he is suffering from a loathesome disease. In fact the natural physical revulsion which is sometimes inevitable is swallowed up by the great desire to help and to heal. When we are confronted with someone who has made a mistake, our first feeling must be, not, " I'll see that this person suffers for this; I'll have nothing more to do with someone who could act like that," but, " What can I do to help? What can I do to restore? What can I do to undo the consequences of this mistake?" Quite simply, we must always extend to others the same compassionate pity as we would wish to be extended to us, if we were involved in a like situation.

(iii) It is very important that we should understand just how Jesus did treat this woman. It is very easy to use this passage to draw the wrong lesson altogether, and to give the impression that Jesus forgave lightly and easily, as if the sin did not matter. What Jesus did say was: " I am not going to condemn you just now; *go, and sin no more.*" In effect what Jesus was doing was not to abandon judgment, and not to say, " Don't worry; it's quite all right." To put it in human terms, what He did was *to defer sentence.* He said, " I am not going to pass a final judgment and a condemnation *now*; go out, and prove that you can do better. You have sinned; go out and sin no more and I'll help you all the time. At the end of the day we will still see how you have lived." Jesus' attitude to the sinner involved a number of things.

(*a*) It involved *the second chance.* It is as if Jesus said to the woman: " I know you have made a mess of things; but life is not finished yet; I am giving you another chance, the chance to redeem yourself." Someone has written the lines:

> " How I wish that there was some wonderful place
> Called the Land of Beginning Again,
> Where all our mistakes and all our heartaches
> And all our poor selfish grief
> Could be dropped like a shabby old coat at the door,
> And never put on again."

In Jesus there is the gospel of the second chance. Jesus was always intensely interested, not only in what a person had been, but also in what a person could be. He did not say that what they had done did not matter; broken laws and broken hearts always matter; but Jesus was sure that every man has a future as well as a past.

(b) It involved *pity*. The basic difference between Jesus and the Scribes and Pharisees was they they wished to condemn; He wished to forgive. If we read between the lines of this story it is quite clear that these Scribes and Pharisees wished to stone this woman to death, and they were going to take a pleasure in doing so. They knew the thrill of exercising power to condemn; Jesus knew the thrill of exercising power to forgive. Jesus regarded the sinner with pity born of love; the Scribes and Pharisees regarded the sinner with disgust born of self-righteousness.

(c) It involved *challenge*. The challenge with which Jesus confronted this woman was the challenge of the sinless life. He did not say: " It's all right; don't worry; just go on as you are doing." He said: " It's all wrong; go out and fight; change your life from top to bottom; go, and sin no more." Here was no easy forgiveness. Here was a challenge which pointed a sinner to heights of goodness of which she had never dreamed. Jesus confronts the bad life with the challenge of the good life.

(d) It involved *belief in human nature*. When we come to think of it, it is a staggering thing that Jesus should say to a woman taken in adultery, a woman of loose morals: " Go, and sin no more." The amazing, heart-uplifting

9

thing about Jesus was His belief in men and women. When He was confronted with someone who had gone wrong, He did not say: " You are a wretched and a hopeless creature." He said: " Go, and sin no more." Obviously He believed that with His help the sinner has it in him to become the saint. Jesus' method was not to blast men with the knowledge—of which they were well aware— that they were miserable sinners, but to inspire them with the unglimpsed discovery that they were potential saints.

(e) It involved *warning*. There is the unspoken but implied warning here. Here we are face to face with the eternal situation of the gospel, the eternal choice. Jesus confronted that woman with a choice that day—she could go back to her old ways or she could reach out to the new way with Him. This story is an unfinished story, for every life is unfinished until it stands before God.

[It is to be noted that this story of the woman taken in adultery involves a series of very difficult textual questions. A discussion of these textual questions will be found at the end of this book].

THE LIGHT MEN FAILED TO RECOGNIZE

John 8: 12-20

So Jesus again continued to speak to them. " I am the Light of the World," He said. " He who follows me will not walk in darkness, but he will have the light of life." So the Pharisees said to Him: " You are bearing witness about yourself. Your witness is not true." Jesus answered: " Even if I do bear witness about myself, my witness is true, because I know where I came from and where I am going to. You do not know where I came from and where I am going to. You form your judgments on purely human grounds. I do not judge anyone. But if I do form a judgment, my judgment is true, because I am not alone in my judgment, but I and the Father who sent me join in such a judgment. It stands written in your law, that the witness of two persons is to be accepted as true. It is I who witness about myself, and the Father who sent me also witnesses about me." They said to Him: "Where is your Father?" Jesus answered: "You know neither me nor my Father. If you had known me you would know my Father too." He spoke these words in the Treasury while He was teaching in the Temple precincts; and no one laid violent hands upon Him, because His hour had not yet come.

THE scene of this argument of Jesus with the Jewish authorities is laid in the Temple treasury. The Temple treasury was in the Court of the Women, which was the second of the Temple courts. The first court was the Court of the Gentiles; the second was the Court of the Women. It was so called because women might not pass beyond it unless they were actually about to offer sacrifice on the altar which was in the Court of the Priests. Round the Court of the Women there was a colonnade or porch; and, in that porch, set against the wall, there were thirteen treasure chests into which people dropped their offerings. These treasure chests were called *The Trumpets* because they were shaped like trumpets, narrow at the top and swelling out towards the foot. The thirteen treasure chests all had their allotted offering. Into the first two were dropped the half shekels which every Jew had to pay towards the upkeep of the Temple. Into the third and fourth were dropped sums which would purchase the two pigeons which a woman had to offer for her purification after the birth of a child (*Leviticus* 12: 8). Into the fifth were put contributions towards the cost of the wood which was needed to keep the altar fire alight. Into the sixth were dropped contributions towards the cost of the incense which was used at the Temple services. Into the seventh went contributions towards the upkeep of the golden vessels which were used at the Temple services. Sometimes a man or a family set apart a certain sum to make some trespass- or thank-offering. Into the remaining six trumpets people dropped any surplus money which remained after the offering had been bought or made, or anything extra which they wished to offer. Clearly the Temple treasury would be a busy place, with a constant flow of worshippers coming and going, for there would always be a stream of devout Jews desiring to give their offerings to God. There would be no better place to collect an audience of devout people and to teach them than the Temple treasury.

It is in this passage that Jesus makes the great claim: ' I am the Light of the World." And it is very likely that the background against which Jesus made this claim made it doubly vivid and impressive. The Festival with which John connects these discourses and arguments was the Festival of Tabernacles (*John* 7: 2). We have already seen (*John* 7: 37) how the ceremonies of that Festival lent drama to Jesus' claim to give to men the living water. But there was also another ceremony connected with this Festival. On the evening of the first day of the Festival there was a ceremony called The Illumination of the Temple. It took place in the Court of the Women in the Temple. The Court was surrounded with deep galleries, erected to hold the spectators. In the centre of the court four great candelabra were prepared. When the dark came the four great candelabra were lit and, it was said, that they sent such a blaze of light throughout Jerusalem that every courtyard in the city was lit up with their brilliance. And then all night long, until cock-crow the next morning, the greatest and the wisest and the holiest men in Israel danced before the Lord and sang psalms of joy and praise to God while the people watched. The Festival of Tabernacles was a time then that the blaze of the Temple lights illumined the city and pierced the darkness of its squares and courts and lanes. Jesus is saying: " You have seen the blaze of the Temple illuminations piercing the darkness of the night. *I am the Light of the World*, and, for the man who follows me there will be light, not only for one exciting night, but for all the pathway of his life. The light in the Temple is a brilliant light, but in the end it flickers and dies. I am to men the Light which lasts for ever and for ever."

THE LIGHT MEN FAILED TO RECOGNIZE

John 8: 12-20 (*continued*)

JESUS said: " He who follows me will not walk in darkness, but he will have the light of life." The phrase *the light of life* means two things. In the Greek it can mean, either, the light which issues from the source of life, or, the light which gives life to men. In this passage it means both things. Jesus is the very light of God come among men; and Jesus is the light which gives men life. Just as the flower can never blossom when it never sees the sunlight, so our lives can never flower with the grace and beauty they ought to have until they are irradiated with the light of the presence of Jesus Christ.

In this passage Jesus talks of *following* Himself. We often speak of following Jesus; we often urge men to follow Him. When we speak of following Jesus, what do we mean? The Greek word for *to follow* is *akolouthein*; and when we investigate its meanings they combine to shed a flood of light on what it means *to follow* Jesus and to become a *follower* of His. *Akolouthein* has five different but closely connected meanings.

(i) It is often used of a soldier following his captain and his leader. On the long route marches, into battle, in campaigns in strange lands, the soldier follows his captain wherever the captain may lead. The Christian is the soldier whose commander is Christ.

(ii) It is often used of a slave accompanying his master. Wherever the master goes the slave is in attendance upon him. Always the slave is ready to spring to the master's service, and to carry out the tasks the master gives him to do. He is literally at his master's beck and call. The Christian is the slave whose joy it is always to serve Christ.

(iii) It is often used of accepting a wise counsellor's opinion or verdict or judgment. When a man is in doubt, he goes to the man of wisdom and of skill, the man of knowledge, the expert, and if he is a wise man he accepts the judgment and the verdict which he receives. The Christian is the man to whom Christ is counsellor and expert. The Christian is the man who guides his life and conduct by the counsel of Christ.

(iv) It is often used of giving obedience to the laws of a city or a state. If a man is to be an acceptable and useful member of any society or citizen of any community, he must agree to abide by the laws of that society or community. The Christian is the citizen of the Kingdom of Heaven, and he has accepted the law of the Kingdom and the law of Christ as the law which governs his life.

(v) It is often used of following a teacher's line of argument, or of following the gist of someone's speech or address. The Christian is the man who has understood the meaning of the teaching of Christ. He has not listened in dull incomprehension; he has not listened with slack inattention; he has not listened in such a way that the message goes in at one ear and out at the other. He listens, and takes the message into his mind and understands, and receives the words into his memory and remembers, and hides them in his heart and obeys.

To be a follower of Christ is to give oneself body, soul and spirit into the obedience of the Master. And to enter upon that following is to walk in the light. When we walk alone we are bound to stumble and grope, for so many of life's problems are beyond our solution, and, if we try to settle them ourselves, we are bound to go wrong. When we walk alone we are bound to take the wrong way, because we have no secure map of life. We need the heavenly wisdom to walk the earthly way. The man who has a sure guide and an accurate map is the man who is bound to come in safety to his journey's end. Jesus Christ is that guide; He alone possesses the map to life. To follow

Him is to walk in safety through life and afterwards to enter into glory.

THE LIGHT MEN FAILED TO RECOGNIZE

John 8: 12-20 (*continued*)

WHEN Jesus made His claim to be the Light of the World the Scribes and Pharisees reacted with hostility. That claim of Jesus would sound to them even more astonishing than it sounds to us. To them it would sound like a claim—as indeed it was—to be the Messiah, and, even more, to do the work that only God could do. The word *light* was specially associated in Jewish thought and language with God. " The Lord is my *light* " (*Psalm* 27: 1). " The Lord shall be thy everlasting *light* " (*Isaiah* 60: 19). " By His *light* I walked through darkness " (*Job* 29: 3). " When I sit in darkness the Lord shall be a *light* to me " (*Micah* 7: 8). The Rabbis declared that the name of the Messiah is Light. When Jesus made the claim that He was the Light of the World, He was making a claim than which none could possibly be higher.

The argument of this passage is difficult and complicated and compressed, but it involves three strands.

(i) The Jews first insisted that a statement such as Jesus made could not be regarded as accurate because it was backed by insufficient witness. It was, as they saw it, backed by His word alone. Now it was Jewish law that any statement must be founded on the evidence of two witnesses before it could be regarded as true. " One witness shall not rise up against a man for any iniquity, or for any sin, in any sin that he sinneth, at the mouth of two witnesses, or at the mouth of three witnesses, it shall be established " (*Deuteronomy* 19: 15). " At the mouth of two witnesses, or three witnesses, shall he that is worthy of death be put to death; but at the mouth of one witness he shall not be put to death " (*Deuteronomy*

17: 6). " One witness shall not testify against any person to cause him to die " (*Numbers* 35: 30). The Jewish accusation was that Jesus' statement could not be accepted, because it was unsupported by any witness except Himself. Jesus' answer was twofold. First, He answered that His own witness was enough. He was so conscious of His own authority, of His own close relationship with God, that no other witness was necessary. This is not pride or self-confidence. It is simply the supreme instance of the kind of thing which happens every day in life. A great surgeon or physician is confident in his own verdict; he does not need anyone to support him; his witness is his own skill. A great lawyer or judge is sure of his own interpretation and application of the law. It is not that he is proud of his own knowledge; it is simply that he knows that he knows. Jesus was so sure and so aware of His closeness to God that He needed no other authority for His claims than His own relationship to God. But second, Jesus says that in point of fact He *has* a second witness, and *that second witness is God*. How can we say that God bears witness to the supreme authority of Jesus? (*a*) The witness of God is in Jesus' *words*. No man could speak with such wisdom unless God had given him knowledge. (*b*) The witness of God is in Jesus' *deeds*. No man could do such things unless God was with him and acting through him. (*c*) The witness of God is in *the effect of Jesus upon men*. Christ works changes in men which are obviously beyond human power to work. No human power can make the bad man good; Jesus did that; therefore the power of Jesus is divine. The very fact that Jesus can do for men what men can never do for themselves is the final proof that His power is not simply a man's power. It is God's. (*d*) The witness of God is in *the reaction of men to Jesus*. Wherever and whenever Jesus has been full displayed to men, wherever and whenever the Cross has been preached in all its grandeur and its splendour, there has been an immediate and an overwhelming response in the hearts of men. What wakened that response? That response is the Holy Spirit of God working and witnessing in the hearts of men. It is God in our hearts who enables us to see God in Jesus. So, then, Jesus dealt with the argument of the Scribes and Pharisees that His words could not be accepted because the witness to Him was inadequate. His words were backed by a double witness, the witness of His own consciousness of authority and the witness of God.

(ii) Second, Jesus deals with His right to judge. His coming into the world was not primarily for judgment; His coming into the world was for love; it was because God so loved the world that Jesus came. Yet at the same time a man's reaction to Jesus is in itself a judgment. If he sees no beauty in Jesus, by that very reaction he has condemned himself. Here Jesus draws a contrast between two kinds of judgment. (*a*) There is the judgment that is based on human knowledge and human standards, the judgment which never sees below the surface. That was the judgment of the Scribes and Pharisees; and, in the last analysis, that is any human judgment, for in the nature of things men can never see below the surface of things. (*b*) There is the judgment that is based on full knowledge, not superficial knowledge, but knowledge which knows *all* the facts, even the hidden facts, and that judgment can only belong to God, for only God has that knowledge. Now it is Jesus' claim that any judgment He passes is not a human judgment; it is God's judgment; because He is so one with God. Therein lies at once our comfort and our warning. Only Jesus knows all the facts. That very fact makes Him merciful as none other can ever be merciful; but it also enables Him to see the sins in us which are hidden from the eyes of men. The judgment of Jesus is perfect because it is made with the knowledge which belongs to God.

(iii) Lastly, Jesus bluntly told the Scribes and Pharisees that they had no real knowledge of God. The fact that they did not recognize Him for who and what He was was the proof that they did not really know God. The tragedy was that the whole history of Israel was so designed that the Jews should have recognized the Son of God when He came; all their history was leading up to that coming. But they had become so involved with their own ideas, so intent on their own way, so sure of their own conception of what religion was that they had become blind to God. The tragedy of the Jews was that they thought that they knew better than God.

THE FATAL INCOMPREHENSION

John 8: 21-30

So He said to them again: " I am going away, and you will search for me, and you will die in your sin. You cannot come where I am going." So the Jews said: " Surely He is not going to kill Himself, because He is saying: ' You cannot come where I am going '? " He said to them: " You are from below, but I am from above. You belong to this world, but I do not belong to this world. I said to you that you will die in your sins. For if you will not believe that I am who I am, you will die in your sins." They said to Him: " Who are you? " Jesus said to them: " Anything I am saying to you is only the beginning. I have many things to say about you, and many judgments to deliver on you; but He who sent me is true, and I speak to the world what I have heard from Him." They did not know that it was about the Father that He was speaking to them. So Jesus said to them: " When you lift up the Son of Man, then you will know that I am who I am, and that I do nothing on my own authority, but that I speak these things as the Father has taught me. And He who sent me is with me. He has not left me alone, because I always do the things that are pleasing to Him." As He said these things, many believed in Him.

THIS is one of these passages of argument and debate which are so characteristic of the Fourth Gospel and which are so difficult to elucidate and to understand. In this passage there are various strands of argument all woven together.

Jesus begins by telling His opponents that He is going away; and that, after He is gone, they will realize what they have missed, and they will search for Him and not find Him, and will discover their mistake too late. This is the true prophetic note. It reminds us of three things. (i) There are certain opportunities which come and which do not return. To every man there is given the opportunity to decide for Christ and to accept Christ as Saviour and Lord. But that is an opportunity which can be refused and lost. (ii) Implicit in this argument of Jesus is the truth that life and time are limited. No man has all the time in the world; no man has unlimited life; our span and our time are necessarily limited. It is within that allotted span that we must make this decision. The time we have to make the decision for Christ is limited—and no man knows what his limit is. There is therefore every reason for making that decision now. (iii) Just because there is opportunity in life there is also judgment. The lost opportunity involves judgment. And the greater that opportunity was, the more clearly it beckoned, the oftener it came, the greater the judgment if it be refused and missed. This passage brings us face to face with the glory of our opportunity, and the limitation of time in which to seize it.

When Jesus spoke about going away, He was speaking about His return to His Father and to His glory. That was precisely where His opponents could not follow Him, because by their continuous disobedience, and by their refusal to accept Him, they had shut themselves off from God. His opponents met His words with a grim and mocking jest. Jesus said that they could not follow where He went; and they suggested that perhaps He was going to kill Himself. The point is that, according to Jewish thought, the depths of hell were reserved for suicides, for those who took their own lives. So in effect, with a kind of grim and terrible blasphemy, these Jews said of Jesus: " Maybe

He will take His own life; maybe He is on the way to the depths of Hell; it is very true that we cannot and will not follow Him there."

Jesus said that if they continued to refuse Him they would *die in their sins*. That is a prophetic phrase (cp. *Ezekiel* 3: 18; 18: 18). There are two things involved there. (i) The word for sin is *hamartia*, which is a word which originally had to do with shooting and which literally means *a missing of the target*. The man who refuses to accept Jesus as Saviour and Lord has missed the target in life. He dies with life frustrated, unfinished, incomplete, unrealized; and he therefore dies unfitted by himself to enter into the higher life with God. (ii) The essence of sin is that it separates a man from God. When Adam, in the old story, committed the first sin, his first instinct was to hide himself from God (*Genesis* 3: 8-10). The man who dies in sin dies at enmity and in fear of God. The man who accepts Christ already walks with God, and death only opens the way to a closer walk. To refuse Christ is to be a stranger to God; to accept Christ is to be the friend of God; and in that friendship the fear of death is for ever banished.

THE FATAL INCOMPREHENSION

John 8: 21-30 (*continued*)

JESUS goes on to draw a series of contrasts. His opponents belong to earth; He is from Heaven. They are of the world; He is not of the world.

John frequently talks about the world; the word in Greek is *kosmos*. He uses the word in a way that is all his own.

(i) The *kosmos, the world,* is the opposite of heaven. Jesus came from Heaven into the world (*John* 1: 9). He was sent by God into the world (*John* 3: 17). He is not of the world; His opponents are of the world (*John* 8: 23). The *kosmos* is the changing, passing, transient

20

life that we live; the *kosmos* is all that is human as opposed to all that is divine.

(ii) And yet the *kosmos, the world*, is not separated from God. First and foremost, the world is God's creation (*John* 1: 10). It was through God's word that God's world was made. Different as the world is from heaven human as one is and divine as the other is, there is yet no unbridgeable gulf between them.

(iii) More than that, the *kosmos, the world*, is the object of God's love. God so loved the world that He sent His Son (*John* 3: 16). However different the world may be from all that is divine, God has never abandoned the world; it is the object of His love and the recipient of His greatest gift.

(iv) But at the same time there is something wrong with the *kosmos*. There is a *blindness* in the world; when the Creator of the world came into the world, the world did not recognize Him (*John* 1: 10). The world cannot receive the Spirit of truth (*John* 14: 17). The world does not know God (*John* 17: 25). In the world there is a terrible and tragic blindness which does not recognize God, or God's truth, or God's Son. There is an hostility to God in the *kosmos*. The world is hostile to God and to God's people. The world hates Christ and hates the followers of Christ (*John* 15: 18, 19). In the hostility of the world Christ's followers can only look for trouble and tribulation (*John* 16: 33).

(v) Here we have a strange sequence of facts. The world is separate from God; and yet between God and the world there is no gulf which cannot be spanned. God created the world; God loves the world; God sent His Son into the world. And yet in the world there is this blindness and this hostility to God.

There is only one possible conclusion. G. K. Chesterton once said that there was only one thing certain about man—that man is not what he was meant to be. There is only one thing certain about the *kosmos, the world*—the *kosmos* is not what it was meant to be. Something has gone wrong. What is that something? It is sin. It is sin which separated the world from God; it is sin which blinds the world to God; it is sin which is fundamentally hostile to God.

Now into this world which has gone wrong comes Christ; and Christ comes with the cure. He brings forgiveness for sin; He brings cleansing from sin; He brings strength and grace to live as man ought and to make the world what it ought to be. But a man can refuse a cure. A doctor may offer a patient a cure; he may tell the patient that a certain treatment, a certain operation is able to restore the patient to health and strength again. He may actually tell the patient that if he does not accept the treatment, death is inevitable. That is precisely what Jesus is saying Jesus said: " If you will not believe that I am who I am you will die in your sins." If men do not accept the cure which Jesus brings then they die.

There is something wrong with the world—anyone can see that. The cure is to recognize Jesus Christ as the Son of God, to recognize that only obedience to His perfect wisdom can cure the world, and only acceptance of Him as Saviour and Lord can cure the individual soul.

We are only too well aware of the disease which haunts and wrecks the world; the cure lies before us. The responsibility is ours if we refuse to accept it.

THE TRAGIC INCOMPREHENSION

John 8: 21-30 *(continued)*

THERE is no verse in all the New Testament more difficult to translate than *John* 8: 25. No one can really be sure what the Greek means. It could mean: " I am that which I have spoken into you from the beginning," which is the meaning the Authorised Version takes. Other suggested translations are: " Primarily, essentially, I am what I am telling you." " I declare to you that I am the beginning."

" How is it that I even speak to you at all? " which is the translation of Moffatt and the Authorised Version. It is suggested in our translation that it may mean: " Every thing I am saying to you now is only a beginning." If we take it in that way, the passage goes on to say that men will see the real meaning of Christ in three ways.

(i) They will see it in the Cross. It is when Christ is lifted up that we really see what Christ is. It is there we see the love that will never let men go, and which loves them to the end.

(ii) They will see it in the Judgment. He has many judgments still to pass. At the moment He might look like the outlawed carpenter of Nazareth; but the day would come when they would see Him as judge and know what He is.

(iii) When that happens they will see in Him the embodied will of God. " I *always* do the things that are pleasing to Him," Jesus said. Other men however good are spasmodic in their obedience. The obedience of Jesus is continuous, perfect and complete. The day must come when men see and admit that in Jesus is embodied the very mind of God.

THE TRUE DISCIPLESHIP

John 8: 31-32

> So Jesus said to the Jews who had come to believe in Him: " If you remain in my word, you are truly my disciples: and you will know the truth; and the truth will make you free."

THERE are few New Testament passages which have such a complete picture of discipleship as this passage has. Herein is set out the whole map and goal of the way of discipleship.

(i) *Discipleship begins with belief.* The beginning of the discipleship is the moment when a man accepts what Jesus says as true. When a man accepts all that Jesus says about the love of God, when a man accepts all that Jesus

says about the terror of sin, when a man accepts all that Jesus says about the real meaning of life, then on that day the man begins to be a disciple of Jesus.

(ii) *Discipleship means constantly remaining in the word of Jesus.* What does it mean *to remain* in the word of Jesus? To remain in the word of Jesus involves four things. (*a*) It involves constant *listening* to the word of Jesus. It was said of John Brown of Haddington that when he preached he paused every now and then as if listening for a voice. The Christian is the man who all his life listens for the voice of Jesus. The Christian is the man who will take no decision until he has first listened to what Jesus has to say. (*b*) It involves constant *learning* from Jesus. The disciple (*mathētēs*) is literally *the learner*, for that is what the Greek word means. All his life a Christian should be learning more and more about Jesus. The shut mind is the end of discipleship. (*c*) It involves constant *penetrating* into the truth which the words of Jesus bear. No one can hear the words of Jesus once, no one can read them once, and then say that he understands the full meaning of them. The difference between a great book and an ephemeral book lies precisely in the fact that we read an ephemeral book once, and we never wish to go back to it; whereas we read a great book many times, and go back to it time and time again. To remain in the word of Jesus means constantly to study and think about what He said and is still saying to us, until more and more of its meaning becomes ours. (*c*) It involves constant *obeying* of the word of Jesus. We study the word of Jesus, not simply for academic satisfaction, or for intellectual appreciation, but in order to find out what God wishes us to do. The disciple is the learner who learns in order that he may do. The truth which Jesus brought is truth designed for action.

(iii) *Discipleship issues in knowledge of the truth.* To learn from Jesus is to learn the truth. " You will know the truth," said Jesus. And what is the truth that we will know? There are many possible answers to that question.

but the most comprehensive way to put it is that the truth which Jesus brings to us shows us the real values of life. The fundamental question to which every man has consciously or unconsciously to give an answer is: " To what am I to give my life? " " Am I to give it to a career? Am I to give it to the amassing of material possessions? Am I to give it to pleasure? Am I to give it to the obedience and to the service of God? " The truth which Jesus brings enables us to get our scale of values right; it is in His truth that we see what things are really important and what things are not.

(iv) *Discipleship results in freedom.* " The truth will make you free." " In His service is perfect freedom." Discipleship brings us four freedoms. (*a*) It brings us freedom from *fear*. The man who is a disciple never again has to walk alone. He walks for ever in the company of Jesus, and in that company fear is gone. (*b*) It brings freedom from *self*. Many a man fully recognizes that his greatest handicap and his greatest enemy is his own self. And many a man in despair cries out: " I cannot change myself. I have tried, but it is impossible." The power and the presence of Jesus can recreate a man until he is altogether new. (c) It brings freedom from *other people*. There are many whose lives are dominated by the fear of what other people may think and say. H. G. Wells once said that the voice of our neighbours sounds louder in our ears than the voice of God. The disciple is the man who has ceased to care what people say, because he thinks only of what God says. (*d*) It brings freedom from *sin*. There is many a man who has come to the stage when he sins, not because he wants to, but because he cannot help it. His sins, his habits, his self-indulgences, his weaknesses, his irritabilities have so mastered him that, try as he will, he cannot break away from them. Discipleship breaks the chains which bind us to our sins, and enables us to be the person we know we ought to be.

> " O that a man may arise in me
> That the man I am may cease to be "—

that is the very prayer which the disciple of Christ will find answered.

FREEDOM AND SLAVERY

John 8: 33-36

> They answered Him: " We are the descendants of Abraham and we have never been slaves to any man. How do you say: ' You will become free ' ? " Jesus answered them: " This is the truth I tell you— everyone who commits sin is the slave of sin. The slave is not a permanent resident in the house; the son is a permanent resident. If the son shall make you free you will be really free."

JESUS' talk of freedom annoyed the Jews. They claimed that they had never been slaves to any man. Obviously there was a sense in which this was simply not true. They had been captives in exile in Babylon; and at the moment they were subjects of the Romans. But the Jews set a tremendous value on freedom which they held to be the birthright of every Jew. In the Law it was laid down that no Jew, however poor, must descend to the level of being a slave. " And if thy brother that dwelleth by thee be waxen poor, and be sold unto thee, thou shalt not compel him to serve thee as a bondservant . . . for they are my servants, which I brought forth out of the land of Egypt; they shall not be sold as bondmen " (*Leviticus* 25: 39-42). Again and again Jewish insurrections and rebellions flared up because some fiery leader arose who insisted that the Jews could not obey no earthly ruler and no earthly king, because God was their only King and Lord. Josephus writes of the followers of Judas of Galilee who led a famous revolt against the Romans: " They have an inviolable attachment to liberty, and they say that God is to be their only Ruler and Lord " (Josephus, *Antiquities of the Jews*, 18: 1, 6). When the Jews said that they had been no man's slaves they were saying something which was a

26

fundamental article of their creed of life. And even if it was true that there had been times when they were subject to other nations, even if it was true that at that very moment they were subject to Rome, it was still true that even in servitude they maintained an independence of spirit, which meant that they might be slaves in body but never in spirit. Cyril of Jerusalem wrote of Joseph: " Joseph was sold to be a bond slave, yet he was free, all radiant in the nobility of his soul." Even to suggest to a Jew that he might be regarded as a slave was a deadly insult.

But it was another slavery of which Jesus was speaking. " Everyone," He said, " who commits sin is the slave of sin." Everyone who practises sin is a slave. Here Jesus was reiterating a principle which the wise Greeks had stated again and again. The Stoics said: " Only the wise man is free; the foolish man is a slave." Socrates had demanded: " How can you call a man free when his pleasures rule over him? " Paul later was to thank God that the Christian was freed from slavery to sin (*Romans* 6: 17-20).

There is something very interesting and very suggestive here. Sometimes when a man is rebuked for doing something which is wrong, or when he is warned against such a thing, his answer is: " I will do what I like. Surely I can do what I will with my own life." But the whole point of life is that man who sins does *not* do what he likes; he does what sin likes. A man can let a habit get such a grip of him that he cannot break it. He can allow a pleasure to master him so completely that he cannot do without it. He can let some self-indulgence so dominate him that he is powerless to break away from it. He can get into such a state that in the end, as Seneca said, he hates and loves his sins at one and the same time. So far from doing what he likes, the sinner has lost the power to do what he likes. He is a slave to the habits, the self-indulgences, the wrong pleasures which have mastered him. It is precisely Jesus' point that no man who sins can ever be said to be free. He is in fact the slave of sin.

And then Jesus makes a veiled threat, but a threat which the listening Jews would well understand. The word *slave* reminds him of something. In any household there was a difference between the slave and the son. The son was a permanent dweller in the household; nothing could put him out. But the slave could be ejected at any time. The master could at any time dispense with him and tell him to be gone. No man can unmake a son; a son is always a son. But a slave can be banished at any time. In effect Jesus was saying to the Jews: "You think that you are sons in God's house; you think that nothing can ever banish you from God; have a care; you by your conduct are making yourselves slaves; and the slave can be ejected from the master's presence at any time." Here was a threat. It is a terrible thing to trade on the mercy and the favour of God—and that is what the Jews were doing. There is warning here for more than the Jews.

REAL SONSHIP

John 8: 37-41

> "I know that you are the descendants of Abraham, but you are trying to find a way to kill me, because there is no room in you for my word. I speak what I have seen in the presence of the Father. So you must do what you have heard from the Father." "Our father is Abraham," they answered. "If," answered Jesus, "you are the children of Abraham, act as Abraham acted. But, as it is, you are trying to find a way to kill me, a man who has spoken the truth to you, truth which I heard from God. That Abraham did not do. As for you, you do the works of your father."

IN this passage Jesus is dealing a death-blow to the claim which to the Jews was all-important. For the Jew Abraham was the greatest figure in all religious history; and the Jew considered himself safe and secure in the favour of God simply because he was a descendant of Abraham.

28

The psalmist could address the people as: " O ye seed of
Abraham, His servant, ye children of Jacob, His chosen "
(*Psalm* 105: 6). Isaiah said to the people: " But thou
Israel art my servant, Jacob whom I have chosen, the
seed of Abraham my friend " (*Isaiah* 41: 8). The admiration
which the Jews gave to Abraham was perfectly legitimate,
for Abraham is a giant in the religious history of mankind,
but the deductions they drew from Abraham's greatness
were quite misguided. The Jews believed that Abraham
had gained such merit from his goodness that this merit
was sufficient, not only for himself, but for all his descendants also. Abraham's goodness, so they believed, had
been so great that he had built up a kind of treasury of
merit on which all his descendants could draw. Abraham's
credit balance with God had been so vast that all his
descendants could go on drawing on it for ever and not
exhaust it. Justin Martyr had a discussion with Trypho
the Jew about Jewish religion and the conclusion of the
argument was that, " the eternal kingdom will be given
to those who are the seed of Abraham according to the
flesh, even though they be sinners and unbelievers and
disobedient to God " (Justin Martyr, *The Dialogue with
Trypho*, 140). Quite literally the Jew believed that he
was safe because he was a descendant of Abraham.

There are certain things on which it is impossible to
live, although not a few people try to live on them. The
attitude of the Jews is not completely with parallel in
modern life.

(*a*) There are those who still try to live on a *pedigree and
a name*. At some time in the history of their family someone
performed some really outstanding service to Church or
state, and ever since they have claimed a special place
because of that. A great name should never be an excuse
for a comfortable inaction; it should always be an urge
and an inspiration to new greatness and to new effort.

(*b*) There are those who try to live on *a history and a
tradition*. There is many a Church which has a quite

undue sense of its own importance because at one time it had a famous ministry. There is many a congregation living on the spiritual capital of the past; but if capital be always drawn upon and never built up anew, the day inevitably comes when it is exhausted.

Neither a man, nor a Church, nor a nation can live on the achievements of the past. That is what the Jews were trying to do.

Jesus was quite blunt about this. He declared in effect that the real descendant of Abraham was the man who acted in the way in which Abraham had acted. That is exactly what John the Baptist had said before. John had told the people bluntly that the day of judgment was on the way, and that it was no good pleading that they were descendants of Abraham, for God could raise up descendants to Abraham from the very stones, if He chose to do so (*Matthew* 3: 9; *Luke* 3: 8). It was the argument which again and again Paul was to use. It was not flesh and blood which made a man a descendant of Abraham; it was moral quality and spiritual fidelity.

In this particular matter Jesus ties it down to one thing. They are seeking a way to kill Him; that is precisely the opposite of what Abraham did. When a messenger from God came to Abraham, Abraham welcomed him with all eagerness and with all reverence (*Genesis* 18: 1-8). Abraham had welcomed God's messenger; the Jews of the time of Jesus were trying to kill God's messenger. How could they dare to call themselves descendants of Abraham, when their conduct was so very different?

Here is a great implicit claim of Jesus. By the very calling to mind of the old story in *Genesis* 18, Jesus is saying that He too is the messenger of God. Then He makes that claim explicit: " I speak what I have seen in the presence of the Father." The fundamental thing about Jesus is that He brought to men, not His own opinions, but a message from God. Jesus was not simply a man telling other men what He thought about things;

He was the Son of God telling men what God thought about things. At best men can only tell other men the truth as they see it; Jesus told men the truth as God sees it.

And then at the end of this passage there comes a shattering statement. " You," said Jesus, " do the works of your father." He has just said that Abraham is *not* their father. Who then is their father? For a moment the full impact is held back. It comes in verse 44—their father is the devil. Those who had gloried in the claim that they are the children of Abraham are now devastatingly confronted with the charge that they are children of the devil. Their works had revealed their true sonship, for man can only prove his kinship to God by his conduct.

CHILDREN OF THE DEVIL

John 8: 41-45

> They said to Him: " We were born of no adulterous union. We have one Father—God." " If God was your Father," said Jesus, " you would love me. For it was from God that I came forth and have come here. I had nothing to do with my own coming, but it was He who sent me. Why do you not understand what I am saying? The reason is that you are unable to hear my word. You belong to your father, the devil, and it is the evil desires of your father that you wish to do. He was a murderer from the very beginning, and he never took his stand in the truth, because the truth is not in him. When he speaks falsehood it is his characteristic way of speaking, because he is a liar and the father of falsehood. But because I speak the truth, you do not believe in me."

JESUS had just told the Jews that by their life and conduct and by their reaction to Him they had made it clear that they were no real children of Abraham. The reaction of the Jews was to make an ever greater claim. They claimed that God was their Father and that they were sons of God. All over the Old Testament there is repeated the fact that God was in a special way the Father of His people Israel. It was God's command to Moses that he should say to Pharaoh: " Thus saith the Lord, Israel is my son, even my firstborn " (*Exodus* 4: 22). When Moses was chiding the people for their disobedience, his appeal was: " Do ye thus requite the Lord, O foolish people and unwise? Is not He thy Father that hath bought thee? " (*Deuteronomy* 32: 6). Isaiah speaks of his trust in God: " Doubtless Thou art our Father, though Abraham be ignorant of us, and Israel acknowledges us not: Thou O Lord art our Father, our Redeemer " (*Isaiah* 63: 16). " But now, O Lord, Thou art our Father " (*Isaiah* 64: 8). " Have we not all one Father? " demanded Malachi. " Hath not one God created us? " (*Malachi* 2: 10). So the Jews claimed that God was their Father.

" We," they said proudly, " were born of no adulterous union." There may be two things there. In the Old Testament one of the loveliest descriptions of the nation of Israel is that which sees in her the Bride of God. Because of that when Israel forsook God and went after strange gods, she was said to go awhoring after strange gods. Her infidelity was spiritual adultery, the breaking of the marriage bond with God. When the nation was thus faithless, the apostate people were said to be " children of whoredoms " (*Hosea* 2: 4). So when the Jews said to Jesus that they were not the children of any adulterous union, they meant that they did not belong to a nation of idolaters; they had always worshipped the true God. It was a claim that they had never gone astray from God—a tremendous claim to make, and a claim that only a people steeped in self-righteousness would ever have dared to make. But when the Jews spoke like this, there may have been something much more personal in it. It is certainly true in later times that the Jews spread abroad a most malicious and evil-minded slander against Jesus. The Christians very early preached the miraculous birth of Jesus. The Jews put it about that Mary had been unfaithful to Joseph; that her paramour had been a Roman soldier called

Panthera; and that Jesus was the child of that adulterous union. It is just possible that the Jews were flinging at Jesus even then an insult at His birth, as if to say: " What right have you to speak to the like of us as you do? "

Jesus' answer to the claim of the Jews is that it is false; and the proof is that if God was really their Father, they would have loved and welcomed Him. Here again is the key thought of the Fourth Gospel. The test of a man is his reaction to Jesus. If a man sees in Jesus the altogether lovely, that man at least has it in him to become a real son of God. If a man sees in Jesus nothing lovely, and if a man's only desire is to eliminate Jesus from life, that man is not a child of God. To be confronted with Jesus is to be confronted with judgment. Jesus is the touchstone of God by which all men are judged.

So Jesus' close knit indictment goes on. He asks the question: " Why do the Jews not understand and recognize the truth of what He is saying? " The answer is a terrible answer. The answer is, not that they are intellectually stupid, but that they are spiritually deaf. It is not that they are not able to hear; it is not that they are not able to understand; it is that they refuse to hear and they refuse to understand. A man can stop his ears to any warning; a man can deliberately refuse to listen to the voice of conscience. If he goes on doing that long enough, he becomes spiritually deaf. In the last analysis, a man will only hear what he wishes to hear. And if for long enough he attunes his ears to his own wishes and desires, and to the wrong voices, in the end he will be unable to tune in at all to the wavelength of God. That is what the Jews had done.

Then comes the scarifying accusation. The real father of the Jews is the devil. Jesus chooses two characteristics of the devil.

(i) The devil is <u>characteristically a murderer</u>. There may be two things in Jesus' mind. He may be thinking back to the old Cain and Abel story. Cain was the first murderer and Cain was inspired by the devil. He may be thinking of something even more serious than that. It was the devil who first tempted man, in the old *Genesis* story. Through the devil sin entered into the world; and through sin came death (*Romans* 5: 13). If there had been no temptation, there would have been no sin; and, if there had been no sin, there would have been no death; and therefore, in a sense, the devil is the murderer of the whole human race. But, even apart from the old stories, the fact remains that Christ leads to life, the devil leads to death. The devil murders goodness, chastity, honour, honesty, beauty, all that makes life lovely. The devil murders peace of mind and happiness and even love. The devil is essentially a killer. Evil characteristically destroys; Christ characteristically brings life. At that very moment the Jews were plotting and planning how to kill Christ. They were trying to become successful murderers. They were taking the devil's way.

(ii) The devil characteristically loves falsehood. The false word, the false thought, the twisting of the truth, the lie belong to the devil. Every lie is begotten and inspired by the devil and does the devil's work. Falsehood always hates the truth, and always tries to destroy the truth. That is why the Jews hated Jesus. When the Jews and Jesus met, the false way met the true, and inevitably the false tried to destroy the true.

Jesus indicted the Jews as children of the devil because their thoughts were bent on the destruction of the good and the maintaining of the false. Every man who tries to destroy the truth is doing the devil's work.

THE GREAT INDICTMENT AND THE SHINING FAITH

John 8: 46-50

" Who of you can convict me of sin? If I speak the truth, why do you not believe in me? He who is from God hears God's words. That is why you do not hear, because you are not from God." The Jews answered:

34

" Are we not right in saying that you are a Samaritan, and that you have a devil? " Jesus answered: " It is not I who have a devil. I honour my Father, but you dishonour me. I do not seek my own glory. There is One who seeks and judges."

THIS is one of these passages when we must actually try to see the scene happening before our eyes. There is drama here, and the drama is not only in the words, but in the pauses between them. Jesus begins with a tremendous claim. " Is there anyone here," He demands, " who can accuse me of any sin? Is there anyone here who can point the finger at any evil in my life? " Then there must have followed a silence during which the eyes of Jesus ranged round the crowd waiting for anyone to accept the extraordinary challenge that He had thrown down. The silence went on, and there was none who could accept it. Say what they like and search as they like, there was none who could formulate a charge against this amazing Jesus. Then when He had given them their chance Jesus spoke again. " You admit," He said, " that you can find no charge against me. Then why do you not accept what I say? " Again there was that uncomfortable silence. Then Jesus answers His own question. " You do not accept my words," He said, " because you are not from God and there is nothing of the Spirit of God in your hearts."

What did Jesus mean when He levelled this charge against the Jews? Think of it this way. No experience can enter into a man's mind and heart unless there is something there to answer to it. And it is quite possible that a man may lack the something essential which will enable him to have the experience. A man who is tone deaf cannot ever experience the thrill of music. A man who is colour blind cannot ever appreciate a picture. A man with no sense of time and rhythm cannot ever appreciate ballet or dancing. Now the Jews had a very wonderful way of thinking of the Spirit of God. They believed that the Spirit of God had two great functions.

The Spirit revealed God's truth to men; and the Spirit enabled men to recognize and grasp that truth when they saw it. That quite clearly means that unless the Spirit of God is in a man's heart he *cannot* recognize God's truth when he sees it. And it also means that if a man shuts the door of his heart against the Spirit of God, if he so follows his own ideas and desires that the Spirit cannot gain an entry into his heart, then, even when the truth is full displayed before his eyes, he is quite unable to see it and recognize it and grasp it and make it his. Jesus was saying to the Jews: "You have gone your own way; you have followed your own ideas; you have manufactured a god of your own; the Spirit of God has been unable to gain an entry into your hearts; that is why you cannot recognize me and that is why you will not accept my words." The Jews believed they were religious people; but because they clung to their idea of religion instead of to God's idea of it they had in the end drifted so far from God that they had become godless. They were in the terrible position of men who were godlessly serving God.

To be told that they were strangers to God stung the Jews to the quick. They hurled their invective against Jesus. As our present form of the words has it they accused Him of being a Samaritan and of being mad. What did they mean by calling Him a Samaritan? If that is what they did call Him they meant that he was a foe of Israel, for there was deadly enmity between the Jews and the Samaritans, that He was a law breaker because He did not observe the law, and above all that He was a heretic, for the word Samaritan and the word heretic had become synonymous. It would be an extraordinary position that the Son of God should be branded as a heretic. And beyond a doubt it would happen to Him again if He returned to this world and its Churches. But it is just possible that the word Samaritan is really a corruption of something else. To begin with, we note that Jesus did reply to the charge that He was mad, that He had a devil, but He did not reply to the charge that He was a Samaritan. That makes us wonder if we do have the charge of the Jews rightly stated. In the original Aramaic the word for Samaritan would be *Shomeroni*. Now the word *Shomeron* was also a title for the prince of the devils, who is also called Ashmedai and Sammael and Satan. In point of fact the *Koran*, which is the Mohammedan bible, actually says that the Jews were seduced into idolatry by Shomeron, the prince of the devils. So the word *Shomeroni* could quite well mean *a child of the devil*. It is very likely that what the Jews said to Jesus was: " You are a child of the devil; you have a devil; you are mad with the madness of the Evil One."

Jesus' answer was that, so far from being a servant of the devil, His one aim was to honour God, while the whole conduct of the Jews was a continual dishonouring of God. He says in effect: " It is not *I* who have a devil; it is *you*. It is not *my* work which is essentially evil; it is *yours*."

Then there comes the radiance of the supreme faith of Jesus. He says: " I am not looking for honour in this world: I know that I will be insulted and rejected and dishonoured and crucified. But there is One who will one day assess things at their true value; there is One who will one day assign to men their true honour; that One is God; and He will give me the honour which is real because it is His." Of one thing Jesus was sure—ultimately, in the light of the eternities, God will protect the honour of His own. In time Jesus saw ahead nothing but pain and dishonour and rejection; in eternity Jesus saw ahead only the glory which He who is obedient to God will some day receive. In *Paracelsus* Browning wrote:

> " If I stoop
> Into a dark tremendous sea of cloud,
> It is but for a time; I press God's lamp
> Close to my breast; its splendour, soon or late,
> Will pierce the gloom: I shall emerge one day."

Jesus had the supreme optimism which is born of supreme faith, the optimism which is rooted in God.

THE LIFE AND THE GLORY

John 8: 51-55

> " This is the truth I tell you—if anyone keeps my
> word, he will not see death for ever." The Jews said
> to Him: " Now we are certain that you are mad.
> Abraham died and so did the prophets, yet you are
> saying: ' If anyone keeps my word, he will not taste
> of death for ever.' Surely you are not greater than
> our father Abraham who did die? And the prophets
> died too. Who are you making yourself out to be? "
> Jesus answered: " If I glorify myself, my glory is
> valueless. It is my Father who glorifies me, that
> Father, who, you claim, is your God, and yet you
> know nothing about Him. But I know Him. If I
> were to say that I do not know Him, I would be a
> liar, like you. But I know Him and I keep His word."

THIS is a chapter which passes from lightning flash to
lightning flash of astonishment. In it Jesus makes claim
after claim, each one more tremendous than the one which
went before. Here he makes the claim that if anyone keeps
His words, he will never know death. The thing shocked
the Jews. Zechariah had said: " Your fathers, where
are they? And the prophets, do they live for ever? "
(*Zechariah* 1: 5). Abraham was dead; the prophets were
dead; and had they not, in their day and generation,
kept the word of God? Who was Jesus to set Himself
above the great ones of the faith? It was the literal-
mindedness of the Jews which blocked their intelligence.
It was not physical life and physical death of which Jesus
was thinking. He meant that, for the man who fully
accepted Him, there was no such thing as death. Death
had lost its finality. The man who enters into fellowship
with Jesus has entered into a fellowship which is independent of time. The man who accepts Jesus has entered
into a relationship with God which neither time nor eternity
can sever. Such a man goes, not from life to death, but
from life to life. Death is only the introduction to the
nearer presence of God.

From that Jesus goes on to make a great statement—

all true honour must come from God. It is not difficult to honour oneself. One can quite easily surround oneself with a kind of synthetic halo. It is easy enough—in fact, it is fatally easy—to bask in the sunshine of one's own approval. It is not over difficult to win honour from men. The world honours the successful and the ambitious man. But the real honour is the honour which only eternity can reveal; and the verdicts of eternity are not the verdicts of time.

Then Jesus makes the two essential claims which are the very foundation of His life.

(i) He claims *unique knowledge of God.* He claims to know God as no one else ever has known Him or ever will know Him. Nor will He lower that claim, for to lower it would be a lie. The only way to full knowledge of the heart and mind of God is through Jesus Christ. With our own minds we can reach fragments of knowledge about God. Only in Jesus Christ is the full orb of truth, for only in Him do we see what God is like.

(ii) He claims *unique obedience to God.* He keeps God's word. To look at Jesus is to be able to say: "This is how God wishes me to live." To look at His life is to say: "This is serving God."

In Jesus alone we see what God wants us to know and what God wants us to be.

THE TREMENDOUS CLAIM

John 8: 56-59

"Abraham your father rejoiced to see my day; and he saw it and was glad." The Jews said to Him: "You are not yet fifty years old, and have you seen Abraham?" Jesus said to them: "This is the truth I tell you—before Abraham was I am." So they lifted stones to throw them at Him, but Jesus slipped out of their sight, and went out of the Temple precincts.

ALL the previous lightning flashes flicker and pale into significance before the blaze of this passage. When Jesus said to the Jews that Abraham rejoiced to see His day, He was talking language that the Jew could understand. The Jews had many beliefs about Abraham which would enable them to see what Jesus was implying. There were altogether five different ways in which the Jews themselves would interpret this passage.

(*a*) Abraham was living in Paradise and was able to see what was happening on earth. Jesus used that idea in the Parable of Dives and Lazarus (*Luke* 16: 22-31). That is the simplest way to interpret this saying.

(*b*) But that is not really the correct interpretation. Jesus said Abraham *rejoiced* to see my day. It is the past tense that he uses. Now the Jews interpreted many passages of scripture in a way that explains this. They took the great promise to Abraham in *Genesis* 12: 3: " In thee shall all families of the earth be blessed," and they said that when that promise was made, Abraham knew that it meant that the Messiah of God was to come from his line, and he rejoiced at the magnificence of the promise.

(*c*) Some of the Rabbis held that in the vision which is recounted in *Genesis* 15: 8-21 Abraham was given a vision of the whole future of the nation of Israel, and that therefore he had a vision beforehand of the time when the Messiah would come.

(*d*) Some of the Rabbis took *Genesis* 17: 17, which tells how Abraham laughed when he heard that a son would be born to him, not as the laugh of unbelief, but as the laugh of sheer joy that from him the Messiah would come.

(*e*) Some of the Rabbis had a fanciful interpretation of *Genesis* 24: 1. There the Authorised Version has it that Abraham was " well stricken in age." The margin of the Authorised Version tells us that the Hebrew literally means that Abraham had " gone into days." Some of the Rabbis held that that meant that in a vision given by God Abraham had *entered into the days which lay ahead*, and had seen the whole history of the people and the coming of the Messiah.

From all this we see clearly that the Jews did believe that somehow Abraham, while he was still alive, did have a vision of the history of Israel and the coming of the Messiah. So then when Jesus said that Abraham had seen His day, He was making a deliberate claim that He was the Messiah. He was saying: " You believe that Abraham was given a vision by God in which He saw the Messiah come. It was this day, it was I, that Abraham saw in that vision."

Immediately after that statement Jesus goes on to say of Abraham: " He saw it (my day) and was glad." Some of the early Christians had a very fanciful interpretation of that. In I *Peter* 4: 18-22 and 5: 6 we have the two passages which are the basis of the doctrine which is called The Descent into Hell. That doctrine became embedded in the creed in the phrase, " He descended into Hell." It is to be noted that the word *Hell* gives the wrong idea; it ought to be *Hades*. The idea is not that Jesus went to the place of the tortured and the damned, as the word Hell suggests. Hades was the land of the shadows where all the dead, good and bad alike, went; Hades was the shadowy land in which people believed before the full belief in immortality came to them. The Apocryphal work called The Gospel of Nicodemus or the Acts of Pilate has a passage where it is told that Abraham rejoiced to see the light of Christ on that day when Jesus descended into the land of the dead. The passage runs like this: " O Lord Jesus Christ, the resurrection and the life of the world, give us grace that we may tell of Thy resurrection and of Thy marvellous works, which Thou didst in Hades. We, then, were in Hades together with all them that have fallen asleep since the beginning. And at the hour of midnight there rose upon those dark places as it were the light of the sun, and shined, and all we were enlightened and beheld one another. And straightway our father Abraham, together with the patriarchs and the prophets, were at once filled with joy and said to one another : ' This light cometh of the great lightening.' " So the strange story tells how the dead saw Jesus and were given the chance to believe and to repent. And at that sight Abraham rejoiced.

To us these ideas are strange; to a Jew they were quite normal, for the Jew believed that Abraham had already seen the day when the Messiah would come.

But the Jews, although they knew better, chose to take this literally. " How," they demanded, " can you have seen Abraham when you are not yet fifty? " Why fifty? Fifty was the age at which the Levites retired from their service (*Numbers* 4: 3). The Jews are saying to Jesus: " You are a young man, still in the prime of life, not even old enough to retire from service. How can you possibly have seen Abraham? This is mad talk." It was then that Jesus made that most staggering statement: " Before Abraham was, I am." Now we must note carefully that Jesus did not say: " Before Abraham was, I *was*," but, " Before Abraham was, I *am*." Here is the claim that Jesus is *timeless*. There never was a time when He came into being; there never will be a time when He is not in being. We cannot say of Jesus, *He was*. We must always say, *He is*. What did He mean? Obviously He did not mean that He, the human figure Jesus, had always existed. We know that Jesus was born into this world at Bethlehem. There is more than that here. Think of it this way. There is only one person in the universe who is timeless. There is only one person who is above and beyond time, and who can always say, *I am. And that one person is God.* What Jesus is saying here is nothing less than that the life in Him is the life of God; that in Him the timeless eternity of God had broken into the time of man; He is saying, as the writer of the Hebrews put it more simply, that He is the same yesterday, to-day and forever. In Jesus we see, not simply a man who came and lived and died; in Jesus we see the timeless God, who was the God of Abraham and of Isaac and of Jacob, who was before time and who will be after time, who always *is*. In Jesus the eternal God showed Himself to men.

LIGHT FOR THE BLIND EYES

John 9: 1-5

> As Jesus was passing by, He saw a man who was blind from the day of his birth. " Rabbi," His disciples said to Him, " who was it who sinned that he was born blind—this man or his parents?" " It was neither he nor his parents who sinned," answered Jesus, " but it happened that in him there might be a demonstration of what God can do. We must do the works of Him who sent me while day lasts; the night is coming when no man is able to work. So long as I am in the world, I am the light of the world."

THIS is the only miracle in the gospels in which the sufferer is said to have been afflicted from his birth. In *Acts* we twice hear of people who had been helpless from their birth (the lame man at the Beautiful Gate of the Temple in *Acts* 3: 2, and the impotent man at Lystra in *Acts* 14: 8), but this man is the only man in the gospel story who had been afflicted from the day of his birth. He must have been a well-known character, for the disciples knew all about him. When they saw him, they used the opportunity to put to Jesus a problem with which Jewish thought had always been deeply concerned, and a problem which is still a problem. The Jews unhesitatingly connected suffering and sin. They worked on the basic assumption that wherever there was suffering, somewhere there was sin. So they asked Jesus their question. " This man," they said, " is blind. Is his blindness due to his own sin, or to the sin of his parents?" How could the blindness be possibly due to the man's own sin, when he had been blind *from his birth?* To that question the Jewish theologians gave two answers. (i) Some of them had the strange notion of pre-natal sin. They actually believed that a man could begin to sin while he was still in his mother's womb. In the imaginary conversations between Antoninus and Rabbi Judah the Patriarch, Antoninus asks: " From what time does the evil influence bear sway over a man, from the formation of the embryo in the womb or from the moment of birth? " The Rabbi first answered: " From the for- mation of the embryo." Antoninus objected to this view and convinced Judah by his arguments, for Judah admitted that, if the evil impulse began with the formation of the embryo, then the child would kick in the womb and break his way out. Judah found a text to support his view. He took the saying in *Genesis* 4: 47: " Sin lieth at the door." And he put the meaning into it that sin awaited man at the door of the womb, as soon as he was born. But the argument does show us that the queer idea of pre-natal sin was known. (ii) In the time of Jesus the Jews believed in the pre-existence of the soul. They really got that idea from Plato and the Greeks. They believed that all souls existed before the creation of the world in the garden of Eden, or that they were in the seventh heaven, or in a certain chamber, waiting to enter into a body. The Greeks had believed that such souls were good, and that it was the entry into the body which contaminated them; but there were certain Jews who believed that these souls were already good and bad. The writer of *The Book of Wisdom* says: " Now I was a child good by nature, and a good soul fell to my lot " (*Wisdom* 8: 19). In the time of Jesus there were certain Jews who did believe that a man's affliction, even if it be from birth, might come from sin that he had committed even before he was born. It is a strange idea, and it may seem to us almost fantastic; but at the heart of it there lies the idea of a sin-infected universe.

The alternative was that the man's affliction was due

to the sin of his parents. The idea that children inherit the consequences of the sin of their parents is woven into the thought of the Old Testament. " I the Lord Thy God am a jealous God, visiting the iniquity of the fathers upon the children unto the third and fourth generation " (*Exodus* 20: 5: cp. *Exodus* 34: 7, *Numbers* 14: 18). Of the wicked man the psalmist says: " Let the iniquity of his fathers be remembered before the Lord; and let not the sin of his mother be blotted out " (*Psalm* 109: 14). Isaiah talks about your iniquities and the " iniquities of your fathers," and goes on to say: " Therefore will I measure their former work into their bosom " (*Isaiah* 65: 6, 7). One of the key-notes of the Old Testament is that the sins of the fathers are always visited upon the children. It is a thing which must never be forgotten that no man lives to himself and no man dies to himself. When a man sins he sets in motion a train of consequences which has no end.

LIGHT FOR THE BLIND EYES

John 9: 1-5 (*continued*)

As we go on to consider this passage, we find that in it there are two great eternal principles.

(i) Jesus does not try to follow out or to explain the connection of sin and suffering. He says that this man's affliction came to him to give an opportunity of showing what God can do. There are two senses in which that is true. (*a*) For John the miracles are always a sign of the glory and the power of God. The writers of the other gospels had a different point of view. They regarded the miracles as a demonstration of the compassion of Jesus. When Jesus looked on the hungry crowd He had *compassion* on them, because they were as sheep not having a shepherd (*Mark* 6: 34). When the leper came with his desperate request for cleansing Jesus was *moved with compassion*

(*Mark* I: 41). It is often urged that in this the Fourth Gospel is quite different from the others. The other gospels stress the compassion of the miracles; the Fourth Gospel stresses the fact that the miracles are manifestations of power and glory. Surely there is no real contradiction here. It is simply two ways of looking at the same thing. And at the heart of it there is the supreme truth that the glory of God lies in His compassion, and that God never so fully reveals His glory as when He reveals His pity. (*b*) But there is another sense in which the man's affliction shows what God can do. Affliction, sorrow, pain, disappointment, loss always enable any man to show what God can do. First, it enables the sufferer to show what God can do. When trouble and disaster fall upon a man who does not know God then that man may well collapse; but when they fall on a man who lives and walks with God they bring out the strength and the beauty, and the endurance and the nobility, which are within man's heart when God is there. It is told that when an old saint was dying in an agony of pain, he sent for his family, saying: " Come and see how a Christian can die." It is when life hits us a terrible blow that we can show the world how a Christian can live, and, if need be, die. Any kind of suffering is a God-given opportunity to demonstrate the glory of God in our own lives. Second, by helping those who are in trouble and in pain, we can demonstrate to others the glory of God. Frank Laubach has the great thought that when Christ, who is the Way, enters into us " we become part of the Way. God's highway runs straight through us." When we give and spend ourselves to help those in trouble, in distress, in pain, in sorrow, in affliction, God is using us as the highway by which He sends His help into the hearts of His people. To help a fellow-man who needs that help is to manifest the glory of God, for it is to show what God is like.

Then Jesus goes on to say that He and all His followers must do God's work while there is time to do it. God gave men the day for work, and the night for rest. The day comes to an end, and the time for work is also ended. For Jesus it was true that He had to press on with God's work in the day for the night of the Cross lay close ahead. But it is true for every man. We are only given so much time. Whatever we are to do must be done within it. There is in Glasgow a sundial with the motto: " Tak' tent of time ere time be tint." " Take thought of time before time is ended." We can never put things off until another time, for another time may never come. The Christian's bounden duty is to fill the time he has—and no man knows how much that will be—with the service of God and of his fellow-men. There is no more poignant sorrow than the tragic discovery that it is now too late to do something which we might have done.

But there is another opportunity which we may miss. Jesus said: " So long as I am in the world I am the light of the world." When Jesus said that He did not mean that the time of His life and work were limited; what He did mean was that our opportunity of laying hold on that life, and light and work are limited. There comes to every man a chance to decide for Christ, to accept Christ, to give His life to Christ, to accept Christ as His Saviour, His Master and His Lord. And if that opportunity is not seized it may well never come back. E. D. Starbuck, in his book *The Psychology of Religion* has some interesting and warning statistics about the age at which conversion normally occurs. Conversion can occur as early as seven or eight; it increases gradually to the age of ten or eleven; it increases rapidly to the age of sixteen; it declines steeply up to the age of twenty; and after thirty it is very rare. God is always saying to us: " *Now* is the time." It is not that the power of Jesus grows less, or that His light grows dim; it is that if we put off the great decision we become ever less able to take it as the years go on. Work must be done, decisions must be taken, while it is day, and before the day ends and the night comes down.

THE METHOD OF A MIRACLE

John 9: 6-12

When He had said this He spat on the ground, and made clay from the spittle, and He smeared the clay on his eyes and said to him: " Go, wash in the Pool of Siloam." (The word " Siloam " means " sent.") So he went away and washed, and he came able to see. So the neighbours and those who formerly knew him by sight and knew that he was a beggar, said: " Is this not the man who sat begging? " Some said: " It is he." Others said: " It is not he, but it is some- one like him." The man himself said: " I am he." " How then," they said to him, " have your eyes been opened? " " The man they call Jesus made clay," he said, " and smeared it on my eyes, and said to me: ' Go to the Pool of Siloam and wash.' So I went and washed, and sight came to me." They said to him: " Where is this man you are talking about? " He said: " I don't know."

THERE are two miracles in which Jesus is said to have used spittle to effect a cure. The other is the miracle of the deaf stammerer (*Mark* 7: 33). The use of spittle seems to us strange and repulsive and unhygienic; but in the ancient world it was quite common. Spittle, and especially the spittle of some distinguished person, was believed to possess certain curative qualities. Tacitus tells us how, when Vespasian visited Alexandria, there came to him two men, one with diseased eyes and one with a diseased hand, who said that they had been advised by their god to come to him. The man with the diseased eyes wished Vespasian " to moisten his eye-balls with spittle "; the man with the diseased hand wished Vespasian " to trample on his hand with the sole of his foot." Vespasian was very unwilling to do so. He was finally persuaded to do as the men asked. " The hand immediately recovered its power; the blind man saw once more. Both facts are attested to this day, when falsehood can bring no reward, by those who were present on the occasion " (Tacitus, *Histories* 4: 81). Pliny, the famous Roman collector of what was then called scientific information, has a whole chapter on the use of spittle. He says that it is a sovereign preservative against the poison of serpents; a protection against epilepsy; that lichens and leprous spots can be cured by the application of fasting spittle; that ophthalmia can be cured by anointing, as it were, the eyes every morning with fasting spittle; that carcinomata and crick in the neck can be cured by the use of spittle. Spittle was held to be very effective in averting the evil eye. Persius tells how the aunt or the grandmother, who fears the gods, and who is skilled in averting the evil eye will lift the baby from his cradle and " with her middle finger apply the lustrous spittle to his forehead and slobbering lips." The use of spittle was very common in the ancient world. To this day, if we burn a finger our first instinct is to put it into our mouth; and to this day there are many who believe that warts can be cured by licking them with fasting spittle.

The fact is that Jesus took the methods and the customs of his time and used them. He was a wise physician. He had to gain the confidence of his patient. It was not that Jesus believed in these things, but He kindled expectation by doing what the patient would expect a doctor to do. After all, to this day the efficacy of any medicine or treatment depends at least as much on the patient's faith in it as in the treatment or the drug itself.

After anointing the man's eyes with spittle, Jesus sent him to wash in the Pool of Siloam. The Pool of Siloam was one of the landmarks of Jerusalem; and, in its day, it was the result of one of the great engineering feats of the ancient world. The water supply of Jerusalem had always been precarious in the event of a siege. It came mainly from The Virgin's Fountain or the Spring Gihon, which was situated in the Kidron Valley. To that spring there had been built a staircase of thirty-three rock-cut steps leading down to it; and there, from a stone basin, people drew the water. But, in the event of a siege, the spring was completely exposed and could be completely cut off, with consequences which would have been disastrous. When Hezekiah realized that Sennacherib was about to invade Palestine he determined to cut through the solid rock a tunnel or conduit from the spring into the city (2 *Chronicles* 32: 2-8, 30; *Isaiah* 22: 9-11; 2 *Kings* 20: 20). The distance was through solid rock. If the engineers had cut straight it would have been a distance of 366 yards; but because they cut in a zig-zag, either because they were following a fissure in the rock, or to avoid sacred sites, the conduit is actually 583 yards. The tunnel is at places only about two feet wide, but its average height is about six feet. The engineers began their cutting from both ends and met in the middle—a truly amazing feat for the equipment of the time. In 1880 a tablet was discovered commemorating the completion of the conduit. It was accidently discovered by two boys who were wading in the pool. It runs like this: " The boring through is completed. Now this is the story of the boring through. While the workmen were still lifting pick to pick, each towards his neighbour, and while three cubits remained to be cut through, each heard the voice of the other who called his neighbour, since there was a crevice in the rock on the right side. And on the day of the boring through the stone-cutters struck, each to meet his fellow, pick to pick; and there flowed the waters to the pool for a thousand and two hundred cubits, and a hundred cubits was the height of the rock above the heads of the stone-cutters." The Pool of Siloam was the place where the conduit from the Virgin's Fountain issued in the city. It was an open air basin twenty by thirty feet. That is how the pool got its name. It was called *Siloam*, which, it was said, meant *sent*, because the water in it had been *sent* through the conduit into the city. So Jesus sent this man to wash in this pool which was one of the landmarks of the city; and the man washed and saw.

Having been cured, he had some difficulty in persuading

the people that a real cure had been effected. But he stoutly maintained the miracle which Jesus had wrought. Jesus is always doing things which seem to the unbeliever far too good and far too wonderful to be true.

PREJUDICE AND CONVICTION

John 9: 13-16

> They brought him, the man who had been blind, to the Pharisees. The day on which Jesus had made the clay and opened his eyes was the Sabbath day. So the Pharisees asked him again how sight had come to him. He said to them: " He put clay on my eyes; and I washed; and now I can see." So some of the Pharisees said: " This man is not from God, because He does not observe the Sabbath." But others said: " How can a man who is a sinner perform such signs? " And there was a division of opinion among them. So they said to the blind man: " What is your opinion about Him, in view of the fact that He opened your eyes? " He said: " He is a prophet."

And now there comes the inevitable trouble. It was the Sabbath day on which Jesus had made the clay and had healed the man. Now, undoubtedly, Jesus had broken the Sabbath law, as the Scribes had worked it out. He had in fact broken it in three different ways.

(i) By making clay He had been guilty of working on the Sabbath day. To do even the simplest acts on the Sabbath day was to be guilty of working on it. Here are some of the things which were forbidden by the law, and which a man must not do on the Sabbath. " A man may not fill a dish with oil and put it beside a lamp and put the end of the wick in it." " If a man extinguishes a lamp on the Sabbath to spare the lamp or the oil or the wick, he is culpable." " A man may not go out on the Sabbath with sandals shod with nails." (The weight of the nails would have constituted a burden, and to carry a burden was to break the Sabbath.) A man might not cut his finger nails or pull out a hair of his head or his beard. Obviously in the eyes of such a law to make clay was to work and to break the Sabbath.

(ii) It was forbidden to heal on the Sabbath. Medical attention could only be given if life was in actual danger. And even then it must be such as to keep the patient from getting worse, and it must not make him any better. For instance, a man with toothache might not suck vinegar through his teeth. It was forbidden to set a broken limb. " If a man's hand or foot is dislocated he may not pour cold water over it." The cold water would help to heal the sprain. Clearly the man who was born blind was in no danger of his life; therefore Jesus broke the Sabbath when He healed him.

(iii) It was quite definitely laid down in the law in regard to the Sabbath and healing that: " As to fasting spittle, it is not lawful to put it so much as upon the eyelids."

It was by observation of these petty rules and details that the Scribes and Pharisees sought to honour God; to Jesus they were fantastic and irrelevant; therefore, in their eyes, He was guilty of breaking the Sabbath.

The Pharisees are typical of the people in every generation who condemn anyone whose idea of religion is not theirs. The Pharisees were the kind of people who thought that there was only one way of serving God, and that that was their way. There were some of them who thought otherwise, and who declared that no one could do the things which Jesus did and be a sinner.

So they brought the man and examined him. When he was asked what his opinion of Jesus was, he gave it without hesitation. He said that Jesus was a prophet. In the Old Testament a prophet was often tested by the signs he could produce. Moses guaranteed to Pharaoh that he really was God's messenger by the signs and wonders which he performed (*Exodus* 4: 1-17). Elijah proved that he was the prophet of the real God by doing things the prophets of Baal could not do (I *Kings* 18). No doubt the man's thoughts were running on these things when he said that in his opinion Jesus was a prophet.

One thing is true of this man—whatever else he was, he was a brave man. He knew quite well what the Pharisees thought of Jesus. He knew quite well that if he came out as a follower of Jesus he was certain to be excommunicated. But he made his statement and took his stand. It was as if he said: " I am bound to believe in Him, I am bound to take my stand by Him because of all that He has done for me." Therein he is our great example.

THE PHARISEES DEFIED

John 9: 17-35

Now the Jews refused to believe that he had been blind and had become able to see, until they called the parents of the man who had become able to see, and asked them: " Is this your son? And do you say that he was born blind? How, then, can he now see? " His parents answered: " We know that this is our son; and we know that he was born blind; how he has now come to see we do not know; or who it was who opened his eyes we do not know. Ask himself. He is of age. He can answer his own questions" His parents said this because they were afraid of the Jews; for the Jews had already agreed that if anyone acknowledged Jesus to be the Anointed One of God, he should be excommunicated from the Synagogue. That is why his parents said: " He is of age. Ask him." A second time they called the man who used to be blind. " Give the glory to God," they said. " We know that this man is a sinner." " Whether he is a sinner or not," the man answered, " I do not know. One thing I do know—I used to be blind and now I can see." " What did He do to you?" they said. " How did He open your eyes? " " I have already told you," the man said, " and you did not listen. Why do you want to hear the story all over again? Surely you can't want to become His disciples? " They heaped abuse on him. " It is you who are His disciple," they said. " We are Moses' disciples. We know that God spoke to Moses; but,

as for this man, we do not know where he comes from."
The man answered: " It is an astonishing thing that
you do not know where He comes from, when He
opened my eyes. It is a fact known to all of us that
God does not listen to sinners. But if a man is a
reverent man and does His will, God hears him. Since
time began no one has ever heard of anyone who
opened the eyes of a man born blind. If this man was
not from God, He could not have done anything."
" You were altogether born in sins," they said to him,
" and are you trying to teach us? " And they ordered
him to get out.

THERE is not a more vivid bit of character drawing in all
literature than this. With deft and revealing touches
John draws the pictures of all the people involved so that
they live before us.

(i) First of all, there is the blind man himself. He begins
by being irritated at the persistence of the Pharisees.
" Say what you like," he says, " about this man. I don't
know anything about him except that he made me able
to see." It is the simple fact of Christian experience that
many a man may not be able to put into theologically
correct language what he believes Jesus to be, but in spite
of that he can witness to what Jesus has done for his soul.
A man need not be a theologian to experience the benefits
of Jesus Christ. Even when a man cannot understand with
his intellect, he can still feel with his heart. It is better to
love Jesus Christ than to love theories about Jesus Christ.

(ii) There are the man's parents. They are obviously
unco-operative, but at the same time they are afraid.
The Jewish Synagogue authorities had one powerful
weapon, the weapon of excommunication, the weapon
whereby a man was shut off from the congregation of
God's people. Away back in the days of Ezra we read of a
decree that whosoever did not obey the command of
the authorities " his substance should be forfeited and
himself separated from the congregation " (*Ezra* 10: 8).
Jesus warned His disciples that their name would be cast
out for evil (*Luke* 6: 22). He told them that they would

be put out of the Synagogues (*John* 16: 2). Many of the
rulers in Jerusalem really believed in Jesus, but they were
afraid to say so " lest they should be put out of the Synagogue " (*John* 12: 42). There were two kinds of excommunication. There was the ban, the *cherem*, by which a man
was banished from the Synagogue for life. In such a case he
was publicly anathematized. He was cursed in the presence
of the people, and he was cut off from God and from man.
There was sentence of temporary excommunication which
might last for a month, or for some other fixed period.
The terror of such a situation was that a Jew would regard
it as shutting him out, not only from the Synagogue
but from God. That is why the man's parents answered
that their son was quite old enough to be a legal witness
and to answer his own questions. The Pharisees were so
venomously embittered against Jesus that they were
prepared to do what ecclesiastics at their worst have
sometimes done—they were prepared to use ecclesiastical
procedure to further their own ends.

(iii) There were the Pharisees. They did not believe
at first that the man had been blind. That is to say, they
suspected collusion. They thought that this was a miracle
faked between Jesus and the man. Further, they were well
aware that the law had recognized that a false prophet
could produce false miracles for his own false purposes
(*Deuteronomy* 13: 1-5 warns against the false prophet
who produces false signs in order to lead people away
after strange gods). So the Pharisees began with suspicion.
They went on to try to browbeat the man. " Give the
glory to God," they said. " We know that this man is a
sinner." " Give the glory to God," was a phrase used in
cross-examination which really meant: "Speak the truth
in the presence and the name of God." When Joshua
was cross-examining Achan about the sin which had
brought disaster to Israel, he said to him: " Give, I pray
thee, glory to the Lord God of Israel, and make confession

unto Him; and tell me now what thou hast done; hide it not from me " (*Joshua* 7: 19).

They were annoyed and helpless because they could not meet the man's arguments which were based on scripture The man's argument was: " Jesus has done a very wonderful thing; the fact that He has done it means that God hears Him; now God never hears the prayers of a bad man; therefore Jesus cannot be a bad man; He must be good." The fact that God did not hear the prayer of a bad man is a basic thought of the Old Testament. When Job is speaking of the hypocrite, he says: " Will God hear his cry when trouble cometh upon him ? " (*Job* 27: 9). The psalmist says: " If I regard iniquity in my heart, the Lord will not hear me " (*Psalm* 66: 18). Isaiah hears God say to the sinning people: " When ye spread forth your hands (the Jews prayed with the hands stretched out, palms upwards), I will hide mine eyes from you; yea, when you make many prayers, I will not hear; your hands are full of blood " (*Isaiah* 1: 15). Ezekiel says of the disobedient people: " Though they cry in mine ears with a loud voice, yet will I not hear them " (*Ezekiel* 8: 18) Conversely they believed that the prayer of a good man was always heard. " The eyes of the Lord are upon the righteous, and His ears are open to their cry " (*Psalm* 34: 15). " He will fulfil the desire of them that fear Him; He will also hear their cry and will save them " (*Psalm* 145: 19). " The Lord is far from the wicked; but He heareth the prayer of the righteous " (*Proverbs* 15: 29). The man who had been blind presented the Pharisees with an argument which they could not answer.

Now when they were confronted with such an argument, see what they did. First, they resorted to *abuse*. " They heaped abuse on him." Second, they resorted to *insult*. They accused the man of being born in sins. That is to say, they accused him of pre-natal sin. Third, they resorted to *threatened force*. They ordered him out of their presence.

Often we have our differences with people, and it is

well that it should be so. But the moment insult and abuse and threat enter into an argument, it ceases to be an argument and becomes a contest in bitterness. If in argument we become angry, and we resort to wild words and hot threats, then all that we prove is that our case is too weak to be stated as a case ought to be stated.

REVELATION AND CONDEMNATION

John 9: 35-41

> Jesus heard that they had put him out, so He found him and said to him: " Do you believe in the Son of God? " " But who is He, sir," he answered Him, " that I might believe in Him? " Jesus said to him: " You have both seen Him, and He who is talking with you is He." " Lord," he said, " I believe." And he knelt before Him. Jesus said: " It was for judgment that I came into this world that those who do not see might see, and that those who see might become blind." Some of the Pharisees who were with Him heard this. " Surely," they said, " *we* are not blind? " Jesus said to them: " If you were blind, you would not have sin. As it is, your claim is, ' We see.' Your sin remains."

THIS section begins with two great and precious spiritual truths.

(i) Jesus looked for the man. As Chrysostom put it: " The Jews cast Him out of the Temple; the Lord of the Temple found him." Jesus never leaves any man to bear his witness alone. If any man's Christian witness separates him from his fellow-men, it brings him nearer to Jesus Christ. When a man is cast out from men because of his fidelity to Christ, it brings him closer to Christ than ever he was before. Jesus is always true to the man who is true to Him.

(ii) To this man there was made the great revelation that Jesus was the Son of God. Here is a tremendous truth. Loyalty always brings revelation. It is to the man

who is true to Him that Jesus most fully reveals Himself.
The penalty of loyalty may well be persecution and
ostracism at the hands of men; the reward of loyalty
is a closer walk with Christ, and an increasing knowledge
of the wonder of Christ.

John finishes this story with two of his favourite thoughts.

(i) Jesus came into this world for judgment. Whenever
a man is confronted with Jesus, that man at once passes
a judgment on himself. If he sees in Jesus nothing to
desire, nothing to admire, nothing to love, then he has
condemned himself. If he sees in Jesus something to wonder
at, something to respond to, something to reach out to,
then that man is on the way to God. The man who is
conscious of his own blindness, and who longs to see better
and to know more, is the man whose eyes can be opened
and who can be lead more and more deeply into the truth.
The man who thinks he knows it all, the man who does
not realize that he cannot see, is the man who is truly
blind, and who is beyond hope and help. Only the man
who realizes his own weakness can become strong. Only
the man who realizes his own blindness can learn to see.
Only the man who realizes his own sin can be forgiven.

(ii) The more knowledge a man has the more he is to
be condemned if he does not recognize the good when he
sees it. If the Pharisees had been brought up in ignorance,
then they could not have been condemned. Their condemnation lay in the fact that they knew so much, and
they claimed to see so well, and yet they failed to recognize
God's Son when He came. The law that responsibility
is the other side of privilege is written into life.

GREATER AND GREATER

John 9

BEFORE we leave this very wonderful chapter we would do
well to read it again, this time straight through from start
to finish. If we do so read it with care and attention, we

will see the loveliest progression in the blind man's idea of Jesus. The blind man's idea of Jesus goes through three stages, each one higher than the last.

(i) He begins by calling Jesus a *man*. " A man that is called Jesus opened mine eyes " (verse 11). He began by thinking of Jesus as a very wonderful man. Anyone may well begin there. The blind man had never met any man who could do the kind of things Jesus did. He had never met anyone like Jesus. And he began by thinking of Jesus as supreme among men. We do well sometimes to think of the sheer magnificence of the manhood of Jesus. In any gallery of the world's heroes Jesus must find a place. In any anthology of the loveliest lives ever lived, the life of Jesus would have to be included. In any collection of the world's greatest literature His parables would have to be included. Shakespeare makes Mark Antony say of Julius Caesar:

> " His life was gentle, and the elements
> So mix'd in him that Nature might stand up
> And say to all the world, ' This was a man.' "

Whatever else is in doubt, there is never any doubt that Jesus was a man among men.

(ii) He goes on to call Jesus a *prophet*. When he was asked what his opinion of Jesus was in view of the fact that He had given him his sight, his answer was: " He is a prophet " (verse 17). Now a prophet is a man who brings God's message to men. " Surely the Lord God will do nothing," said Amos, " but He revealeth His secret unto His servants the prophets " (*Amos* 3: 7). A prophet is a man who lives close to God. A prophet is a man who has penetrated into the inner councils of God. When we read the wisdom of the words of Jesus, when we listen to His voice speaking these immortal sayings, we are bound to say: " This is a prophet." Whatever else is in doubt, this is true—if men followed the teachings of Jesus, all personal, all social, all national, all international problems would be solved. If ever any man had the right to be called a prophet, who spoke to men with the voice of God, Jesus has.

(iii) Finally the blind man came to confess that Jesus was the *Son of God*. He came to see that human categories were not adequate to describe Jesus. He came to see that Jesus did things which are beyond human power to do, and knew things which are beyond human knowledge to know. Napoleon was once in a company in which a number of clever sceptics were discussing Jesus. They dismissed Jesus as a very great man and nothing more. " Gentlemen," said Napoleon, " I know men, and Jesus Christ was more than a man."

> " If Jesus Christ is a man
>   And only a man—I say
> That of all mankind I cleave to Him
>   And to Him will I cleave alway.
>
> If Jesus Christ is a god—
>   And the only God—I swear
> I will follow Him through heaven and hell,
>   The earth, the sea, and the air! "

The tremendous thing about Jesus is that the more we know Him the greater He becomes. The trouble with human relationships is that it so often happens the better we know a person the more we know his weaknesses, his faults, his failings, his feet of clay; but the more we know Jesus, the greater the wonder becomes; and that will be true, not only in time, but also in eternity.

THE SHEPHERD AND HIS SHEEP

John 10: 1-6

> Jesus said: " This is the truth I tell you; he who does not enter the sheepfold through the door, but climbs in some other way, is a thief and a robber. But he who comes in through the door is the shepherd of the sheep. The keeper of the door opens the door to him; and the sheep hear his voice; and he calls his own sheep by name and leads them out. Whenever he puts his

own sheep out, he walks in front of them; and the sheep follow him, because they know his voice. But they will not follow a stranger, but they will run away from him, because they do not know the voice of strangers." Jesus spoke this parable to them, but they did not know what He was saying to them.

THERE is no better loved picture of Jesus than the picture of Him as the Good Shepherd. The picture of the shepherd is deeply woven into the language and the imagery of the Bible. It could not be otherwise. The main part of Judaea is a central plateau. It stretches from Bethel to Hebron for a distance of about 35 miles. It varies from 14 to 17 miles across. The ground, for the most part, is rough and stony. Judaea was, therefore, naturally much more a pastoral than an agricultural country. It was, therefore, inevitable that the most familiar figure of the Judaean uplands was the shepherd. The life of the Palestinian shepherd was very hard. In Palestine no flock ever grazes without a shepherd, and the shepherd is never off duty. There is little grass, and the sheep are bound to wander far afield. There are no protecting walls, and the sheep have ever to be watched. On either side of the narrow plateau the ground dips sharply down to the craggy deserts and the sheep are always liable to wander away and to get lost. The shepherd's task was constant and dangerous, for, in addition, he had to guard the flock against wild animals, especially against wolves, and there were ever thieves and robbers ready to steal the sheep. Sir George Adam Smith, who travelled in Palestine, writes: " On some high moor, across which at night the hyaenas howl, when you meet him, sleepless, far-sighted, weather-beaten, leaning on his staff, and looking out over his scattered sheep, every one of them on his heart, you understand why the shepherd of Judaea sprang to the front in his people's history; why they gave his name to their king, and made him the symbol of providence; why Christ took him as the type of self-sacrifice." Constant vigilance, fearless courage, patient love for his flock, were the necessary characteristics of the shepherd.

In the Old Testament God is often pictured as the shepherd, and the people as His flock. " The Lord is my shepherd: I shall not want " (*Psalm* 23: 1). " Thou leadest Thy people like a flock by the hand of Moses and Aaron " (*Psalm* 77: 20). " We Thy people and sheep of Thy pasture will give Thee thanks for ever " (*Psalm* 79: 13). " Give ear, O Shepherd of Israel, Thou that leadest Joseph like a flock " (*Psalm* 80: 1). " He is our God, and we are the people of His pasture, and the sheep of His hand " (*Psalm* 95: 7). " We are His people, and the sheep of His pasture " (*Psalm* 100: 3). God's Anointed One, the Messiah, was also pictured as the shepherd of the sheep. " He shall feed His flock like a shepherd: He shall gather the lambs with His arm, and carry them in His bosom, and shall gently lead those that are young " (*Isaiah* 40: 11). " He will be shepherding the flock of the Lord faithfully and righteously, and will suffer none of them to stumble in their pasture. He will lead them all aright " (*Psalms of Solomon* 17: 45). The leaders of the people are described as the shepherds of God's people and nation. " Woe be unto the pastors that destroy and scatter the sheep of my pasture! " (*Jeremiah* 23: 1-4). Ezekiel has a tremendous indictment of the false leaders who seek their own good rather than the good of the flock. " Woe be unto the shepherds of Israel that do feed themselves! Should not the shepherds feed the flock? " (*Ezekiel* 34).

This picture passes over into the New Testament. Jesus is the Good Shepherd. He is the shepherd who will risk His life to seek and to save the one straying sheep (*Matthew* 18: 12; *Luke* 15: 4). He has pity upon the people because they are as sheep without a shepherd (*Matthew* 9: 36; *Mark* 6: 34). His disciples are His little flock (*Luke* 12: 32). When He, the shepherd, is smitten the sheep are scattered (*Mark* 14: 27; *Matthew*

26: 31). He is the Shepherd of the souls of men (I *Peter* 2: 25), and the great Shepherd of the sheep (*Hebrews* 13: 20).

Just as in the Old Testament picture, the leaders of the Church are the shepherds and the people are the flock. It is the duty of the leader to feed the flock of God, to accept the oversight willingly and not by constraint, to do it eagerly and not for love of money, not to use the position for the exercise of power and to be an example to the flock (I *Peter* 5: 2, 3). Paul urges the elders of Ephesus to take heed to all the flock over which the Holy Spirit had made them overseers (*Acts* 20: 28). It is Jesus' last command to Peter that he should feed His lambs and His sheep (*John* 21: 15-19). The very word *pastor* (*Ephesians* 4: 11) is the Latin word for *shepherd*.

The Jews had a lovely legend to explain why God chose Moses to be the leader of His people. " When Moses was feeding the sheep of his father-in-law in the wilderness, a young kid ran away. Moses followed it until it reached a ravine, where it found a well to drink from. When Moses got up to it he said: ' I did not know that you ran away because you were thirsty. Now you must be weary.' He took the kid on his shoulders and carried it back. Then God said: ' Because you have shown pity in leading back one of a flock belonging to a man,' you shall lead *my* flock Israel.' "

When we think of the word shepherd it should paint a picture to us of the unceasing vigilance and patience of the love of God; and it should remind us of our duty towards our fellow-men, especially if we hold any kind of office in the Church of Christ.

THE SHEPHERD OF THE SHEEP

John 10: 1-6 (*continued*)

THE Palestinian shepherd had different ways of doing things from the shepherds of our country; and, to get the full meaning of this picture, we must look at the shepherd and the way in which he worked.

The shepherd's equipment was very simple. He had his *scrip*. The scrip was a bag made of the skin of an animal, in which he carried his food. In his scrip he would have no more than bread, dried fruit, some olives and cheese. He had his *sling*. The skill of many of the men of Palestine was such that they " could sling stones at an hair breadth and not miss " (*Judges* 20: 16). The shepherd used his sling as a weapon of offence and defence; but he made one curious use of it. There were no sheep dogs in Palestine, and, when the shepherd wished to call back a sheep which was straying away, he fitted a stone into his sling and landed the stone just in front of the straying sheep's nose as a warning to turn back. He had his *staff*. His staff was a wooden club. It was quite short; it had a lump of wood at the end often studded with nails. It usually had a slit in the handle at the top, through which a thong passed; and by the thong the staff swung at the shepherd's belt. His staff was the weapon with which he defended himself and his flock against marauding beasts and robbers. He had his *rod*. His rod was like the shepherd's crook. With it he could catch and pull back any sheep which was moving to stray away. At the end of the day, when the sheep were going into the fold, the shepherd held his rod across the entrance, quite close to the ground; and every sheep had to pass under the rod (*Ezekiel* 20: 37; *Leviticus* 27: 32); and, as the sheep passed under the rod, the shepherd quickly examined it to see if it had received any kind of hurt or injury throughout the day.

The relationship between sheep and shepherd is quite different in Palestine. In Britain the sheep are largely kept for killing; but in Palestine the sheep are largely kept for their fleece for making wool. It thus happens that in Palestine the sheep are often with the shepherd for years. Often the sheep have names by which the shepherd calls them. Usually these names are descriptive—

" Brown-leg," " Black-ear."   In Palestine the shepherd did go before the sheep and the sheep did follow him. The shepherd went first to see that the path was safe, and that there were no dangers.   Sometimes the sheep had to be encouraged to follow.   A traveller tells how he saw a shepherd leading his flock come to a ford across a stream. The sheep were unwilling to cross.   The shepherd finally solved the problem by carrying one of the lambs across. When the ewe who was the mother of the lamb saw her lamb on the other side she crossed too, and soon all the rest of the flock had followed her.

It is strictly true that the sheep know and understand the eastern shepherd's voice; and that they will never answer to the voice of a stranger.   H. V. Morton has a wonderful description of the way in which the shepherd talks to the sheep.   " Sometimes he talks to them in a loud sing-song voice, using a weird language unlike anything I have ever heard in my life.   The first time I heard this sheep and goat language I was on the hills at the back of Jericho.   A goat-herd had descended into the valley and was mounting the slope of an opposite hill, when turning round, he saw his goats had remained behind to devour a rich patch of scrub.   Lifting his voice, he spoke to the goats in a language that Pan must have spoken on the mountains of Greece.   It was uncanny because there was nothing human about it.   The words were animal sounds arranged in a kind of order.   No sooner had he spoken than an answering bleat shivered over the herd, and one or two of the animals turned their heads in his direction.   But they did not obey him.   The goat-herd then called one word, and gave a laughing kind of whinny.   Immediately a goat with a bell round his neck stopped eating, and, leaving the herd, trotted down the hill, across the valley, and up the opposite slopes.   The man, accompanied by this animal, walked on and disappeared round a ledge of rock.   Very soon a panic spread among the herd.   They forgot to eat. They looked up for their shepherd.   He was not to be seen.

They became conscious that the leader with the bell at his neck was no longer with them. From the distance came the strange laughing call of the shepherd, and at the sound of it the entire herd stampeded into the hollow and leapt up the hill after him " (H. V. Morton, *In the Steps of the Master*, pp. 154, 155). W. M. Thomson in *The Land and the Book* has the same story to tell. " The shepherd calls sharply from time to time, to remind them of his presence. They know his voice, and follow on; but, if a stranger call, they stop short, lift up their heads in alarm, and if it is repeated, they turn and flee, because they know not the voice of a stranger. I have made the experiment repeatedly." That is exactly John's picture.

H. V. Morton tells of a scene that he saw in a cave near Bethlehem. Two shepherds had sheltered their flocks in the cave during the night. How were the flocks to be sorted out? One of the shepherds stood some distance away and gave his peculiar call which only his own sheep knew, and soon his whole flock had run to him, because they knew his voice. They would have come for no one else, but they knew the call of their own shepherd. An 18th century traveller actually tells how Palestinian sheep could be made to dance, quick or slow, to the peculiar whistle, or the peculiar tune on the flute that their own shepherd would play to them.

Every detail of the shepherd's life lights up the picture of the Good Shepherd whose sheep hear His voice, and whose constant care is for His flock.

THE DOOR TO LIFE

John 10: 7-10

So Jesus said to them again: " This is the truth I tell you—I am the door of the sheep. All who came before me are thieves and robbers, but the sheep did not listen to them. I am the door. If any man enter in through me, he will be saved, and he will go in and out, and he will find pasture. The thief comes only to kill and to steal and to destroy; I am come that they might have life, and that they might have it more abundantly."

THE Jews did not understand the meaning of the story of the Good Shepherd. So Jesus, openly, plainly and without concealment, took it and applied it to Himself.

He began by saying: " I am the door." In this parable Jesus spoke about two kinds of sheep-folds. In the villages and towns themselves there were communal sheep-folds where all the village flocks were sheltered when they returned home at night. These folds were protected by a strong door of which only the guardian of the door held the key. It is to that kind of fold that Jesus refers in verses 2 and 3. But when the sheep were out on the hills in the warm season, when they did not return at night to the village at all, at night they were collected into sheep-folds out on the hillside. These hillside sheep-folds were just open spaces enclosed by a wall. In them there was an opening by which the sheep came in and went out; but there was no door of any kind. What happened was that at night the shepherd himself lay down across the opening and entrance, and no sheep could get out or in except over his body. In the most literal sense the shepherd was the door; there was no access to the sheep-fold except through him.

That is what Jesus was thinking of when He said: " I am the door." Through Him, and through Him alone, men find access to God. " Through Him," said Paul, " we have access unto the Father " (*Ephesians* 2: 18). " He," said the writer to the Hebrews, " is the new and living way " (*Hebrews* 10: 20). Jesus opens the way to God. Until Jesus came men could only think of God as, at best, a stranger and as, at worst, an enemy. But Jesus came to tell men and to show men what God was like, and to open the way to God. It is as if Jesus gave us the introduction to God which by ourselves we could never have obtained or discovered. Jesus opened the door for men

to God. He is the door through whom alone entrance to
God becomes possible for men.

To describe something of what that entrance to God
means Jesus uses a well-known Hebrew phrase. He says
that through Him *we can go in and come out.* To be able
to come and go out unmolested was the Jewish way of
describing a life that is absolutely secure and safe. When
a man can go in and out without fear, it means that his
country is at peace, that the forces of law and order are
supreme, and that he enjoys a perfect security for his
life. The leader of the nation is to be one who can bring
them out and lead them in (*Numbers* 27: 17). Of the man
who is obedient to God it is said that he is blessed when he
comes in and blessed then he goes out (*Deuteronomy* 28: 6).
A child is one who is not yet able by himself to go out
and to come in (I *Kings* 3: 7). It is the Psalmist's certainty
that God will keep him in his going out and in his coming
in (*Psalm* 121: 8). Once a man discovers, through Jesus
Christ, what God is like, a new sense of safety and of
security enters into life. If life is in the hands of a God
like that, the worries and the fears are gone.

There is a contrast between Jesus and those who came
before. Jesus said that those who came before Him were
thieves and robbers. When He said this He was of course
not referring to the great succession of the prophets and
the heroes. He was referring to these adventurers who
were continually arising in Palestine and promising that
if people would follow them, they would bring in the golden
age. All these claimants were revolutionaries and insur-
rectionists. They believed that men would have to wade
through blood to the golden age. At this very time Josephus
speaks of there being ten thousand disorders in Judaea;
tumults caused by men of war. He speaks of men like the
Zealots who did not mind dying themselves, and who did
not mind slaughtering their own loved ones if their schemes
and hopes of victory and conquest could be achieved.
Jesus is saying: " There have been men who claimed that

they were leaders sent to you from God. They believed in war, murder, assassination, death. And their way only leads for ever farther and farther away from God. My way is the way of peace, and love and life. And my way, if you will only take it, leads ever closer and closer to God." There have been, and still are, those who believe that the golden age must be brought in with violence, class warfare, bitterness, destruction. It is the message of Jesus that the only way that leads to God in heaven and to the golden age on earth is the way of love.

It is Jesus' claim that He came that men might have life, and that they might have it more abundantly. The phrase which is used for *having it more abundantly* is the Greek phrase which means to have *a surplus, a super-abundance of a thing*. To be a follower of Jesus, to know who He is and what He means, is to have a superabundance of life. There is a story of a Roman soldier who came to Julius Caesar with a request for permission to commit suicide and to end his life. He was a wretched, miserable, dispirited creature with no vitality. Caesar looked at him. "Man," he said, "were you ever really alive?" When we try to live our own lives, life is a dull, dispirited thing. When we walk with Jesus, when we know His presence in our lives, there comes into life a new vitality, a super-abundance of life. It is only when we live with Christ that life becomes really worth living, and that we begin to live at all in the real sense of the word.

THE TRUE AND THE FALSE SHEPHERD
John 10: 11-15

"I am the good shepherd; the good shepherd gives his life for the sheep. The hireling, who is not a real shepherd, and to whom the sheep do not really belong, sees the wolf coming, and leaves the sheep, and runs away; and the wolf seizes them and scatters them. He abandons the sheep because he is a hireling, and the sheep are nothing to him. I am the good shepherd,

> and I know my own sheep, and my own sheep know me, just as the Father knows me and I know the Father. And I lay down my life for the sheep."

THIS passage draws the contrast between the good and the bad, the faithful and the unfaithful shepherd. In Palestine the shepherd was absolutely responsible for the sheep. If anything did happen to the sheep, he had to produce some kind of proof that it was not his fault. Amos speaks about the shepherd rescuing two legs or a piece of an ear out of a lion's mouth (*Amos* 3: 12). The law laid it down: " If it be torn in pieces, then let him bring it for witness " (*Exodus* 22: 13). The idea is that the shepherd must bring home proof that the sheep had died, and that he had been unable to prevent the death. David tells Saul how when he was keeping his father's sheep, he had the battle with the lion and the bear (I *Samuel* 17: 34-36). Isaiah speaks of the crowd of shepherds being called out to deal with the lion (*Isaiah* 31: 4). To the shepherd it was the most natural thing to risk his life in the defence of the flock which was his flock. Sometimes the shepherd had to do more than risk his life for the sheep: he had to lay down his life for the sheep. This specially happened when thieves and robbers came to despoil the flock. Dr. W. M. Thomson in *The Land and the Book* writes: " I have listened with intense interest to their graphic descriptions of downright and desperate fights with these savage beasts. And when the thief and the robber come (and come they do), the faithful shepherd has often to put his life in his hand to defend his flock. I have known more than one case where he had literally to lay it down in the contest. A poor faithful fellow last spring, between Tiberias and Tabor, instead of fleeing, actually fought three Bedawin robbers until he was hacked to pieces with their khanjars, and died among the sheep he was defending." The true shepherd never hesitated to risk, and even to lay down, his life for his sheep.

But, on the other hand, there was the false and unfaithful

shepherd. The difference was this. A real shepherd was born to his task. He was sent out with the flock as soon as he was old enough to go; he grew into the calling of being a shepherd; the sheep became his friends and his companions; and it became second nature to him to think of them before he thought of himself. But the false shepherd came into the job, not as a calling, but as a means of making money. He was in it simply and solely for the pay he could get out of it. He might even be a man who had taken to the hills because the town was too hot to hold him. He had no sense of the height and the responsibility of his calling. He was only a hireling. The wolves were a threat to the flock. Jesus said of His disciples that He was sending them out as sheep in the midst of wolves (*Matthew* 10: 16); Paul warned the elders of Ephesus that grievous wolves would come, not sparing the flock (*Acts* 20: 29). These wolves attacked, and the hireling shepherd forgot everything but the saving of his own life and ran away. Zechariah marks it as the characteristic of a false shepherd that he made no attempt to gather together the scattered sheep (*Zechariah* 11: 6). Carlyle's father once took this imagery caustically to his speech. In Ecclefechan they were having trouble with their minister; and it was the worst of all kinds of such trouble—it was trouble about money. Carlyle's father rose and said bitingly: " Give the hireling his wages and let him go."

Jesus' point is that the man who works only for reward thinks more of the money than anything else; the man who works for love thinks more of the people he is trying to serve than anything else. Jesus was the good shepherd, who so loved His sheep that for their safety He would risk, and one day give, His life.

We may note two further points before we leave this passage. Jesus describes Himself as the *good* shepherd. Now, in Greek, there are two words for good. There is the word *agathos* which simply describes the moral quality of a thing; there is the word *kalos* which means that a thing or a person is not only good; but in the goodness there is a quality of winsomeness, loveliness, attractiveness which makes it a lovely thing. Now, when Jesus is described as the *good* shepherd, the word is *kalos*. In Jesus there is more than efficiency, and more than fidelity; there is a certain loveliness. Sometimes in a village or town people speak about *the good doctor*. When they speak like that they are not thinking only of the doctor's efficiency and skill as a physician; they are thinking of the sympathy and the kindness and the graciousness which he brought with him, and which made him the friend of all. In the picture of Jesus as the Good Shepherd there is loveliness as well as strength and power.

The second point is this. In the parable the flock is the Church of Christ. And the flock suffers from a double danger. It is always liable to attack from outside from the wolves and the robbers and the marauders. It is always liable to trouble from the inside from the false shepherd. The Church runs a double danger. It is always under attack from outside. It often suffers from the tragedy of bad leadership, from the disaster of shepherds who see their calling as a career and not as a means of service. The second danger is by far the worse; because, if the shepherd is faithful and good, there is a strong defence from the attack from outside; but if the shepherd is faithless and a hireling, then the foes from outside can penetrate into and destroy the flock. The Church's first essential is a leadership which is based on the example of Jesus Christ.

THE ULTIMATE UNITY

John 10: 16.

> " But I have other sheep which are not of this fold. These too I must bring in, and they will hear my voice; and they will become one flock, and there will be one shepherd."

ONE of the hardest things in the world to unlearn is exclusiveness. Once a people, or a section of a people, gets the idea that they are specially privileged and that they are different from other people, it is very difficult for them to realize that the privileges which they believed belonged to them and to them only are in fact open to all men. That is what the Jews never learned. They believed that they were God's chosen people and that God had no use for any other people or for any other nation. They believed that, at the best, other nations were designed to be their slaves, and, at the worst, that other nations were destined for elimination and obliteration from the scheme of things. But here Jesus is saying that there will come a day when He will gather in all men and when all men will know Him as their shepherd.

Even the Old Testament is not without its glimpses of that day. One great prophet whom we know as Isaiah had that very dream. It was his conviction that God had given Israel for *a light to the Gentiles* (*Isaiah* 42: 6; 49: 6; 56: 8). Always there had been some lonely voices which insisted that God was not the exclusive property of Israel, but that Israel's destiny was to make God known to all men.

At first sight, it might seem that the New Testament speaks with two voices on this subject. It may well be that there are some passages of the New Testament which trouble us and perplex us a little as we read them. As Matthew tells the story, when Jesus sent out His disciples, He said to them: " Go not into the way of the Gentiles, and into any city of the Samaritans enter ye not; but go rather to the lost sheep of the house of Israel" (*Matthew* 10: 5, 6). When the Syro-Phœnician woman appealed to Jesus for help, His first answer was that He was not sent but unto the lost sheep of the house of Israel (*Matthew* 15: 24). But there is so much that is to be set on the other side. Jesus Himself stayed and taught in Samaria (*John* 4: 40); He declared that descent from Abraham was no guarantee of entry into the kingdom (*John* 8: 39). It was of a Roman centurion that Jesus said that He had never seen such faith in Israel (*Matthew* 8: 10); it was a Samaritan leper who alone returned to give thanks (*Luke* 17: 19); it was the Samaritan traveller who showed the kindness that all men must copy (*Luke* 10: 37); many would come from the east and the west and the north and the south to sit down in the Kingdom of God (*Matthew* 8: 11; *Luke* 13: 28); the command in the end was to go out and to preach the gospel to all nations (*Mark* 16: 5; *Matthew* 28: 19); Jesus was, not the light of the Jews, but the light of the world (*John* 8: 12). Why the difference? What is the explanation of the sayings which seem to limit the work of Jesus to the Jews? The explanation is in reality very simple. The *ultimate* aim of Jesus was the world for God. But any great commander knows that he must in the first instance limit his objectives. If he tries to attack on too wide a front, if he tries to strike everywhere at the one time, he only scatters his forces, diffuses his strength, and gains success nowhere. In order to win an ultimately complete victory he must begin by concentrating his forces at certain limited and chosen objectives. That is what Jesus did. When He came Himself, and when He sent out His disciples, He deliberately chose the limited objective. Had He gone here, there and everywhere, had He sent His disciples out with no limitation to their sphere of work, nothing would have happened and nothing would have been achieved. At the moment He consciously and deliberately concentrated on the Jewish nation, but the ultimate aim was the gathering of the whole world into His love.

There are three great truths in this passage.

(i) It is only in Jesus Christ that the world can become one. Egerton Young was the first missionary to the Red Indians. In Saskatchewan he went out to find them and he told them of the love of God, the Father. To the Indians it was like a new revelation. When the missionary had told his message, an old chief said: " When you spoke of the

great Spirit just now, did I hear you say, ' Our Father '? "
" Yes," said Egerton Young. " That is very new and
sweet to me," said the chief. " We never thought of the
great Spirit as Father. We heard Him in the thunder; we
saw Him in the lightning, the tempest and the blizzard, and
we were afraid. So when you tell us that the great Spirit is
our Father, that is very beautiful to us." The old man
paused, and then he went on, as a glimpse of glory suddenly
shone on him. " Missionary, did you say that the great
Spirit is *your* Father? " " Yes," said the missionary'
" And," said the chief, " did you say that He is *the Indians*'
Father? " " I did," said the missionary. " Then," said
the old chief, like a man on whom a dawn of joy had burst,
" *you and I are brothers!*" The only possible unity for men
is in their common sonship with God. In the world there is
the division between nation and nation; in the nation there
is the division between class and class. There can never be
one nation; and there can never be one class. The only
thing which can cross the barriers and wipe out the dis-
tinctions is the gospel of Jesus Christ telling men of the
universal fatherhood of God.

(ii) In the Authorised Version, as it stands, there is a
mistranslation. The Authorised Version has it: " There
shall be one *fold* and one shepherd." That mistranslation
goes back to Jerome and the Vulgate. And on that mistranslation the Roman Catholic Church has based the
teaching that, since there is only one fold, there can only
be one Church, the Roman Catholic Church, and that,
outside the Church, there is no salvation. But the real
translation beyond all possible doubt is: " There shall be
one *flock*, and one shepherd," or, even better, " They shall
become one flock and there shall be one shepherd." The
unity comes from the fact, not that all the sheep are forced
into one fold, but that all the sheep hear, and answer and
obey one shepherd. The unity is not an ecclesiastical unity;
the unity is a unity of loyalty to Jesus Christ. There is an
obvious human illustration of that. The British Common-

wealth of Nations is not a unity in which each nation has the same form of government, and is under the same administration. The countries which compose the Commonwealth are quite independent; they can do what they like; they have their own government; but they are united by a common loyalty to the Queen and to the Crown. The fact that there is one flock does not mean that there can only be one Church, one method of worship, one form of ecclesiastical administration. But it does mean that all the different Churches are united by and in a common loyalty to Jesus Christ. The Christian unity is not based on obedience to any kind of ecclesiastical procedure; it is based on loyalty to a person, to Jesus Christ.

(iii) But this saying of Jesus becomes very personal; for this is a dream of Jesus which every one of us can help Him to realise. Men cannot hear without a preacher. The other sheep cannot be gathered in unless someone goes out to bring them in. Here there is set before us the tremendous missionary task of the Church. And we must not think of that only in terms of what we call *foreign* missions. If we know someone here and now who is outside the love of Christ, Christ wants that man, and we can find him for Christ. The dream of Christ depends on us. It is we who can help Him to make the world one flock whose Shepherd is Christ.

LOVE'S CHOICE

John 10: 17, 18.

> " The reason why my Father loves me is that I lay down my life that I may take it again. No one takes it from me, but I lay it down of my own free will. I have full authority to lay it down, and I have full authority to take it again. I have received this injunction from my Father."

THERE are few passages in the New Testament which in so short a compass tell us so much about Jesus.

(i) It tells us that Jesus saw His whole life as an act of obedience to God. God had given Him a task to do, and He was prepared to carry out that task to the end, even if the doing so meant death. Jesus was in a unique relationship to God. We can only describe that relationship by saying that He was the Son of God. But that relationship did not give Him the right to do what He liked; it depended on the fact that, cost what it may, He always did what God liked. For Jesus, to be the Son of God was at one and the same time the greatest of privileges and the greatest of responsibilities. Sonship for Him, and sonship for us, can never be based on anything except obedience.

(ii) It tells us that Jesus always saw the Cross and the glory together. He never doubted that He must die; and He equally never doubted that He would rise again. The reason for this confidence was Jesus' confidence in God. He never believed that God would abandon Him. He believed that obedience to God was bound to bring suffering; but He also believed that obedience to God was bound to bring glory. And further, He believed that that suffering was but for a moment, and that the glory was for all eternity. All life is based on the fact that anything worth getting is hard to get. There is a price to be paid for anything. Scholarship can only be bought at the price of study; skill in any craft or technique can only be bought at the price of practice; eminence in any sport can only be bought at the price of training and discipline. The world is full of people who have missed their destiny because they would not pay the price. No one can take the easy way and enter into any kind of glory or greatness; no one can take the hard way and fail to find glory and greatness.

(iii) It tells us in a way that we cannot possibly mistake that Jesus' death was entirely voluntary. That is a fact that Jesus stresses again and again. In the garden He bade His would-be defender to put up his sword. If He had wished to do so, He could have called in the hosts of heaven to His defence (*Matthew* 26: 53). Before Pilate Jesus made it quite clear that Pilate was not condemning Him, but that He was accepting death (*John* 19: 9, 10). Jesus was not the victim of circumstance. He was not like some animal, dragged to the sacrifice, unwilling to go, struggling against the hands of the priest, unknowing what was happening. Jesus voluntarily laid down His life because He chose to do so. It is told that in the First World War there was a young French soldier who was seriously wounded. His arm was so badly smashed that it had to be amputated. He was a magnificent specimen of young manhood, and the surgeon was grieved that the lad must go through life maimed. So he waited beside the bedside of the lad to tell him the bad news when he recovered consciousness. When the lad's eyes opened, the surgeon said to him: " I am sorry to tell you that you have lost your arm." " Sir," said the lad, " I did not lose it; I gave it—for France." Jesus was not helplessly caught up in a mesh of circumstances from which He could not break free. Apart from anything else, apart from any divine power and aid that He might have called in, it is quite clear that to the end He could have turned back and saved His life. He did not lose His life: He gave it. He was not killed: He chose to die. The Cross was not thrust upon Him: He willingly accepted it—for us.

MADMAN OR SON OF GOD

John 10: 19-21

> There was again a division among the Jews because of these words. Many of them said: " He has an evil spirit, and He is mad. Why do you listen to Him? " Others said: " These are not the words of a man possessed by an evil spirit. Can a man with an evil spirit open the eyes of the blind? "

THE people who listened to Jesus on this occasion were confronted with a dilemma which is for ever confronting men. Either Jesus was a megalomaniac madman, or He was the Son of God. There is no escape from that choice.

If a man speaks about God and about himself in the way in which Jesus spoke, either that man is completely deluded, or else he is profoundly right. The claims which Jesus made are either the claims of insanity or the claims of divinity. How can we assure ourselves that the claims of Jesus were indeed justified, and were not the claims of the world's greatest delusion?

(i) The words of Jesus are not the words of a madman. We could cite witness after witness to prove that men have always been well aware that the teaching of Jesus is in fact the supreme sanity. In a book entitled *What I believe* certain people set down the beliefs which they held to be central. Lionel Curtis said that he believed that the aim of mankind should be to make the world what he calls *The Commonwealth of God*. He goes on, " When asked what I mean by such a commonwealth, I reply: ' The Sermon on the Mount reduced to political principles.' " Madame Chiang Kai-shek said: " How then are we to follow the tenets of the moral law in order to build a more moral world? The Sermon on the Mount is my answer, and, to me, the whole answer." The truth is that it is the witness of thinking men and women in every generation that the teaching of Jesus is the one sane thing which brings sanity into a mad world. He is the one voice which speaks God's sense in the midst of man's delusions. There is no madness there.

(ii) The deeds of Jesus are not the deeds of a madman. He healed the sick and fed the hungry and comforted the sorrowing. The madness of megalomania is essentially selfish. It seeks for nothing but its own glory and its own prestige. But Jesus' life was spent in doing things for others. As the Jews themselves said, a man who was mad would not be able to open the eyes of the blind.

(iii) The effect of Jesus is not the effect of a madman. The simple undeniable fact is that there have been millions upon millions of people whose lives have been changed by the power of Jesus Christ, weak who have become strong, selfish who have become selfless, defeated who have become victorious, worried who have become serene, bad who have become good. It is not madness which produces such a change, but perfect wisdom and perfect sanity.

The choice remains—Jesus was either mad or divine. And no honest person can review the evidence and come to any other conclusion than that Jesus brought into the world, not a deluded madness, but the perfect sanity of God.

THE CLAIM AND THE PROMISE

John 10: 22-28

It was the Festival of the Dedication in Jerusalem. I was wintry weather, and Jesus was walking in the Temple precincts in Solomon's Porch. So the Jews surrounded Him. " How long," they said to Him, " are you going to keep us hanging in suspense? If you really are God's Anointed One, tell us plainly." Jesus answered them: " I did tell you and you did not believe me. The works that I do in the name of my Father, these are evidence about me. But you do not believe because you are not among the number of my sheep. My sheep hear my voice, and I know them, and tney follow me. And I give them eternal life, and they will never perish, and no one will snatch them from my hand."

JOHN begins by giving us both the date and the place of this discussion. The date was the Festival of the Dedication. The Festival of the Dedication was the latest of all the great Jewish Festivals to be founded. It was sometimes called The Festival of Lights; and its Jewish name was *Hanukkah*. Its date is the 25th of the Jewish month called Chislew. Chislew corresponds with the English month December; and therefore this Festival falls very near our Christmas time. It is still universally observed by the Jews.

The origin of the Festival of the Dedication lies in one of the greatest times of ordeal and heroism in Jewish history. There was a king of Syria called Antiochus Epiphanes who reigned in Syria from 175 to 164 B.C. He was a lover and a devotee of all things Greek. He decided that he would eliminate the Jewish religion once and for all, and introduce Greek ways and Greek thoughts, Greek religion and Greek gods into Palestine. At first he tried to do so by peaceful penetration of ideas. Some of the Jews welcomed these new ways, but most of them were stubbornly loyal to their ancestral faith. It was in 170 B.C. that the deluge really broke. In that year Antiochus attacked Jerusalem. It was said that 80,000 Jews perished, and as many were sold into slavery. 1,800 talents—a talent is equal to £240— were stolen from the Temple treasury. It became a capital offence to possess a copy of the law, or to circumcise a child; and mothers who did circumcise their children were crucified with their children hanging round their necks. The Temple Courts were profaned; the Temple chambers were turned into brothels; and finally Antiochus took the dreadful step of turning the great altar of the burnt-offering into an altar to Olympian Zeus; and on it he proceeded to offer swine's flesh to the pagan gods. The Temple courts were deliberately and terribly polluted. It was then that Judas Maccabaeus and his brothers arose to fight their epic fight for freedom and to deliver their country. It was in 164 B.C. that the struggle was finally won; and in that year the Temple was cleansed and purified. The altar was rebuilt; the robes and the utensils were replaced, after three years of pollution. It was to commemorate that purification of the Temple that the Feast of the Dedication was instituted. Judas Maccabaeus enacted that " the days of the dedication of the altar should be kept in their season from year to year, by the space of eight days, from the five and twentieth day of the month of Chislew, with gladness and joy" (I *Maccabees* 4: 59). For that reason the Festival was sometimes called The Festival of the Dedication of the Altar, and sometimes the Memorial of the Purification of the Temple.

But as we have already seen, it had still another name. It was often called The Festival of Lights. There were great illuminations in the Temple; and there were also illuminations—which can be seen to this day—in every Jewish home. In the window of every Jewish house there were set lights. According to Shammai, eight lights were set in the window, and the lights were reduced each day by one until on the last day one was left burning. According to Hillel, one light was kindled on the first day, and it was increased each day by one until on the last day eight were burning. We can still see these lights in the windows of every devout Jewish home to this day.

These lights had two significances. First, they were said to be a reminder that at the first celebrating of the Festival the light of freedom had come back to Israel. Second, they were traced back to a very old legend. It was told that when the Temple had been purified, and when the great seven-branched candlestick came to be re-lit, only one little cruse of unpolluted oil for the lamps could be found. This one cruse was still intact, and still sealed with the impress of the ring of the High Priest. By all normal measures, there was only oil enough in that cruse to light the lamps for one single day. But by a miracle the oil in that one little cruse lasted for eight days, until the new oil had been prepared according to the correct formula and had been consecrated for its sacred use. So it was said that for eight days the lights burned in the Temple and in the homes of the people in memory of the cruse which God had made to last for eight days instead of one.

It is not without significance that it must have been very close to this time of illumination that Jesus said: " I am the Light of the world." When all the lights were being kindled in the city in memory of the freedom which had been won to worship God in the only true way, Jesus said: " I am the Light of the world; I alone can light men into the knowledge and the presence of God."

John also gives us the place of this discussion. It took

place in Solomon's Porch. The first court which he who entered the Temple precincts came to was the Court of the Gentiles. Along two sides of it there ran two magnificent colonnades called the Royal Porch and Solomon's Porch. They were rows of magnificent pillars almost forty feet high, and roofed over. People walked there to pray and meditate; and Rabbis strolled there as they talked to their students and expounded the doctrines of the faith. It was there that Jesus was walking, because, as John says with a pictorial touch, " it was wintry weather." So at this time of national memory and thanksgiving, and among the Rabbis and their students, this discussion took place.

THE CLAIM AND THE PROMISE

John 10: 22-28 (*continued*)

As Jesus walked in Solomon's Porch the Jews came to Him. " How long," they said to Him, " are you going to keep us in suspense? Tell us plainly, Are you or are you not God's promised Anointed One? " There is no doubt that behind that question there were two attitudes of mind. There were those who genuinely wished to know. They were on an eager tip-toe of expectation. Their idea of God's Anointed One would not be Jesus' idea. But they were eager to know if at last the promised and longed-for deliverer had come. But there were others; and beyond a doubt they asked the question as a trap. They wished to inveigle Jesus into making a statement which could be twisted, either into a charge of blasphemy with which their own courts could deal, or a charge of insurrection with which the Roman governor would deal.

Jesus' answer was that He had already told them who He was. True, He had not done so in so many words; for, as John tells the story, Jesus' two great claims had been made in private. To the Samaritan woman He had revealed Himself as the Messiah (*John* 4: 26) and to the man born blind He had claimed to be the Son of God (*John* 9: 37). But there are some claims which do not need to be made in words, especially to an audience well-qualified and trained to perceive them. There were two things about Jesus which left His claim beyond all doubt whether He stated it in words or not. First, there were His *deeds*. It was Isaiah's dream of the golden age: " Then the eyes of the blind shall be opened, and the ears of the deaf shall be unstopped. Then shall the lame man leap as an hart, and the tongue of the dumb sing " (*Isaiah* 35: 5, 6). That is exactly what Jesus was doing; every one of His miracles was a claim which shouted out that the age of God had dawned, that the Messiah had come. Second, there were His *words*. It had been Moses' promise and forecast that God would raise up the Prophet who must be listened to (*Deuteronomy* 18: 15). The very accent of authority with which Jesus spoke, the way in which He regally abrogated the old law and put His own teaching in its place, was a claim that God was speaking in Him, that in Him the incarnate voice of God had come to men. Anyone who listened to Jesus speak, and who watched Jesus act, had no need of any verbal claim. The words and deeds of Jesus were one continuous claim to the Anointed One of God.

But the great majority of the Jews had not accepted that claim. As we have seen, in Palestine the sheep knew their own shepherd's special call and answered it. They belonged to the shepherd and they knew his voice. These Jews were not of Jesus' flock. In the Fourth Gospel there is behind it all a doctrine of predestination. Things were happening all the time as God meant them to happen. John is really saying that these Jews were predestined not to follow and not to answer to Jesus. Somehow or other the whole New Testament keeps two opposite ideas in balance—the fact that everything happens within the purpose of God, and yet everything happens in such a way that man's free-will is responsible. These Jews had made themselves such that they were predestined not to accept Jesus; and yet, as

John sees it, that does not make them any the less to be condemned.

But though they did not accept Jesus there were those who did; and to those who did Jesus offered and promised three things.

(i) He promised them *eternal life*. He promised them a foretaste of the life which is the very life of God. He promised that if they accepted Him as Master and Lord, if they became members of His flock, all the littleness of earthly life would be gone, and they would know the splendour and the magnificence of the life of God.

(ii) He promised them a *life that would know no end*. They would never perish. Death for them would be nothing; death would not be the end but the beginning. They would never be obliterated or go out into the dark. They would know the glory of indestructible life.

(iii) He promised them a *life that was secure*. Nothing could snatch them from His hand. This would not mean that they would be saved from sorrow, saved from suffering and saved from death; but it would mean that in the sorest moment and the darkest hour they would still be conscious of the everlasting arms underneath and about them. They would know a security which not all earth's perils and alarms could shake. Even in a world crashing to disaster they would know the serenity of God.

THE TREMENDOUS TRUST AND THE TREMENDOUS CLAIM

John 10: 29, 30.

> My Father, who gave them to me, is greater than all; and no one can snatch them from the hand of the Father. I and the Father are one.

THIS passage shows us at one and the same time the tremendous trust and the tremendous claim of Jesus.

Jesus' trust was something which traced everything back to God. He has just been speaking about *His* sheep and

His flock; He has just been saying that no one will ever snatch His own from *His* hand, that He is the shepherd who will keep the sheep for ever safe. At first sight, and if He had stopped there, it would have seemed that Jesus put His whole trust in His own attraction and in His own keeping power. But now we see the other side of it. It is His Father who gave Him His sheep; it is in His Father's hand that both He and His sheep are. Jesus was so sure of Himself because He was so sure of God. Jesus' attitude to life was not self-confidence, but God-confidence. Jesus was secure, not in His own power, but in God's power. Jesus was so certain of ultimate safety and ultimate victory, not because he arrogated all power to Himself, but because He assigned all power to God.

And now we come to the supreme claim. " I and the Father are one," said Jesus. What did Jesus mean by this? Is it indeed absolute mystery, or can we understand at least a little of it? Are we driven to interpret this in terms of essence and hypostasis and all the rest of the metaphysical and philosophic notions about which the makers of the creeds fought and argued, and struggled and battled? Has one to be a profound theologian and a trained philosopher to grasp even a fragment of the meaning of this tremendous statement?

If we will go to the Bible itself for the interpretation of this statement, we will find that it is in fact so simple that the simplest mind can grasp it. What did Jesus mean by saying that He and the Father are one? Let us go on ahead and turn to the seventeenth chapter of John's gospel. There John tells us of the prayer of Jesus for His own people before He went to His death. He prayed thus: " Holy Father, keep through Thine own name those whom Thou hast given me, *that they may be one as we are* " (*John* 17: 11). There it is clear that Jesus conceived of the unity of Christian with Christian as the same as His own unity with God. He says so in so many words. In the same passage He goes on: " Neither pray I for these alone, but for them also which shall believe on me through their word; *that they all may be one,* as Thou Father art in me, and I in Thee; *that they also may be one in us;* that the world may believe that Thou hast sent me. And the glory which Thou gavest me I have given them; *that they may be one even as we are one* " (*John* 17: 20-22). There Jesus is saying with simplicity and with clarity which none can mistake that the end of the Christian life is that Christians should be one as He and His Father are one.

Now what is the unity which should exist between Christian and Christian? What is it that makes the Christian one with his fellow Christians? The secret of that unity is *love*. " A new commandment give I unto you, That ye love one another; as I have loved you, that ye also love one another " (*John* 13: 34). Christians are one because they love one another. Even so, Jesus is one with God because of His love of God. But we can go further. What is the only test and proof and guarantee of love? Let us go again to the words of Jesus. " If ye keep my commandments, ye shall abide in my love; even as I have kept my Father's commandments and abide in His love " (*John* 15: 9, 10). " If any man love me, he will keep my words " (*John* 14: 23, 24). " If ye love me, keep my commandments " (*John* 14: 15). " He that hath my commandments and keepeth them, he it is that loveth me " (*John* 14: 21).

Here is the essence of the matter. The bond of unity is love; the proof of love is obedience. Christians are one with each other when they are bound by the bond of unity, and obey the words of Christ. Jesus is one with God, because as no other person ever did, He obeyed God and He loved God. His unity with God is a unity of perfect love, issuing in a perfect obedience.

When Jesus said: " I and the Father are one," He was not moving in the world of philosophy and metaphysics and abstractions; He was moving in the world of *personal relationships.* No one can really understand what a phrase like "a unity of essence" means; but any one can understand what a unity of heart means. Jesus' unity with God came from the twin facts of perfect love and perfect obedience. He was one with God because He loved God perfectly and obeyed God perfectly. And He came to this world to make us what He is.

INVITING THE ACID TEST

John 10: 31-39

> The Jews again lifted up stones to stone Him. Jesus said to them: " I have showed you many lovely deeds, which came from my Father. For which of these deeds are you trying to stone me?" The Jews answered Him: " It is not for any lovely deed that we propose to stone you; it is for insulting God, and because you, being a man, make yourself God." " Does it not stand written in your law," Jesus answered them, " ' I said you are gods'? If He called those to whom the word came gods—and the scripture cannot be destroyed— are you going to say about me, whom the Father consecrated and despatched into the world: ' You insult God,' because I said: ' I am the Son of God '? If I do not do the works of my Father, do not believe me. But if I do, even if you do not believe me, believe the works, that you may know and recognize that the Father is in me, and I am in the Father." They again tried to lay violent hands on Him, but He evaded their grasp.

To the Jews Jesus' statement that He and the Father were one was blasphemy, insult against God. It was the invasion by a man of the place which belonged to God alone. It was a human being claiming equality with God. The Jewish law laid down the penalty of stoning for blasphemy. " And he that blasphemeth the name of the Lord, he shall surely be put to death, and all the congregation shall certainly stone him " (*Leviticus* 24: 16). So the Jews made their preparations to stone Jesus. The Greek really means that they went and fetched stones to fling at Him. Jesus met their hostility with three arguments.

(i) He told them that He had spent all His days doing lovely things, healing the sick, and feeding the hungry, and comforting the sorrowing, deeds so full of help and power and beauty that they obviously came from God. For which of these deeds did they wish to stone Him? Their answer was that it was not for anything He did they wished to stone Him, but for the claims that He was making.

(ii) What was that claim? The claim was that He was the Son of God. To meet that claim Jesus used two arguments. The first is a purely Jewish argument which is difficult for us to understand. Jesus quoted *Psalm 82: 6.* That psalm is a warning to unjust judges; it is a warning to those to whom judgment has been committed that they should cease from unjust ways and that they should defend the poor and the innocent. The appeal concludes: " I have said, Ye are gods; and all of you are the children of the most High." The judge is commissioned by God to bring God's help and justice to men. He is God to men. This idea comes out very clearly in certain of the regulations in *Exodus. Exodus* 21: 1-6 tells how the Hebrew servant may go free in the seventh year. Verse 6 says: " Then his master shall bring him unto the *judges.*" But in the Hebrew, the word which is translated *judges* is actually *elohim,*which means *gods.* The same form of expression is used in *Exodus* 22: 9, 28. Even scripture said of men who were specially commissioned to some task by God that they were gods. So Jesus said: " If scripture can speak like that about men, why should I not speak so about myself? "

Jesus claimed two things for Himself. (*a*) He was *consecrated* by God to a special task. The word for *to consecrate* is *hagiazein.* It is the verb from which there comes the adjective *hagios,* which means *holy.* Now this word always has the idea of rendering a person or a place or a thing different from other persons and places and things, because it is set aside for a special purpose or task. A thing or a person is *holy* because it or he has been set aside for a special task which is different from the ordinary tasks of everyday

life. So, for instance, the Sabbath is *holy* (*Exodus* 20: 11).
It is different from other days, because it is set aside for a
special purpose. The altar is *holy* (*Leviticus* 16: 19). The
altar is not like any other piece of stone, or any other
structure, because it is constructed and set apart for a
special task. The priests are *holy* (2 *Chronicles* 26: 18).
They are different from other men, in that they are separated for a special work and a special task. The prophet is
holy (*Jeremiah* 1: 5). He is different from other men because he has been given a different and a special task.
When Jesus said that God had *consecrated* Him, made Him
holy, He meant that God had set Him apart from other men,
made Him different from other men, because He had given
Him a special task to do. The very fact that Jesus used
this word shows how conscious He was of a special task
given Him by God to do. (*b*) Jesus said that God had
despatched Him into the world. The word that is used is
the word which would be used for sending a messenger, or
an ambassador, or an army, or a task-force. When Jesus
used the word He showed that He did not so much think of
Himself as *coming* into the world, as being *sent* into the
world. His coming was an act of God; He came to re
present God; He came to do the task which God had given
Him to do.

So Jesus said: " In the old days it was possible for
scripture to speak of judges as gods, because they were
commissioned by God to bring His truth and justice into
the world. Now I have been set apart for a special task;
I have been despatched into the world by God; how can you
then object if I call myself the Son of God? I am only
doing what scripture does." That is one of those biblical
arguments the force of which it is difficult for us to feel.
But it is an argument which to a Jewish Rabbi would have
been entirely convincing. It was just the kind of argument,
an argument founded on a word of scripture, which the
Rabbis loved to use and found most unanswerable.

(iii) Then Jesus went on to invite the acid test. " I do not ask you," He said in effect, " to accept my words. But I do ask you to accept my deeds." A word is something about which a man can argue; but a deed is something about which there is no argument. A man's verbal claims for himself may well be doubted and discussed; but a man's deeds admit of no discussion. Jesus is the perfect teacher in that He does not base His claims on what He said, but on what He is and does. He invites the acid test, the test of deeds. His invitation to the Jews was to base their verdict on Him, not on what He said, but on what He did. And that is a test which all His followers ought to be able to meet. The tragedy of the Church is that so few can meet it, still less invite it.

PEACE BEFORE THE STORM

John 10: 40, 41

> And He went away again to the other side of Jordan, to the place where John first used to baptize; and He stayed there. And many came to Him, and they kept saying: " John did no sign; but everything John said about this man is true." And then many believed in Him.

FOR Jesus the time was running out; but Jesus knew His time. He would not recklessly court danger and throw His life away; nor would He in cowardice avoid danger and preserve His life. But He desired to retire to quietness before the final struggle. Jesus always came out of the presence of God into the presence of men. He always nerved and armed Himself to meet men by first meeting God. That is why He retired to the other side of Jordan. He was not running away: He was preparing Himself for the final contest.

But the place to which He went is most significant. He went to the place where John had been accustomed to baptize; He went to the place where He Himself had been baptized. It was there that the voice of God had come to

Him and had assured Him that He had taken the right decision and was on the right way. There is everything to be said for a man returning every now and then to the place where he had the supreme experience of his life. When Jacob was up against it, when things had gone wrong and badly wrong, Jacob went back to Bethel (*Genesis* 35: 1-5). When he needed God, he went back to the place where he had found God. Jesus, before the end, went back to the place at which the beginning had happened. It would often do our souls a world of good if we made a pilgrimage to the place where God found us and where we found God.

Even on the far side of Jordan the Jews came to Jesus, and they too thought of John. They remembered that John had spoken with the words of a prophet; but he had done no mighty deeds. They saw that there was a difference between Jesus and John. To John's proclamation Jesus added God's power. John could diagnose the situation; Jesus brought the power to deal with the situation. These Jews had looked on John as a prophet. Now they saw that what John had foretold of Jesus was true; and many of them believed.

It so often happens that a man for whom a great future is painted, and who sets out with the hopes of men upon him, disappoints that future and belies these hopes. But the greatness of Jesus was that He was even greater than John had said that He would be. Jesus is the one person who never disappoints those who set their hopes upon Him. He is the one person in whom the dream always comes true.

ON THE ROAD TO GLORY

John 11: 1-5

> There was a man Lazarus, who came from Bethany from the village where Mary and her sister Martha lived, and he was ill. It was Mary who had anointed the Lord with perfumed ointment, and who had wiped His feet with her hair, and it was her brother Lazarus who was ill. So the sisters sent a message to Jesus.

" Lord," they said, " See! The one you love is ill."
When Jesus heard the message, He said: " This
illness is not going to prove fatal; rather it has
happened for the sake of the glory of God, so that
God's Son should be glorified by means of it." Jesus
loved Martha and her sister and Lazarus.

IT is one of the most precious things in the world to have
a house and a home into which one can go at any time
and find rest and understanding and peace and love.
That was doubly true for Jesus, for He had no home of
His own. He had nowhere to lay His head (*Luke* 9: 58).
In the home at Bethany Jesus had just such a place.
There, there were three people who loved Him; and there
He could go for rest from the tension of life.

The greatest gift that any human being can give to
another is the gift of understanding and of peace. To have
someone to whom we can go at any time, and know that
they will not laugh at our dreams, or misunderstand our
confidences is a most wonderful thing. To have somewhere
to go to where the tensions of life are relaxed in peace is a
lovely thing. It is open to us all to make our own homes
like that. This is something which does not cost money,
and which does not need lavish and costly hospitality. It
costs only the understanding heart. Sir William Watson,
in his poem *Wordsworth's Grave,* paid a great tribute to
Wordsworth:

" What hadst thou that could make so large amends,
      For all thou hadst not and thy peers possessed?
Motion and fire, swift means to radiant ends?—
      Thou hadst for weary feet, the gift of rest."

No man can have a greater gift to offer to his fellow men
than the gift of rest for weary feet; and that is the gift
which Jesus found in the house in Bethany, where Martha
and Mary and Lazarus lived.

The name *Lazarus* means *God is my help,* and is the same
name as the name *Eleazar*. Lazarus fell ill, and the sisters
sent to Jesus a message that it was so. It is a lovely thing

93

to note that the sisters' message included no request to Jesus to come to Bethany. They knew that such a request was unnecessary. They knew that the simple statement that they were in need would bring Him to them. Augustine noted this, and said that it was sufficient that Jesus should know; for it is not possible that any man should at one and the same time love a friend and desert him. C. F. Andrews, somewhere, tells of two friends who served together in the First World War. One of them was wounded and left lying helpless and in pain in no man's land between the trenches. The other, in the dark, at peril of his life crawled out to help his friend; and, when he reached him, the wounded man looked up and said simply: " I knew you would come." The simple fact of human need brings Jesus to our side in the twinkling of an eye.

When Jesus came to Bethany He knew what he was doing. He knew that whatever was wrong with Lazarus He had power to deal with it. But He went on to say something. He said that this sickness had happened for God's glory and for His. Now this was true in a double sense—and Jesus knew it. (i) The cure would undoubtedly enable men to see the glory of God in action. (ii) But there was more to it than that. Again and again in the Fourth Gospel Jesus talks of His glory in connection with the Cross. John tells us in 7: 39 that the Spirit had not yet come because Jesus was not yet *glorified*, that is to say, because Jesus had not yet died upon His Cross. When the Greeks came to Him, Jesus said: " The hour is come when the Son of Man should be *glorified* " (*John* 12: 23). And it was of His Cross that He spoke, for He went straight on to speak of the corn of wheat which must fall into the ground and die. In *John* 12: 16 John says that the disciples remembered these things after Jesus had been *glorified*, that is after He had died and risen again. In the Fourth Gospel it is clear that Jesus regarded the Cross both as His supreme glory and as the way to glory. So when Jesus said that the cure of Lazarus would glorify Him, He was showing that He knew perfectly well that to go to Bethany and to cure Lazarus was to take a step which would end in the Cross—as indeed it did.

Jesus, with open eyes, accepted the Cross to help His friend. Jesus knew the cost of helping man, and Jesus was well prepared to pay it.

When some trial or some affliction comes upon us, especially if that trial and affliction are the direct result of fidelity to Jesus Christ, it would make all the difference in the world if we saw the Cross we have to bear as our glory and the way to a greater glory still. Surely it is true that a man can have no greater glory than suffering for Christ. And surely, if we believe what Jesus told us, we can be sure that he who takes up his cross and follows Jesus, will in the end receive the glory and the crown. For Jesus there was no other way to glory than through the Cross; and so it must ever be with those who follow Him.

TIME ENOUGH BUT NOT TOO MUCH

John II: 6-10

> Now, when Jesus had received the news that Lazarus was ill, He continued to stay where He was for two days. But after that He said to His disciples: " Let us go to Judaea again." His disciples said to Him: " Rabbi, things had got to a stage when the Jews were trying to find a way to stone you, and do you propose to go back there?" Jesus answered: " Are there not twelve hours in the day? If a man walks in the day-time, he does not stumble because he has the light of this world. But if a man walks in the night-time, he does stumble because the light is not in him."

WE may find it strange that John shows us Jesus staying two whole days where He was when He received the news about Lazarus. Different commentators have advanced different reasons to explain this delay. (i) It has been suggested that Jesus waited so that when He arrived Lazarus would be indisputably dead. (ii) It has therefore been suggested that Jesus waited because the delay would make the miracle which He proposed to perform all the more impressive. The glory of raising to life a man who had been dead for four days would be all the greater. (iii) The real reason why John tells the story in this way is that John always shows us Jesus taking action entirely on His own initiative, and not on the persuasion of anyone else. In the story of the turning of the water into wine at Cana of Galilee (*John* 2: 1-11) John shows us Mary coming to Jesus and telling Him of the problem. Jesus' first answer to Mary is: " Don't bother about this. Let me handle it in my own way." He takes action, not because He is persuaded or compelled to do so, but entirely on his own initiative. When John tells the story of Jesus' brothers trying to date Him into going to Jerusalem (*John* 7: 1-10), he shows us Jesus at first refusing to go to Jerusalem and then going in His own good time. It is always John's aim to show that Jesus did things, not because He was pressed or persuaded or compelled to do them, but because He chose to do them in His own good time. That is what John is doing here. He is showing us Jesus doing things in His own chosen time. It is a warning to us. So often we would like Jesus to do things in our way; we must leave Him to do them in His own way.

When Jesus finally announced that He was going to Judaea, His disciples were shocked and staggered. They remembered that the last time He was there the Jews had tried to find a way to kill Him. To go to Judaea at that time seemed to them—as indeed humanly speaking it was—the surest way to commit suicide.

Then Jesus said something which contains a great and permanent truth. " Are there not," He asked, " twelve hours in the day? " There are three great truths implied in that question.

(i) A day cannot finish before it ends. There are twelve hours in the day, and these twelve hours will be played out no matter what happens. The day's period is fixed, and nothing will shorten or lengthen it. If a man chooses to serve God, then that man's day will not end before God wishes it to end. In God's economy of time a man has his day, whether that day be short or long.

(ii) If there are twelve hours in the day there is time enough for everything a man should do. There is no need for a rushed haste. If a man uses these twelve hours all that he ought to do can be done in them. Put it that way, and twelve hours is a long time, time enough to do the work which God has given us to do.

(iii) But, even if there are twelve hours in the day, there are *only* twelve hours. They cannot be extended. And, therefore, time cannot be wasted. There is time enough, but there is not too much time. The time we have must be used to the fullest and to the utmost. The legend of Dr. Faustus was turned into great drama and poetry by Christopher Marlowe. Faustus had struck a bargain with the devil. For twenty-four years the devil would be his servant, and his every wish would be realized, but at the end of the years the devil would claim his soul. The twenty-four years have run their course and the last hour has come, and Faustus now sees what a terrible bargain he has struck.

> " O Faustus,
>   Now hast thou but one bare hour to live,
>   And then thou must be damned perpetually!
>   Stand still, you ever-moving spheres of heaven,
>   That time may cease and midnight never come;
>   Fair nature's eye, rise, rise again and make
>   Perpetual day; or let this hour be but
>   A year, a month, a week, a natural day,
>   That Faustus may repent and save his soul!
>   *O lente, lente currite noctis equi !*
>   The stars move still, time runs, the clock will strike,
>   The devil will come and Faustus must be damned."

Nothing in the world would give Faustus more time. That is one of the great salient, threatening facts in the life of man. There are twelve hours in the day—but there are *only* twelve hours in the day. There is no necessity for haste; but, equally, there is no room for waste. There is time enough in life, but there is never time to spare.

THE DAY AND THE NIGHT

John II: 6-IO (*continued*)

JESUS goes on to develop what He has just said about time. He says that if a man walks in the light, he will not stumble; but if he tries to walk in the night, he will stumble and he cannot walk then.

It is John's custom, again and again, to say things which have two meanings. There is so often a meaning which lies on the surface, and which is true, and also a meaning which lies below the surface which is truer yet. It is so here.

(i) There is a surface meaning which is perfectly true, and which we must learn. The Jewish day, as was the Roman day, was divided into twelve equal hours, from sunrise to sunset. That of course means that the length of an hour varied according to the length of the day, and the season of the year. The day ran with the sun, and the time the sun gave was divided into twelve hours of equal length. Now, when Jesus says that a man will not stumble when he has the light of this world, on the surface He simply means that a man will not stumble when the sun is shining; but when the dark comes down he cannot see the way. There was no street lighting in those days, at least in the country places. With the dark, the time for journeying was done. Here we have Jesus saying that a man must finish the day's work within the day, for the night comes when work is ended. If a man had one wish it might well be that he might come to the end of each day with that day's work completed and done. The unrest, and the unease and the hurry of life, is so often simply due that we are trying to catch up on work which should have been done before. A man should so spend his precious capital of time that he does not dissipate it on useless extravagances, however pleasant, but that he should spend it on essentials, so that at the end of each day he is never in debt to time.

(ii) But below the surface meaning of this there is another meaning. Who can hear the phrase *the light of the world* without thinking of Jesus? Again and again John uses the words the *dark* and the *night* to describe life without Christ, life dominated by evil. In his dramatic account of the last meal together John describes how Judas went out to make the dreadful last arrangements for the betrayal. " He then having received the sop went immediately out; *and it was night* " (*John* 13: 30). The night is the time when a man goes out from Christ, and when evil has him.

The whole gospel is based on the love of God; but whether we like it or not, there is a threat also at the heart of the gospel. A man has only so much time to make his peace with God through Christ; and if he does not do so then the judgment must follow. So Jesus says: " Finish your greatest work; finish the work of getting yourself right with God while you have the light of the world; for the time comes when for you, too, the dark must come down and then it will be too late."

There is no gospel which is so sure that God so loved the world as the Fourth Gospel is; but there is also no gospel which is so sure that that love of God may be refused and missed and disregarded. The gospel has in it two notes—the glory of being *in time*; and the tragedy of being *too late*.

THE MAN WHO WOULD NOT QUIT

John 11: 11-16

> Jesus said these things, and then He went on to say: " Our friend Lazarus is sleeping; but I am going to waken him up." " Lord," the disciples said to Him, " if he is sleeping he will recover." But Jesus had

> spoken about his death. They thought that He was
> speaking about the sleep of natural sleep. So Jesus
> then said to them plainly: " Lazarus has died, and,
> for your sakes, I am glad that I was not there, because
> it is all designed in order that you may come to believe.
> But let us go to him." Thereupon Thomas, who was
> called Didymus, said: " Let us, too, go that we may
> die with Him."

JOHN here uses his normal method of relating a conversation of Jesus. In the Fourth Gospel, when Jesus talks to people, the conversation always follows the same pattern. Jesus says something which sounds quite simple. That saying is misunderstood, and then Jesus goes on to explain more fully and unmistakably what He meant. That is the way in which the conversation with Nicodemus about being born again ran (*John* 3: 3-8); and the way in which the conversation with the woman at the well about the water of life ran (*John* 4: 10-15). So Jesus here began by saying that Lazarus was sleeping. To the disciples that sounded good news, for there is no better medicine than sleep. But the word *sleep* has always had a deeper and a more serious meaning. Jesus said of Jairus' daughter that she was asleep (*Matthew* 9: 24); at the end of Stephen's martyrdom we are told that he fell asleep (*Acts* 7: 60). Paul speaks about those who sleep in Jesus (I *Thessalonians* 4: 13). Paul speaks of those who were witne ses of the Resurrection, and who are now fallen asleep (I *Corinthians* 15: 6). So Jesus had to tell them plainly that Lazarus was dead; and then He went on to say that for their sake, this was a good thing, because it would produce an event which would buttress them even more firmly in the faith.

The final proof of the power of Christianity is the sight of what Jesus Christ can do. Words may fail to convince, but there is no argument against God in action. It is the simple fact that the power of Jesus Christ has made the coward into a hero, the doubter into a man of certainty, the selfish man into the servant of all. Above all, it is the plain fact of history that again and again the power of Christ has made the bad man good. That is what lays so tremendous a responsibility on the individual Christian. The design of God is that every one of us should be a living, walking proof of His power. Our task is not to commend Christ to others in words—against which there is always an argument, for no one can ever write Q.E.D. after a Christian verbal proof—but to demonstrate in life what Christ has done for us. Sir John Reith once said: " I do not like crises; but I like the opportunities which they supply." The death of Lazarus brought a crisis to Jesus, and He was glad, because it gave Him the opportunity to demonstrate in the most amazing way what God can do. For us every crisis should be a like opportunity.

At that moment it might well have been that the disciples might have refused to follow Jesus; but then one lonely voice spoke up. They were all feeling that to go to Jerusalem was to go to die, and they were hanging back, for no man likes to undertake a course which is suicide. Then came the grim voice of Thomas: " Let us, too, go that we may die with Him."

All Jews in those days had two names—one was a Hebrew name by which a man was known in his own circle, the other was a Greek name by which he was known in a wider circle. *Thomas* is the *Hebrew*, and *Didymus* is the *Greek* for a *twin*. So *Peter* is the *Greek*, and *Cephas* is the *Hebrew* for a rock. So *Tabitha* is the *Hebrew*, and *Dorcas* is the *Greek* for a *gazelle*. In later days the Apocryphal Gospels wove their stories around Thomas, and they actually in the end came to say that he was the twin of Jesus Himself.

At the moment of this incident Thomas displayed the highest kind of courage. In Thomas' heart, as R. H. Strachan said, " There was not expectant faith, but loyal despair." But of one thing Thomas was determined—come what may, he would not quit. Gilbert Frankau tells of an officer who was a friend of his in the 1914-18 war. This officer was an artillery observation officer. His duty was to go up in a captive balloon, and to mark where the shells from the guns fell; and to indicate to the gunners whether the shells fell short of or over the target. It was one of the most dangerous assignments that could be given to any man. Because the balloon was a captive balloon there was no way to dodge. He was a sitting target for the guns and the planes of the enemy. And Gilbert Frankau said of his friend: " Every time he went up in that balloon he was sick with nerves, but he wouldn't quit." That is the highest form of courage. Courage does not mean not being afraid. If we are not afraid it is the easiest thing in the world to do a thing. Real courage means being perfectly aware of the worst that can happen, being sickeningly afraid of it, and yet doing the right thing. That was what Thomas was like that day. No man need ever be ashamed of being afraid; but he may well be ashamed of allowing his fear to stop him doing what in his heart of hearts he knows he ought to do.

THE HOUSE OF MOURNING

John 11: 17-19

> So, when Jesus came, He found that Lazarus had already been in the tomb for four days. Bethany was near Jerusalem, less than two miles away. Many of the Jews had gone to Martha and Mary to comfort them about their brother.

IN order to visualise this scene we must first see what a Jewish house of mourning was like. Normally in Palestine burial followed death as quickly as possible. The climate made that a necessity. Sometimes of course there was bound to be delay, but as little time as possible elapsed between death and burial. There was a time in Palestine when a funeral and a burial were exceedingly costly things. The finest spices and ointments were used to anoint the body; the body itself was clothed in the most magnificent robes; all kinds of valuable treasures and possessions were buried in the tomb along with the body. By midway through the first century all this had become a ruinous expenditure. Naturally no one wished on such an occasion to be outdone by his neighbour, and the wrappings and robes in which the body was covered, and the treasures left in the tomb, became ever more expensive. The matter had become almost an intolerable burden which no one liked to alter. The man who altered it was a famous Rabbi called Gamaliel the Second. He gave orders that he was to be buried in the simplest possible linen robe, and so broke the extravagance of funeral customs. To this day at Jewish funerals a cup is drunk to Rabbi Gamaliel who rescued the Jews from their own ostentatious extravagance. Thereafter the body was wrapped in a simple linen dress which was sometimes called by the very beautiful name of *the travelling-dress.*

As many as possible attended a funeral. Everyone who could was supposed, in courtesy and respect, to join the procession on its way. There was one curious custom. The women mourners walked first, for it was held that it was woman who by her first sin brought death into the world, and therefore she ought to lead the mourners to the tomb. At the tomb memorial speeches were sometimes made. Everyone was expected to express the deepest sympathy, and, on leaving the tomb, the principal mourners passed between two long lines of mourners. But there was one very curious and very wise rule—mourners were not to be tormented by useless and idle and uninvited talk. They were to be left, at that moment, alone with their sorrow.

In the house of mourning there were set customs. So long as the body was in the house it was forbidden to eat meat or to drink wine, to wear phylacteries or to engage in any kind of study. No food was to be prepared in the house, and such food as was eaten must not be eaten in the presence of the dead. As soon as the body was carried out all furniture was reversed, and the mourners sat on the ground or on low stools.

On the return from the tomb a meal was served, which had been prepared by the friends of the family. It consisted of bread, hard-boiled eggs and lentils. It was coarse fare; and the round eggs and lentils symbolised life which was always rolling to death.

Deep mourning lasted for seven days, of which the first three were days of weeping. During these seven days it was forbidden to anoint oneself, to put on shoes, to engage in any kind of study or business, and even to wash. The week of deep mourning was followed by thirty days of lighter mourning.

So when Jesus found a crowd in the house at Bethany, He found what anyone would expect to find in a Jewish house of mourning. To the Jew it was a sacred duty to come to express loving sympathy with the sorrowing friends and relations of one who had died. The *Talmud* says that whoever visits the sick shall deliver his soul from Gehenna; and Maimonides, the great mediaeval Jewish scholar, declared that to visit the sick takes precedence of all other good works. Visits of sympathy to the sick, and to the sorrowing, were an essential part of Jewish religion. A certain Rabbi expounded the text in *Deuteronomy* 13: 4: " Ye shall walk after the Lord your God." He said that text commands us to imitate the things which God is depicted as doing in scripture. God clothes the naked (*Genesis* 3: 21); God visited the sick (*Genesis* 18: 1). God comforted the mourners (*Genesis* 25: 11); God buried the dead (*Deuteronomy* 35: 6). And in all these things we must imitate the actions of God.

When death came respect for the dead and sympathy for the mourner were an essential part of Jewish duty. As the mourners left the tomb, they turned and said: " Depart in peace," and they never mentioned the name of the one who had died without invoking a blessing on it. In the days of mourning, sympathy was the first of all duties. There is something very lovely in the way in which the Jews stressed the duty of showing sympathy to the mourner.

It would be to a household filled and crowded with sympathisers that Jesus that day came.

THE RESURRECTION AND THE LIFE

John 11: 20-27

> So when Martha heard that Jesus was coming, she went to meet Him, but Mary remained sitting in the house. So Martha said to Jesus: " Lord, if you had been here, my brother would not have died. And even as things are, I know that whatever you ask God, God will give you." Jesus said to her: " Your brother will rise again." Martha said to Him: " I know that he will rise at the resurrection on the last day." Jesus said to her: " I am the Resurrection and the Life. He who believeth in me will live even if he has died; and everyone who lives and believes in me shall never die. Do you believe this? " She said to Him; " Yes, Lord. I am convinced that you are God's Anointed One, the Son of God, the One who is to come into the world."

IN this story, too, Martha is true to character. When Luke tells us about Martha and Mary (*Luke* 10: 38-42), he shows us Martha as the one who loved action, and Mary as the one whose instinct was to sit still. It is so here. As soon as it was announced that Jesus was coming near, Martha was up to meet Him, for she could not sit still, but Mary lingered behind.

When Martha met Jesus her heart spoke through her lips. Here is one of the most human speeches in all the Bible, for Martha spoke, half with a reproach that she could not keep back, and half with a faith that nothing could shake. " If you had been here," she said, " my brother would not have died." Through the words we read her mind. And Martha would have liked to say: " When you got our message, why didn't you come at

once? And now you have left it too late." And then no
sooner are the words out than there come the words of
faith, faith which defied the facts, and defied experience:
" Even yet," she said with a kind of desperate hope,
" even yet, I know that God will give you whatever you
ask."

Then Jesus made a direct statement. " Your brother,"
he said, " will rise again." Martha answered: " I know
quite well that he will rise in the general resurrection on
the last day." Now that is a notable saying. One of the
strangest things in scripture is the fact that the saints of
the Old Testament had practically no belief in any real
life after death. One of the clearest growths in scripture
is the growth of this belief in life after death. In the early
days, the Hebrews believed that the soul of every man,
good and bad alike, went to Sheol. Sheol is wrongly
translated *Hell*; for Sheol was not a place of torture.
It was the land of the shades; to it all alike went. They
lived a vague, shadowy, strengthless, joyless life, like
spectres or ghosts. This is the belief of by far the greater
part of the Old Testament. " In death there is no remem-
brance of Thee: in the grave who shall give Thee thanks? "
(*Psalm* 6: 5). " What profit is there in my blood when I
go down into the pit? Shall the dust praise Thee? Shall it
declare Thy truth?" (*Psalm* 30: 9). The Psalmist speaks
of " the slain that lie in the grave, whom Thou remem-
berest no more; and they are cut off from Thy hand "
(*Psalm* 88: 5). " Shall Thy loving-kindness be declared
in the grave," he asks, " or Thy faithfulness in destruction?
Shall Thy wonders be known to the dark? And Thy
righteousness in the land of forgetfulness?" (*Psalm* 88:
10-12). " The dead praise not the Lord, neither any that
go down into silence " (*Psalm* 115: 17). The preacher
says grimly: " Whatsoever thy hand findeth to do, do it
with thy might; for there is no work, nor device, nor
knowledge, nor wisdom in the grave whither thou goest "
(*Ecclesiastes* 9: 10). It is Hezekiah's pessimistic belief

that: " The grave cannot praise Thee; death cannot celebrate Thee; they that go down into the pit cannot hope for Thy truth " (*Isaiah* 38: 18). After death there came the land of silence, the land of forgetfulness, the land where the shades of men were separated alike from men and from God. As J. E. McFadyen wrote: " There are few more wonderful things than this in the long history of religion, that for centuries men lived the noblest lives, doing their duties and bearing their sorrows, without hop of future reward."

Just very occasionally someone in the Old Testament made a venturesome leap of faith. The Psalmist cries: " My flesh also shall rest in hope; for Thou wilt not leave my soul in Sheol; neither wilt Thou suffer Thine holy one to see corruption. Thou wilt show me the path of life; in Thy presence is fulness of joy; at Thy right hand there are pleasures for ever more " (*Psalm* 16: 9-11). " I am continually with Thee; Thou hast holden me by Thy right hand; Thou shalt guide me with Thy counsel, and afterward receive me to glory (*Psalm* 73: 23, 24). The conviction of the Psalmist was that when a man entered into a real relationship with God, not even death could break it. He felt that the tie between God and the man of God must outlast time. But at that stage it was a desperate leap of faith rather than a settled conviction. Finally in the Old Testament there is the immortal hope we find in *Job*. In face of all his disasters Job cried out:

" I know that there liveth a Champion,
　Who will one day stand over my dust;
Yea, Another shall rise as my Witness,
　And, as Sponsor, shall I behold—God;
Whom mine eyes shall behold, and no stranger's."
(*Job* 14: 7-12; translated by J. E. McFadyen).

Now, here in *Job*, we have the real seed of the Jewish belief in immortality.

The Jewish history was a history of disasters, a history of captivity, of slavery and of defeat. Yet the Jewish people had the utterly unshakable conviction that they were God's own people. This earth had never shown it, and never would show it; inevitably, therefore, they called in the new world to redress the inadequacies of the old. They came to see that if God's design was ever fully to be worked out, that if God's justice was ever completely to be fulfilled, that if God's love was ever finally to be satisfied, another world and another life was necessary. As Galloway (quoted by McFadyen) put it: " The enigmas of life become at least less baffling, when we come to rest in the thought that this is not the last act of the human drama." It was precisely that feeling that lead the Hebrews to a conviction that there was a life to come.

It is true that in the days of Jesus the Sadducees still refused to believe in any life after death. But the Pharisees and the great majority of the Jews did. They said that in the moment of death the two worlds of time and of eternity met and kissed. They said that those who died beheld God, and they refused to call them the dead and called them the living. When Martha answered Jesus as she did she bore witness to the highest reach of her nation's faith.

THE RESURRECTION AND THE LIFE

John 11: 20-27 (*continued*)

WHEN Martha declared her belief in the orthodox Jewish belief in the life to come, Jesus suddenly said something which brought to that belief a new vividness and a new meaning. " I am the Resurrection and the Life," He said. " He who believes in me will live even if he has died; and everyone who lives and believes in me shall never die." What exactly did Jesus mean when He said that? It is not possible that even a lifetime's thinking should reveal the full meaning of this; but we must try to grasp as much of its meaning as we can.

One thing is clear—Jesus was not thinking in terms of physical life; for, speaking physically, it is not true that the man who believes in Jesus will never die. The man who believes in Jesus faces and experiences physical death in the same way as any other man does. The years are not specially suspended for him, and his life in this world will not go on for ever. In this saying we must look for a more than physical meaning.

(i) Jesus was thinking of the death of sin. Jesus was saying: " Even if a man is dead in sin, even if, through his sins, he has lost all that makes life worth calling life, even if that be so, I can make him alive again." This is Jesus' promise, that He can resurrect the life that is dead in sin. In point of historical fact that is abundantly true. A. M. Chirgwin quotes the modern example of Tokichi Ishii. Ishii had an almost unparallelled criminal record. He had murdered men, women and children in the most brutal way. Anyone who stood in his way was pitilessly eliminated. He was in prison awaiting death. While in prison he was visited by two Canadian women who tried to talk to him through the bars, but he only glowered at them like a caged and savage animal. In the end they abandoned the attempt to speak to him; but they gave him a Bible, hoping that it might succeed where they had failed. He began to read it, and, having started, he could not stop. He read on until he came to the story of the Crucifixion. He came to the words: " Father, forgive them, for they know not what they do," and these words broke him. " I stopped," he said. " I was stabbed to the heart, as if pierced by a five-inch nail. Shall I call it the love of Christ? Shall I call it His compassion? I do not know what to call it. I only know that I believed, and my hardness of heart was changed." Later, when the jailer came to lead the doomed man to the scaffold, he found, not the hardened, surly brute he had expected, but a smiling radiant man, for the murderer had been born again. Literally Christ brought Tockichi Ishii to life.

It does not need to be so dramatic as that. A man can become so selfish that he is dead to the needs of others. A man can become so insensitive that he is dead to the feelings of others. A man can become so involved in the petty dishonesties, and the petty disloyalties of life, that he is dead to honour. A man can become so hopeless that he is filled with an inertia, which is spiritual death. Jesus Christ can resurrect that man. The whole witness of history is that He has resurrected millions and millions of people like that, and His touch has never lost its ancient power.

(ii) But Jesus was also thinking of the life to come. He brought into life the certainty that death is not the end of things. The last words of Edward the Confessor were: " Weep not, I shall not die; and as I leave the land of the dying I trust to see the blessings of the Lord in the land of the living." We call this world *the land of the living*; but it would in fact be more correct to call it *the land of the dying*. And through Jesus Christ we know that when death comes we do not pass *out of* the land of the living; we pass *into* the land of the living. Through Jesus Christ we know that we are journeying, not to the sunset, but to the sunrise; we know, as Mary Webb put it, that death is a gate on the sky-line. We know that in the most real sense we are not on our way to death, but we are on our way to life.

How does this happen? It happens when we believe in Jesus Christ. What does that mean? What meaning are we to give this word *believe*? To believe in Jesus means to accept everything that Jesus said as absolutely true, and to stake our lives upon that in perfect trust. When we do that we enter into two new relationships.

(i) We enter into a new relationship with God. When we believe that God is as Jesus told us that He is, then we become absolutely sure of the love of God; we become absolutely sure that God is above all the redeeming God. The fear of death goes, for death means going to the greatest lover of the souls of men the world has ever seen.

(ii) We enter into a new relationship with life. When we accept Jesus' way of life, when we commit ourselves to it; when we take His commands as our laws, and when we realize that He is there to help us to live the life which He has commanded, life becomes a new thing. It is clad with a new beauty, a new loveliness, a new winsomeness, a new strength. Surely we can put it this way—when we accept the way of Christ as the way of our life, then life deserves to go on. It becomes so lovely a thing that we cannot conceive of it ending incomplete.

When we believe in Jesus, when we accept what He says about God and about life, and when we stake everything on it, in truth we are resurrected for we are freed from the fear which is characteristic of the godless life; we are freed from the frustration which is characteristic of the sin-ridden life; we are freed from the futility of the Christless life. Life is raised from sin's death, and life becomes so rich that it cannot die, but must find in death only the transition to a higher life.

THE EMOTION OF JESUS

John 11: 28-33

When Martha had said this, she went away and called Mary her sister. Without letting the rest of the people know, she said to her: " The Teacher has arrived and is calling for you." When she heard this, she rose quickly and began to go to Him. Jesus had not yet come into the village, but He was still in the place where Martha met Him. So when the Jews, who were in the house with Mary, and who were condoling with her, saw her rise quickly and go out, they followed her, for they thought that she was going back to the tomb to weep there. When Mary came to where Jesus was, when she saw Him, she knelt at His feet. " Lord," she said, " if you had been here, my brother would not have died." When Jesus saw her weeping, and when He saw the Jews who had come with her weeping, He was deeply moved in spirit so that an involuntary groan burst from Him, and He trembled with deep emotion.

III

MARTHA went back to the house to tell Mary that Jesus had come. She wanted to give the news to her secretly, without letting the visitors know, because she wanted Mary to have a moment or two alone with Jesus, before the crowds engulfed them and made privacy impossible. But when the visitors saw Mary rise quickly and go out, they immediately assumed that she had gone to visit the tomb of Lazarus. It was the custom, especially for the women, for a week after the body was laid in the tomb to go to the tomb to weep on every possible occasion. Mary's greeting was exactly the same as that of Martha. If only Jesus had come in time this need never have happened and Lazarus might still be alive.

Jesus saw Mary and all the sympathising crowd weeping. We must remember that this would be no gentle, restrained shedding of tears. It would be unrestrained wailing and shrieking almost hysterically, for it was the Jewish point of view that the more unrestrained the weeping was the more honour it paid to the dead.

And now we have a problem of translation. The word which the Authorised Version translates as *deeply moved* in spirit comes from the verb *embrimasthai*. Now, it is very difficult to know how to translate this. It is used three other times in the New Testament. It is used in *Matthew* 9: 30 when it is said that Jesus *straitly charged* the blind men not to publish abroad the fact that He had given them their sight. It is used in *Mark* 1: 43 when Jesus *straitly charged* the leper not to publish the fact that He had healed him. It is used in *Mark* 14: 5 when the spectators are said to *murmur* against the woman who anointed Jesus' head with the costly ointment, because they thought that this deed of love was wastefully extravagant. It can be seen that in every one of these instances the word has a certain sternness, almost anger, in it. It means rather to upbraid, to rebuke, to give a stern order to. Now, there are some who wish to take it in that way. They would translate it: " Jesus was moved to anger in

His spirit." Why the anger? There could have been two reasons. It is suggested that the display of tears and wailing of the Jewish visitors to Bethany was sheer hypocrisy; that they did not really feel their grief; that they were putting on an act; that they had simply turned on this display of emotion as one turns on a tap; and it is suggested that this artificial grief raised Jesus' wrath. It is possible that that is true of the Jewish visitors, although there is no indication in the story that their grief was a synthetic grief. But that is certainly not true of Mary. It can hardly be right here to take *embrimasthai* of anger. Moffatt translates it: " Jesus *chafed* in spirit." But *chafed* is a weak word to apply to Jesus. The American Revised Standard Version translates it: " Jesus was deeply moved in spirit." Again that is a colourless translation for this most unusual word. Rieu translates it: " He gave way to such distress of spirit as made His body tremble." Here we are getting nearer the real meaning. In ordinary classical Greek the usual usage of *embrimasthai* is of a horse *snorting*. Here it can only mean that such deep emotion seized Jesus that an involuntary groan was wrung from His heart.

Now here is one of the most precious things in the gospel. So deeply did Jesus enter into the wounded hearts and the sorrows of people that His heart was wrung with anguish

" In ev'ry pang that rends the heart,
The Man of Sorrows had a part."

But there is more than that. To any Greek reading this— and we must remember that this gospel was written for Greeks—this would be a staggering and incredible picture. John had written his whole gospel on the theme that in Jesus we see the mind of God. Now, to the Greek the primary characteristic of God was what he called *apatheia*. *Apatheia* does not mean what the English word *apathy* means. *Apatheia* means total inability to feel any emotion whatsoever. How did the Greeks come to attribute such a characteristic to God? They argued like this. If we can feel sorrow or joy, gladness or grief, it means that someone can have an effect upon us. Someone else can bring joy or bring sorrow to us. Now, if a person has an effect upon us, it means that for the moment that person has power over us; or, if we like to put it so, that for the moment that person is greater than we are. Now, no one can have any power over God; that would be impossible. And if that is going to be so, it must mean that God is essentially incapable of feeling any emotion whatsoever, for no one must be able to bring joy or sorrow to God. The Greeks believed in their lonely, isolated, passionless and compassionless God. What a different picture Jesus gave of God! Jesus showed us a God whose very heart is wrung with anguish in the anguish of His people, a God who in the most literal way is afflicted in our afflictions. When John drew this picture, he was drawing a completely new picture of God. The greatest thing that Jesus did for us was to bring us the news of a God who cares.

THE VOICE THAT WAKES THE DEAD

John 11: 34-44

Jesus said to them: " Where have you laid him? " " Lord," they said to Him: " Come and see." Jesus wept. So the Jews said: " Look how He loved him! " Some of them said: " Could not this man who opened the eyes of the blind have so acted that Lazarus would not have died? " Again a groan was wrung from Jesus' inner being. He went to the tomb. It was a cave; and a stone had been laid upon it. Jesus said: " Take away the stone." Martha, the dead man's sister, said to Him: " Lord, by this time the stench of death is on him, for he has been in the tomb for four days." Jesus said to her: " Did I not tell you that, if you believe, you will see the glory of God? " So they took the stone away. Jesus lifted up His eyes and said: " Father, I thank you that you have heard me. I knew that you always hear me. But I said this for the sake of the crowd which is standing round, because I want them to believe that you sent me." When He had said this, He cried with a loud voice: " Lazarus, come out! " The man who had been dead came out, bound hand and foot in grave-clothes, and with his face encircled with a napkin. Jesus said to them: " Set him free from his wrappings and let him go! "

So we come to the last scene. Once again we are shown the picture of Jesus wrung with anguish as He shared the anguish of the human heart. To the Greek reader that little sentence: " Jesus wept," would be the most astonishing thing in an astonishing story. That He who was the Son of God could weep would be to a Greek a thing beyond belief.

To get this picture right we must have in our minds a picture of the usual Palestinian tomb. The tombs were either natural caves, or caves hewn out in the rock. They consisted of an entrance in which the bier was first laid. Beyond the entrance there was a cave, usually about six feet long, nine feet wide and ten feet high. In such a tomb there were usually eight shelves cut in the rock, three on each side and two on the wall facing the entrance, and on these shelves the bodies were laid. The bodies were wrapped in a linen garment, but the hands and feet were swathed in bandage-like wrappings, and the head was wrapped in a towel. The tomb had no door, but in front of the opening there ran a groove, and in the groove there was set a great stone like a cartwheel, and the stone was rolled across the entrance so that the cave was sealed.

Jesus asked that the stone should be moved. Martha could only think of one reason for opening the tomb— that Jesus wished to look on the face of His dead friend for the last time. Martha could see no consolation there. What consolation could anyone gain from looking on the grim and repulsive sight of a putrefying corpse? She pointed out that Lazarus had been in the tomb for four days. The point is this. It was Jewish belief that the spirits of the departed hovered around the tombs for four days, seeking an entrance again into the body of the dead.

But after four days the spirits finally left for the face of the body was so decayed that they could no longer recognize it.

Then Jesus spoke His word of command, a command which even death was powerless to oppose.

" He speaks, and, listening to His voice,
New life the dead receive."

And Lazarus came forth. It is a weird picture to think of the bandaged figure staggering out from the tomb. So Jesus bade them unloose the hampering grave-clothes and the wrappings and to let him go.

There are certain things to note here.

(i) Jesus prayed. The power which flowed through Him was not His power; it was the power of God. " Miracles," said Godet, " are just so many answered prayers."

(ii) Jesus sought only the glory of God. He did not do this to glorify Himself. When Elijah had his epic contest with the prophets of Baal, he prayed: " Hear me, O Lord, that this people may know that Thou art God " (I *Kings* 18: 37). Everything that Jesus did was due to the power of God, and designed for the glory of God. How different men are! So much that we do is attempted in our own power and designed for our own prestige. It was by God, and for God, that Jesus acted. It may be that there would be more wonders in our life, too, if we ceased to act by ourselves and for ourselves and set God in the central place.

THE RAISING OF LAZARUS

John 11: 1-44

WE have tried to expound the raising of Lazarus simply as the story stands written in the New Testament. But we can no longer evade the fact that of all the miracles of Jesus this miracle presents the greatest problem. Let us honestly face the difficulties.

(i) In the other three gospels there are accounts of people being raised from the dead. There is the story of the raising of Jairus' daughter (*Matthew* 9: 18-26; *Mark* 5: 21-43; *Luke* 8: 40-56). There is the story of the raising of the widow's son at Nain (*Luke* 7: 11-16). In both these cases the raising from the dead followed *immediately* after death. It would be quite possible to believe that in both these miracles the person raised was in a coma or trance. We have seen how burial had to follow hard upon death in the climate of Palestine; and we know from the evidence of the graves in Palestine that people were not infrequently buried alive, because of the haste with which they were buried. It could well be that these two miracles were miracles of diagnosis in which Jesus saved two young people from a dreadful death. But there is no parallel whatever for the raising of a man who had been dead for four days and whose body had begun to putrefy There is nothing in the gospel story which can in any way parallel the Lazarus story.

(ii) In the other three gospels there is no account, not even a mention, of the raising of Lazarus. If the other gospel writers knew about this miracle, how could they possibly omit it? If it actually happened, how could they possibly fail to know of it? It has been suggested that the answer is this. We know that Mark drew his information from Peter. Now, the fact is that Peter does not appear in the Fourth Gospel at all in chapters 5 and chapters 7 to 12. It has been suggested that Peter was not present. Thomas is, in fact, the spokesman of the disciples. It has been suggested that Peter was not with Jesus at this time, and that he only came up later to the Passover Feast. On the face of it that does not seem likely, and, even if Peter was not there, surely the writers of the gospels must have heard from other sources of so amazing a miracle.

(iii) Perhaps the greatest difficulty is that John sees in this miracle the essential cause which moved the Jewish authorities to take definite steps to have Jesus eliminated

(*John* 11: 47-54). In other words, the raising of Lazarus was the direct cause of the Cross. In the other three gospels the great moving cause of the crucifixion was the Cleansing of the Temple. It is very difficult to understand why the other three gospel writers have nothing to say of it, if indeed it was the immediate cause which made the authorities take steps to crucify Jesus.

(iv) On the other hand, it might well be argued that the Triumphal Entry is inexplicable without this miracle to go before it. Why did Jesus receive that tremendous reception when He arrived in Jerusalem? It could be argued that the reception was due to the fame He had acquired by this very miracle. And yet the fact remains that, in the story as the other three gospel writers tell it, there is just no room and no space into which this miracle can be fitted at all.

If, then, this story is not a record of actual historical fact, how could we explain it?

(i) Renan, the French scholar, suggested that the whole thing was a deliberately designed fraud arranged between Jesus and Martha and Mary and Lazarus. That explanation needs no refutation. It has only to be stated to be dismissed as incredible. And, later, Renan himself departed from it.

(ii) It has been suggested that Lazarus was in a coma or a trance. It would be impossible to argue that from the story as it stands. The details of death are too vivid for that.

(iii) It has been suggested that the story is an allegory written round the saying of Jesus: " I am the Resurrection and the Life," that, in fact, it is a story composed to illustrate that saying and to give it a setting. That may be an oversimplified and overstated version of the truth.

(iv) It has been suggested that the story is to be connected with the Parable of Dives and Lazarus (*Luke* 16: 19-31). That story ends with the saying that even if someone was raised from the dead the Jews would still not believe. It is suggested that the story was produced to show that someone did rise from the dead and the Jews still did not believe. The story is taken as a kind of allegorical development of that parable.

When we consider the difficulties of this story, we are in the end compelled to say that we do not know what happened at Bethany, but undoubtedly something tremendous did happen. It is worth noting that to this day Bethany is still called Azariyeh, which is derived from the name Lazarus. But we do know for certain the truth which this story teaches.

Robert McAfee Brown, an American professor, tells of something which this story did. He was an American army chaplain, and he was on a troopship in which 1,500 marines were returning from Japan to America for discharge. Greatly to his surprise he was approached by a small group to do Bible study with them. He leapt at the opportunity. Near the end of this voyage, they were studying this chapter. After they had studied it a marine came to him. " Everything in that chapter," he said, " is pointing at me." He went on to say that he had been in hell for the last six months. He had gone straight into the marines from college. He had been sent out to Japan. He had been bored with life; and he had gone out and got into trouble—had trouble. Nobody knew about it—but God knew about it. He felt guilty; he felt his life was ruined; he felt he could never face his family although they need never know; he felt he had killed himself and he was a dead man. " And," said this young marine, " after reading this chapter I have come alive again." He said: " I know that this resurrection Jesus was talking about is real here and now, for He has raised me from death to life." That lad's troubles were not finished; he had a hard road to go; but in his sin and his sense of guilt he had found Jesus as the resurrection and the life.

That is the end of the whole matter. It does not really matter whether or not Jesus literally raised a corpse to life in A.D. 30, but it matters intensely that Jesus is the

Resurrection and the Life for every man who is dead in sin and dead to God in A.D. 1955. There may be problems in this story; we may never know what exactly happened at Bethany so many years ago; but we do know for certain that Jesus is still the Resurrection and the Life. That is what this story tells us—and nothing else really matters.

THE TRAGIC IRONY

John 11: 47-53

> The chief priests and Pharisees assembled the Sanhedrin: "What are we going to do?" they said, "because this man does many signs. If we leave Him alone like this, all will believe in Him, and the Romans will come and will take away our place and will destroy our nation." One of them, called Caiaphas, who was High Priest for that year, said to them: "You are witless creatures. You do not think it out that it is to our good that one man should die for the people, rather than that the whole nation should perish." It was not he who was responsible for what he said; but, since he was High Priest for that year, he was really prophesying that Jesus was going to die for the nation, and, not only for the nation, but that the scattered children of God should be gathered into one. So from that day they plotted to kill Him.

IN this passage the Jewish authorities are very vividly sketched before us. The wonderful happening at Bethany had forced the hand of the Jews. It was impossible to allow Jesus to continue unchecked. If He was allowed to go on doing the things which He was doing it was inevitable that the people would follow Him in ever larger numbers. So the Sanhedrin was called to deal with the situation. In the Sanhedrin there were both Pharisees and Sadducees. The Pharisees were not a political party at all; their sole interest was in living according to every detail of the law; and they cared not who governed them so long as they were allowed to continue in meticulous obedience to the law. On the other hand, the Sadducees were an intensely political party. The Sadducees were the wealthy and the aristocratic party. They were also the collaborationist party. So long as they were allowed to enjoy and to retain their wealth, their comfort and their position of authority, they were well content to collaborate with Rome. All the priests were Sadducees. And it is clear that it was the priests who dominated this meeting of the Sanhedrin. That is to say, it was the Sadducees who did all the talking. With a few masterly strokes John delineates their characteristics. First, the Sadducees were notoriously discourteous. Josephus said of them (*The Wars of the Jews* 2: 8, 14) that: " The behaviour of the Sadducees to one another is rather rude, and their intercourse with their equals is rough, as with strangers." " You know nothing at all," said Caiaphas (verse 49). " You are witless, brainless creatures." Here we see the innate, domineering arrogance of the Sadducees in action. This was exactly in character for a Sadducee to say. The contemptuous arrogance of the Sadducee is an implicit contrast to the accents of love of Jesus. Second, the one thing at which the Sadducees always aimed was the retention of their political and social power and prestige. What they feared was that Jesus might gain a following and raise a disturbance against the government. Now, Rome was essentially tolerant, but, with such a vast empire to govern, Rome could never afford civil disorder, and Rome always quelled civil disorder with a firm and merciless hand. If Jesus was the cause of civil disorder, Rome would descend in all her power, and, beyond a doubt, the Sadducees would be dismissed from the positions of authority in which they gloried. It never even occurred to them to ask whether Jesus was right or wrong, or whether this was the will of God or not. Their only question was: " What effect will this have on my ease and comfort and authority? " They judged things, not by the standards of right and wrong, not in the light of principle, but by the standards of their own comfort, and in the light of their own career. It is still possible for a man to set his own career before the will of God.

And then comes the first tremendous example of dramatic irony. Sometimes in a play a character says something, the full significance of which he does not realize. The audience realizes it; but he does not; he is in reality saying something very much more meaningful than he knows, or very much more important than he knows. That is dramatic irony. So the Sadducees insisted that Jesus must be eliminated, or the Romans would come and take their authority away. In A.D. 70 that is exactly what happened. The Romans, weary of Jewish stubbornness and intransigeance, besieged Jerusalem, and, at the end of the siege, Jerusalem was a heap of ruins, and a plough was drawn across the Temple area. How different things might have been if the Jews had accepted Jesus! But the very steps they took to save their nation destroyed their nation. This destruction happened in A.D. 70; John's gospel was written about A.D. 100; and all who read it would see the dramatic irony in the words of the Sadducees.

Then Caiaphas, the High Priest, made his two-edged statement. " If you had any sense," he said, " you would come to the conclusion that it is far better that one man should perish for the nation than that the whole nation should perish." Now it was the Jewish belief that when the High Priest asked God's counsel for the nation, God spoke through him, and sent His message through him, that, in fact, on such occasions the High Priest was also a prophet. In the old story it is told how Moses chose Joshua to be his successor in the leadership of Israel. Joshua was to have a share in his honour, and when Joshua wished for God's counsel he was to go to Eleazar the High Priest: " And he shall stand before Eleazar the priest, who shall ask counsel for him . . . at his word shall they go out, and at his word they shall come in " (*Numbers* 27: 18-21). The High Priest was to be the medium and channel of God's word to the leader and to the nation. That is what Caiaphas was that day. Here, again, is another tremendous example of dramatic irony. Caiaphas meant that it was better that Jesus should die than that there should be trouble with the Romans. He must die to save the nation. That was true—but it was not true in the way that Caiaphas meant it. It was true in a far greater and more wonderful way. God can speak through the most unlikely people. Sometimes God sends His message through a man without the man being aware that God is doing so. God can use even the words of bad men.

Jesus was to die for the nation, and also for all God's people scattered throughout the world. The early Church made a very beautiful use of these words. The first service order book of the Church was called the *Didache*, or *The Teaching of the Twelve Apostles*. It dates back to shortly after A.D. 100. When the bread was being broken, it was laid down that it should be said: " Even as this bread was scattered upon the mountains, and was brought into one, so let Thy Church be brought together from the ends of the earth into the Kingdom " (*Didache* 9: 4). The bread had been put together from the scattered elements of which it was composed; so some day the scattered elements of the Church must be united into one. That is something about which to think as we see the broken bread of the Sacrament.

JESUS THE OUTLAW

John 11: 54-57

> So Jesus walked no longer openly among the Jews, but He went away from them to a place near the wilderness, to a town called Ephraim, and He stayed there with His disciples.
> Now the Passover Feast of the Jews was near; and many from the country areas went up to Jerusalem before the Passover Feast to purify themselves. So they were looking for Jesus; and, as they stood in the Temple precincts, they were talking with each

other and saying: " What do you think? Surely it is impossible that He should come to the Feast? " Now the chief priests and Pharisees had given orders that if anyone knew where Jesus was, he should lodge information with them, that they might seize Him.

JESUS did not unnecessarily court danger. He was ready and willing to lay down His life, but He was not foolishly reckless enough to throw away His life prematurely and before His work was done. There is no virtue in flamboyant recklessness. So He retired to a town called Ephraim. Ephraim was in the mountainous country north of Jerusalem. It was near Bethel, and Bethel and Ephraim are mentioned together in 2 *Chronicles* 13: 19.

By this time Jerusalem was beginning to fill up with people. Before the Jew could attend any feast he had to be ceremonially clean; and uncleanness could be contracted by touching a vast number of things and people. So many of the Jews came up to the city early that they might make the necessary offerings and go through the necessary washings to ensure ceremonial cleanness. The law had it: " Every man is bound to purify himself before the Feast."

These purifications were carried out in the Temple. They took time, and in the time of waiting the Jews gathered in excited little groups. They knew what was going on. They knew about this mortal contest of wills between Jesus and the authorities; and people are always interested in the man who gallantly faces fearful odds. They wondered if He would appear at the Feast; but they came to the conclusion that He could not possibly come. This Galilean carpenter could not take on the whole might of Jewish ecclesiastical and political officialdom. They had under-rated Jesus. When the time came for Him to come nothing on earth would stop Him coming. If God ordered Jesus to go, then the threat of no man could stop Him. Martin Luther was a man who hurled defiance at cautious souls who sought to hold him back from being too venturesome. He took what seemed to him the right course " despite all cardinals, popes, kings and emperors, together with all devils and hell." When he was cited to appear at Worms to answer for his attack on the abuses of the Roman Catholic Church, he was well warned of the danger in which he stood if he went. His answer was: " I would go if there were as many devils in Worms as there are tiles on the housetops." When told that Duke George would capture him, he answered: " I would go if it rained Duke Georges." It was not that Luther was not afraid, for often he made his greatest statements with a voice and with knees that shook; but he had that courage which conquered fear. The Christian does not fear the consequences of doing the right thing; he fears the consequences of *not* doing it.

From the concluding verses of this chapter, it seems that by this time Jesus had been classed as an outlaw. It may be that the authorities had offered a reward for information leading to His apprehension; it may be that it was that reward that Judas sought and received. By this time He was an outlaw with a price upon His head; and yet in spite of that He came to Jerusalem, and He came, not skulking in the back streets, or hiding from the eyes of men. He came openly; He came in such a way as to focus the eyes of men upon Himself. Whatever else we may say of Jesus Christ, we must bow in admiration before His death-defying courage. For the last days of His life Jesus was the greatest outlaw of all time.

LOVE'S EXTRAVAGANCE
John 12: 1-8

Now six days before the Passover Jesus went to Bethany, where Lazarus, whom Jesus raised from the dead, was. So they made Him a meal there, and Martha was serving while Lazarus was one of those who reclined at table with Him. Now Mary took a pound of very precious genuine spikenard ointment, and anointed Jesus' feet, and wiped His feet with her hair; and the house was filled with the perfume of the ointment. But Judas Iscariot, one of His disciples, the one who was going to betray Him, said: " Why

> was this ointment not sold for ten pounds, and the
> proceeds given to the poor?" He said this, not that
> he cared for the poor, but because he was a thief and
> had charge of the money-box, and pilfered from what
> was put into it. So Jesus said: "Let her observe it
> now against the day of my burial. The poor you have
> always with you, but me you have not always."

WE have seen on other occasions that there are many
scholars who believe that certain parts of John's gospel
have become displaced, and that some of the chapters and
verses are out of order. There are some who suspect a
dislocation in this chapter. Moffatt, for instance, prints
this chapter in the order verses 19-29; verses 1-18 and
verse 30; verses 31 to 42. We have retained the order of
the Authorised Version for our studies, but if the reader
will read the chapter in the re-arranged order he will see
the order and connection of events and thought more
clearly.

By this time it was coming very near the end for Jesus. The
very fact that He had come to Jerusalem for the Passover
was an act of the highest courage, for the authorities had
made Him in effect an outlaw (*John* 11: 57). So great were
the crowds who came to the Passover that they could not all
possibly obtain a lodging within the city of Jerusalem itself,
and Bethany was one of the places outside the boundaries
of the city which the law laid down as a place for the over-
flow of the pilgrims to stay.

When Jesus came to Bethany they made Him a feast and
a meal. John does not definitely say so, but it must have
been in the house of Martha and Mary and Lazarus, for
where else would Martha be serving but in her own house ?
It was then that Mary's heart ran over in love. She had a
pound of very precious spikenard ointment. Both John
and Mark describe it by the adjective *pistikos* (*Mark* 14: 3).
Oddly enough, no one really knows what that word means.
There are four possibilities. It may come from the adjective
pistos which means *faithful* or *reliable*, and so may mean
genuine. It may come from the verb *pinein* which

means *to drink*, and so may mean *liquid*. It may be a kind of trade name, and it may have to be translated simply *pistic nard*. It may come from a word meaning the *pistachio nut*, and be a special kind of essence extracted from it. In any event it was a specially valuable kind of perfume. With this perfume Mary anointed Jesus' feet. Judas ungraciously questioned this action as sheer waste. But Jesus silenced him by telling him that money could be given to the poor at any time, but a kindness done to Him must be done now, for soon the chance would never come again.

There is a whole series of little character sketches here.

(i) There is the character of Martha. She was serving at table. Always Martha was true to character. She loved Jesus; she was a practical woman; and the only way in which she could show her love was by the work of her hands. Martha always gave what she could. Many and many a great man, who has stood out in public service and in public eminence, has only been what he was because of someone's loving care for his creature comforts in his home. It is just as possible to serve Jesus in the kitchen as it is on the public platform or in a career which is lived in the eyes of men.

(ii) There is the character of Mary. Mary was the one who above all loved Jesus; and here in this action of Mary we see three things about love.

(a) We see love's extravagance. Mary took the most precious thing she possessed, and spent it all on Jesus. Love is not love if it nicely calculates the cost. Love gives its all, and love's only regret is that it has not still more to give. O. Henry, the master of the short story, has a moving story called *The Gift of the Magi*. There was a young American couple, Della and Jim, who were very poor but very much in love. Each had one unique possession. Della's hair was her glory. When she let it down it almost served her as a robe. Jim had a gold watch which had come to him from his father and which was his pride. It was the day before Christmas, and Della had exactly one dollar eighty-seven cents to buy Jim a present. She did the only thing she could do; she went out and sold her hair for twenty dollars. And with the proceeds she bought a platinum fob for Jim's precious watch. Jim came home at night. When he saw Della's shorn head he stopped as if stupefied. It was not that he did not like it or love her any more. She was lovelier than ever. Slowly he handed her his gift; his gift was a set of expensive tortoise-shell combs with jewelled edges for her lovely hair—and he had sold his gold watch to buy them for her. Each had given the other all he or she had to give. Real love cannot think of any other way to give.

(b) We see love's humility. It was a sign of honour to anoint a person's head. " Thou anointest my head with oil," says the psalmist (*Psalm* 23: 5). But Mary would not look so high as the head of Jesus; she anointed his feet. The last thing that Mary thought of was to confer an honour upon Jesus. She never dreamed that she was good enough for that.

(c) We see love's entire unselfconsciousness. Mary wiped Jesus' feet with the hair of her head. In Palestine no respectable woman would ever appear in public with her hair unbound. On the day a girl was married her hair was bound up, and never again would she be seen in public with her long tresses flowing loose. It was the sign of an immoral woman to appear in public with her hair unbound. But Mary never even thought of that. When two people really love each other they live in a world of their own. They will wander slowly down a crowded street hand in hand, never thinking of what other people think of them. They rejoice that all should see their love. There are many who are self-conscious about showing their Christianity. They are always thinking about what others are thinking about them. Mary loved Jesus so much that it was nothing to her what others thought.

But there is something else about love here. John has

the sentence: " The house was filled with the perfume of the ointment." Now we have seen that so many of John's statements have two meanings, a meaning which lies on the surface and a meaning which is underneath. Many fathers of the Church and many scholars have seen a double meaning here. They have taken this sentence to mean that the whole Church was filled with the sweet memory of Mary's lovely deed. A lovely deed becomes the possession of the whole world. It adds something to the beauty of life in general. A lovely deed brings into the world something permanently precious, something which time cannot ever take away. The love stories are the immortal stories of the world.

LOVE'S EXTRAVAGANCE

John 12: 1-8 (continued)

(iii) THERE is the character of Judas. There are three things here about Judas.

(a) Here we see Jesus' trust in Judas. As far back as *John 6: 70, 71*, John shows us Jesus well aware that there was a traitor within the ranks. It may well be that Jesus tried to touch Judas' heart by making him the treasurer of the apostolic company. It may well be that Jesus tried to appeal to Judas' sense of honour. It may well be that Jesus was saying in effect to Judas: " Judas, here's something that you can do for me. Here is a proof that I need you and want you and trust you." That appeal failed with Judas, but the fact remains that often the best way to reclaim someone who is on the wrong way is not to treat him with suspicion, but to treat him with trust; to treat him, not as if we expected the worst, but as if we expected the best.

(b) Here we see one of the laws of temptation. Jesus would not have put Judas in charge of the money-box unless Judas had some capabilities in that direction.

Westcott in his commentary said: " Temptation commonly comes through that for which we are naturally fitted." If a man is fitted to handle money, the temptation comes to regard money as the most important thing in the world. If a man is naturally fitted to occupy a place of publicity and of prominence, the temptation comes to think first and foremost of reputation. If a man has any particular gift, the temptation comes to take pride or to become conceited in that gift. Judas had a gift for handling money, and Judas became so fond of money that he became first a thief and then a traitor for the sake of money. The Authorised Version says that he *bare* the bag. The verb is *bastazein*; *bastazein* does mean to *bear*, or *carry*, or *lift*. But in colloquial English to *lift* a thing can also mean to *steal* it. We talk, for instance, of a *shop-lifter*. And Judas did not only carry the bag; he pilfered from it. Temptation struck him at the point of his special gift.

(c) Here we see how a man's view of things can be warped. Judas had just seen an action of surpassing loveliness; and he called it an action of extravagant waste. He was an embittered man and he took an embittered view of things. A man's sight depends on what is inside him. He sees only what he is fit to see, and what he is able to see. If we like a person, that person can do no wrong. If we dislike a person, we will misinterpret his finest action. If we are cynically minded, we will impute the lowest motive. to a person even when he has done the finest things. If we are generously minded we will refuse to think ill of any one. The warped mind brings the warped view of things; and, if we find ourselves becoming very critical of others, if we find ourselves imputing unworthy motives to others, we should, for a moment, stop examining them and start examining ourselves.

And, lastly, here there is one great truth about life. There are some things which we can do almost any time; and there are some things which we will never do, unless we grasp the chance to do them when it comes. We are often seized with the desire to do something which is fine and generous and big-hearted. So often we put it off; we will do it to-morrow; and the fine impulse is gone, and the thing is never done. Life is an uncertain thing. Often we are moved to wish to utter some word of thanks or praise or love. We put it off; and it may be that we or the person we were thinking of will be gone from the earth, and the word will never be spoken. There is one tragic instance of how a man realized too late the things he had never said and done. Thomas Carlyle loved Jane Welsh Carlyle, but he was a cross-grained, irritable creature and he never made life happy for her. Unexpectedly she died. J. A. Froude tells us of Carlyle's feelings when he lost her. " He was looking through her papers, her notebooks and journals; and old scenes came mercilessly back to him in the vistas of mournful memory. In his long sleepless nights, he recognized too late what she had felt and suffered under his childish irritabilities. His faults rose up in remorseless judgment, and as he had thought too little of them before, so now he exaggerated them to himself in his helpless repentance . . .' Oh ! ' he cried again and again, ' if I could see her but once more, were it but for five minutes, to let her know that I always loved her through all that. She never did know it, never.' " There is a time for doing and for saying things; and, when that time is past, they can never be said and they can never be done.

It was Judas' ill-natured complaint that the money which that ointment could have raised should have been given to the poor. But as scripture said: " The poor shall never cease out of the land; therefore I command thee saying, Thou shalt open thine hand wide unto thy brother, to thy poor, and to thy needy, in thy land " (*Deuteronomy* 15: 11). To help the poor was something that could be done any time. To show the heart's devotion to Jesus had to be done before the Cross on Calvary took Him to its cruel arms. Let us remember to do things now, for the chance so often never comes again, and the failure to do them, especially the failure to express love, brings the bitterest remorse of all.

A PLAN TO DESTROY THE EVIDENCE

John 12: 9-11

> The mob of the Jews knew that Jesus was there; and they came, not only because of Jesus, but to see Lazarus, whom He had raised from the dead. The chief priests plotted to kill Lazarus too, because many of the Jews were withdrawing from them because of Him and were coming to believe in Jesus.

FOR the leaders of the Jews things were getting into an impossible position. This was specially the case for the Sadducees. All the priests were Sadducees. Now the position for the Sadducees was doubly threatening.

First, they regarded it as threatening from the political point of view. The Sadducees were the wealthy aristocratic class of the Jews; and they were definitely the collaborationist party. They worked in close collaboration with the Roman government. Their aim was to ensure their own wealth and ease and comfort. So long as they were allowed to retain the ruling places in the government they were quite prepared to collaborate. The Romans allowed their subject kingdoms a large amount of freedom. Broadly speaking, under a Roman governor, they allowed them to govern themselves, but at the slightest outbreak of civil disorder Rome's hand came down heavily, and those who were responsible for good government and who had failed to produce it were summarily dismissed. These Sadducees saw Jesus as the possible leader of a rebellion. He was stealing away the hearts of the people. The atmosphere was electric; and the Sadducees were determined to get rid of Him in case there was an uprising of the people, and in case their own ease and comfort and authority was threatened.

Second, they regarded it as theologically intolerable. Unlike the Pharisees, the Sadducees did not believe in the resurrection of the dead. They believed that there was no resurrection; and, as John tells the story, they were confronted with Lazarus who had been raised from the dead. Unless they could do something about it, the foundations of their power, their influence and their teaching, were slipping from beneath their feet.

What then did the Sadducees propose to do about it? *They proposed to destroy the evidence.* They proposed to do away with Lazarus. H. G. Wood tells of a remark of two old ladies in the days when Charles Darwin had made public the conception of evolution, and when men thought that that conception meant that man was sprung from and akin to the beasts. They were heard to say: " Let's hope it's not true, and, if it is, let's hush it up! " When a man has to support a position by destroying the evidence which threatens it, it means that he is prepared to use dishonest methods to support a lie—and he knows it.

The Sadducees were prepared to suppress the truth in order to further their own self-interest. For many people self-interest is the most powerful motive in life. It appears to be a fact that many discoveries which might produce cheaper goods never see the light of day because the patents for them are bought up by those whose products they threaten; and these patents are carefully rendered inoperative. It is, for instance, said, that for years the secret of an everlasting match has existed; but that the rights of it have been acquired and to all intents and purposes suppressed, by those whose interests would be threatened by the marketing of such an article. Whether that actual instance is true or not cannot be stated with certainty, but that kind of thing does happen. Self-interest dictates policy and action.

In order to maintain their own place and their own influence the priests and the Sadducees were prepared to do their best to destroy the evidence for the truth. A man has come to a sorry pass when he is afraid of the truth, and when he sets his personal prestige and profit before the truth.

A KING'S WELCOME

John 12: 12-19

> On the next day the great crowd that was coming to the Feast heard that Jesus was on His way to Jerusalem. They took the branches of palm trees and went out to meet Him. They kept up a shout: " Hosanna! Blessed is He who comes in the name of the Lord, He who is the King of Israel! " Jesus found a young ass and sat on it, as it stands written: " Fear not, daughter of Zion. Look! Your King is coming sitting upon an ass's colt." At first the disciples did not realize the significance of these things; but when Jesus was glorified then they remembered that these things were written about Him, and that they had done these things to Him. The crowd who were with Him testified that He had called Lazarus from the tomb, and had raised him from among the dead. It was because they had heard that He had performed this sign that the crowd went out to meet Him. So the Pharisees said to each other: " You can see that all the steps you have taken have been completely ineffective. See! The whole world has gone off after Him! "

THE Passover, Pentecost and Tabernacles were the three compulsory festivals of the Jews. To the Passover Jews came from the ends of the earth to Jerusalem. Wherever a Jew might live it was his one ambition to observe one Passover in Jerusalem. To this day, when Jews in foreign lands observe the Passover, they say: " This year here; next year in Jerusalem." At such a time Jerusalem and the villages round about were crowded. On one occasion a census was taken of the lambs slain at the Passover Feast. The number was given as 256,500. There had to be a minimum of ten people per lamb; and if that estimate is correct it means that there must have been as many as

2,700,000 people at a Passover Feast. Even if that number is exaggerated it still remains true that the numbers must have been immense. News and rumour had gone out that Jesus the man who had raised Lazarus from the dead was on His way to Jerusalem. There were two crowds. There was the crowd which was accompanying Jesus from Bethany, and there was the crowd which surged out from Jerusalem to see Him; and the two crowds must have flowed together in a surging mass like two tides of the sea. Jesus came riding on an ass's colt. As the crowds met Him they received Him like a conqueror. And the sight of this tumultuous welcome sent the Jewish authorities into the depths of despair, for it seemed that nothing they could do could stop the tide of the people who had gone after Jesus. This is an incident which is so important in the life of Jesus that we must try to understand just what was happening.

(i) There were certain of the crowds who were simply sightseeing. Here was a man who, as rumour had it, had raised a man from the dead; and there were many in these crowds who had simply gone out to gaze on a sensational figure. It is always possible to attract people *for a time* by sensationalism, by shrewd publicity, by fixing the glare of the spotlight upon them. It never lasts. The crowd who were that day regarding Jesus as a sensation and a nine days' wonder were within a week shouting for his death.

(ii) There were many in these crowds who were greeting Jesus as a conqueror. That, in fact, is the predominant atmosphere of the whole scene. They greeted Him with the words: " Hosanna! Blessed is He who is coming in the name of the Lord! " The word *Hosanna* is the Hebrew for " Save now ! " And the shout of the people was almost precisely the shout: " God save the King! "

The words with which the people greeted Jesus are illuminating. They are a quotation from *Psalm* 118: 25, 26. Now that Psalm had many connections, and these connections were bound to be in the minds of the people. It was the last Psalm of the group known as the *Hallel*. *Psalms* 113-118 were known as the *Hallel*. The word *Hallel* means *Praise God!* These are all praising psalms. They were part of the first memory work that every Jewish boy had to learn; they were sung often at great acts of praise and thanksgiving in the Temple; they were an integral part of the Passover ritual. Still further, this Psalm was intimately connected with the ritual of the Feast of Tabernacles. At that Feast worshippers carried bundles made up of palm, myrtle and willow branches called *lulabs*. Daily they went with them to the Temple. On each day of the Feast they marched round the great altar of the burnt offering— once on each of the first six days, seven times on the seventh—and as they marched they triumphantly sang verses from this psalm and especially these very verses. In fact it may well be true that this Psalm was written for the first celebration of the Feast of Tabernacles when Nehemiah had rebuilt the shattered walls and the shattered city and when the Jews came home from Babylon and could worship again. (*Nehemiah* 8: 14-18). This was indeed the psalm of the great occasion—and the people knew it. But still further, this was characteristically the conqueror's Psalm. To take but one instance, these very verses were sung and shouted by the crowd of Jerusalem when they welcomed back Simon Maccabaeus after he had conquered Acra and wrested it from Syrian dominion more than a hundred years before. There is no doubt that when the people sang this psalm they were looking on Jesus as God's Anointed One, The Messiah, The Deliverer, The One who was to come. And there is no doubt that they were looking on Him as the Conqueror. To them it must have been only a matter of time until the trumpets rang out and the call to arms sounded and the Jewish nation swept to its long delayed victory over Rome and over the world. Jesus approached Jerusalem with the shout of the mob hailing a conqueror in His ears—and it must have hurt Him, for they were looking in Him for that very thing which He refused to be.

A KING'S WELCOME

John 12: 12-19 (*continued*)

(iii) Now in such a situation it was obviously impossible for Jesus to speak to the crowd. An excited crowd will not stop to listen once they are started on the march. His voice could not have reached that vast assembly of people. So Jesus did something that all could see. He came riding upon an ass's colt. Now that was two things. First, it was a deliberate claim to be God's Anointed One, the Messiah. It was a dramatic enactment of the words of Zechariah the prophet (*Zechariah* 9: 9). John does not quote accurately because obviously he is quoting from memory. Zechariah had said: "Rejoice greatly, O daughter of Zion; shout, O daughter of Jerusalem: behold thy King cometh unto thee; he is just and having salvation; lowly and riding upon an ass, and upon a colt the foal of an ass." There is no doubt at all that Jesus' action was a messianic claim. But second, it was a claim to be a special and particular kind of Messiah. We must not misunderstand this picture. With us the ass is a lowly and despised animal; but it was not so in the East. In the East it was a noble animal. Jair, the Judge, had twenty sons who rode on asses' colts (*Judges* 10: 4). Ahithophel rode upon an ass (2 *Samuel* 17: 23). Mephibosheth, the royal prince, the son of Saul, came to David riding upon an ass (2 *Samuel* 17: 23). But the point is that a king came riding upon a horse when he was bent on *war*; a king came riding upon an ass when he was coming in *peace*. This whole action of Jesus is a sign that He was coming in peace; that He was not the warrior figure men dreamed of, but that He was the Prince of Peace. No one saw it that way at that time. Not even the disciples, who should have known so much better, saw it. The minds of all were filled with a kind of surge of mob hysteria. Here was the one who was to come. But they looked for the Messiah of their own dreams and their own wishful thinking; they did not look for the Messiah whom God had sent. Jesus drew a dramatic picture of what He claimed to be, but there was none who understood the claim.

(iv) In the background there were the Jewish authorities. They felt frustrated and helpless; nothing they could do seemed able to stop the attraction of this Jesus. " The whole world," they said, " is gone off after Him! " Here in the saying of the authorities there is a magnificent example of that irony in which John is so skilled. No writer in the New Testament can say so much with such amazing reticence. It was because God so loved *the world* that Jesus came into the world; and here, all unwittingly, His enemies are saying that the world has gone after Him. In the very next section John is going to tell of the coming of the Greeks to Jesus. The first representatives of that wider world, the first seekers from the outside world, are coming. The Jewish authorities spoke truer than they knew when they said that the whole world was going away from them and after Jesus. Here, on the lips of Jesus' enemies, is a forecast of what is to be.

We cannot leave this passage without noting the simplest thing of all. Seldom in the world's history has there been such a display of magnificently deliberate courage as the Triumphal Entry. We must remember that Jesus was an outlaw, that the authorities were determined to kill Him. All prudence would have warned Him to turn back, and to make for Galilee, or for the desert places. If He was to enter Jerusalem at all, all caution would have demanded that He should enter secretly and go into hiding; but He came in such a way that he focused every eye upon Himself. It was an act of the most superlative courage, for it was the defiance of all that man could do; and it was an act of the most superlative love, for it was love's last appeal before the end.

THE SEEKING GREEKS

John 12: 20-22

> There were some Greeks among those whose practice
> it was to come up to the Feast. Now these came to
> Philip, who came from Bethsaida in Galilee, and made
> a request to him. " Sir," they said, " we wish to see
> Jesus." Philip went and told Andrew, and Andrew
> and Philip went and told Jesus.

NONE of the other gospels tells of this incident, but it is
very fitting and natural to find it in the Fourth Gospel.
The Fourth Gospel was the Gospel which was written to
present the truth of Christianity in a way that the Greeks
could appreciate and understand; and it is natural that in a
gospel with such an aim the first Greeks to come to Jesus
should find a place.

It need not seem strange to us to find Greeks in Jerusalem
at the Passover time. They need not even have been
proselytes. The Greek was an inveterate wanderer. He was
driven by the wanderlust and by the desire to find out new
things. " You Athenians," said one of the ancients, " will
never rest yourselves, nor will you ever let anyone else rest."
" You Greeks," said another, " are like children, always
young in your souls." More than five hundred years before
this Herodotus had travelled the world, as he said himself,
to find things out. Far up the Nile to this day there stands
a great Egyptian statue on which a Greek tourist, even as
modern tourists do, had scratched his name. The Greek
voyaged for trade and for commerce of course. But the
Greek was the first man to wander for the sake of wandering
in the ancient world. There is no need to be surprised to
find a detachment of sight-seeing Greeks even in Jerusalem.

But the Greek was more than that. The Greek was
characteristically a seeker after truth. It was no unusual
thing to find a Greek who had passed through philosophy
after philosophy, and religion after religion, a Greek who
had gone from teacher to teacher in the search for the truth.
The Greek was the man with the seeking mind.

How was it that these Greeks had come to hear of Jesus and to be interested in Him? J. H. Bernard throws out a most interesting suggestion. It was in the last week of His ministry that Jesus cleansed the Temple and swept the money-changers and the sellers of doves from the Temple Court. Now these traders and hucksters had their stance in the Court of the Gentiles, the great court which was the first of the Temple Courts. It was into that Court that Gentiles were allowed to come, and they were not allowed to pass beyond it. Now if these Greeks were in Jerusalem at all they would be certain to visit the Temple and to stand in the Court of the Gentiles. Perhaps they had actually seen that tremendous day when Jesus had driven the traders from the Temple Court; and perhaps they had wished to know more of a man who could do things like that.

However that may be, this is one of the great moments of the gospel story, for here is the first faint hint of a gospel which is to go out to all the world.

The Greeks came with their request to Philip. Why did they choose to come to Philip? No one can say for certain, but it may be that it was because Philip is a Greek name, and they thought that a man with a Greek name would treat them sympathetically. But Philip did not know what to do, and he went to Andrew. And Andrew was in no doubt. He led them to Jesus.

Andrew had discovered one thing about Jesus—he knew well that no one could ever be a nuisance to Jesus. He knew that Jesus would never turn any seeking soul away. Andrew knew that to Jesus' presence there was an open door that no man can ever shut.

THE AMAZING PARADOX

John 12: 23-26

Jesus answered them: " The hour has come that the Son of Man should be glorified. This is the truth I tell you—unless a grain of wheat falls into the ground and dies, it remains all by itself alone; but, if it dies, it bears much fruit. He who loves his life is losing it; and he who hates his life in this world will keep it to life eternal. If anyone will serve me, let him follow me; and where I am, there will my servant also be."

THERE is hardly any passage in the New Testament which would come with such a shock to those who heard it for the first time as this. It begins with a saying which everyone would expect; and it finishes with a series of sayings which were the last things that anyone would expect.

" The hour has come," began Jesus, " when the Son of Man should be glorified." It was quite clear that things had been building up to a crisis and that crisis had now come. But Jesus' idea of what that crisis involved was quite different from anyone else's. When He talked about the *Son of Man,* He did not mean what other people meant. To understand the shocking nature of this short paragraph we must understand something of what the Jews understood by the term Son of Man. That term took its origin in *Daniel* 7: 13. In that passage the Authorised Version mistranslates. The Authorised Version has it that one like unto *the Son of Man* came to the Ancient of Days, and received a kingdom, a glory and a dominion that were to be universal and for ever. The correct translation is not *like the Son of Man,* but *like a son of man.* The point of the passage is this. In *Daniel* 7: 1-8 the writer has been describing the world powers which have held sway, the Assyrians, the Babylonians, the Medes and the Persians. They were so cruel, so savage, so sadistic that they could only be described under the imagery of wild beasts, the lion with the eagle's wings, the bear with the three ribs between its teeth, the leopard with the four wings and the four heads, and the terrible beast with iron teeth and ten horns. These were the symbols of the powers which had hitherto held sway. But it was the dream of the seer that into the world there was going to come a new power, and that power was to be gentle and humane and gracious, so that it could be depicted under the symbol, not of a savage beast, but of a man. In Daniel the whole passage means that the day of savagery would pass and the day of humanity was coming.

Now that was the dream of the Jews; they dreamed of the golden age, when life would be sweet and when they would be masters of the world. But how was that age to come? It became clearer and clearer to them that their nation was so small, and their power so weak, that the golden age could never come by human means and human power; it must come by the direct intervention of God. God would send His champion to bring it in. So they thought back to the picture in the book of *Daniel,* and what more natural than that they should call the champion the *Son of Man*? The phrase which had once been merely a symbol came to describe a person. The Son of Man would be the conquering champion of God. Now in between the Old and the New Testament there arose a whole series of books which were all about the golden age and how it was to come. Amidst their troubles and their sufferings, in their subjections and their slaveries, the Jews never forgot and never gave up their dream. One of these books was specially influential—the *Book of Enoch*. And repeatedly the *Book of Enoch* speaks about *that Son of Man*. In *Enoch* the Son of Man is a tremendous figure who, as it were, is being held in leash by God. But the day will come when God will release that Son of Man and he will come with a divine and superhuman power against which no man and no kingdom can stand and smash the way to world empire for the Jews.

To the Jews the Son of Man stood for the undefeatable world conqueror sent by God. So Jesus says: " The hour has come when the Son of Man must be glorified." When He said that, the listeners would catch their breath. They would believe that the trumpet call of eternity had sounded, and that the might of heaven was on the march, and that the campaign of victory was on the move. But Jesus did not mean by *glorified* what they meant. By *glorified* they meant that the subjected kingdoms of the earth would grovel before the conqueror's feet; by *glorified* He meant *crucified*. When the Son of Man was mentioned they thought of the conquest of the armies of God; when the Son of Man was mentioned He meant the conquest of the Cross.

So then the first sentence which Jesus spoke would excite the hearts of those who heard it; and then began a succession of sayings which must have left them staggered, bewildered, amazed by their sheer incredibility, for they were sayings which spoke, not in terms of conquest, but in terms of sacrifice and death. We will never understand Jesus, and we will never understand the attitude of the Jews to Him, until we understand how He turned their ideas upside down; until we understand how He turned a dream of conquest into a vision of the Cross. No wonder they did not understand Him; the tragedy is that they refused to understand Him.

THE AMAZING PARADOX

John 12: 23-26 (continued)

WHAT then was this amazing paradox which Jesus was teaching? Jesus was saying three things, which are all variations of one central truth, and which are all at the heart of the Christian faith and life.

(i) He was saying that only by death comes life. The grain of wheat was ineffective and unfruitful so long as it was preserved, as it were, in safety and security. It was when it was thrown into the cold ground, and buried there as if in a tomb, that it bore fruit. It was by the death of the martyrs that the Church grew. In the famous phrase: " The blood of the martyrs was the seed of the Church." It was because they died that the Church became the living Church. It is always because men have been prepared to die that the great things have lived. But it becomes more personal than that. It is sometimes only when a man buries his personal aims and ambitions that he begins to be of real use to God. Cosmo Lang became Archbishop of Canterbury. At one time he had had great worldly ambitions. A godly friend's influence made him abandon his worldly ambitions and enter the Church of England. When he was studying for the ministry at Cuddesdon, one day as he was praying in the chapel he heard unmistakably a voice saying to him: " You are wanted! " It was when he had buried his personal ambitions that he became useful to God. By death comes life. By the loyalty which was true to death there have been preserved and born the most precious things which humanity possesses. By the death of personal desire and personal ambition a man becomes a servant of God.

(ii) He was saying that only by spending life do we retain life. The man who loves his life is moved by two aims. He is moved by selfishness and he is moved by the desire for security. His own advancement and his own safety are the two things which are the driving force of life. Not once or twice but many times Jesus insisted that the man who hoarded his life must in the end lose it, and the man who spent his life must in the end gain it. There was a famous evangelist called Christmas Evans. He was always on the move preaching for Christ. His friends advised and besought him to take things easier. His answer always was: " It is better to burn out than to rust out." When Joan of Arc knew that her enemies were strong and her time was short, she prayed to God: " I shall only last a year, use me as you can." Again and again Jesus laid down this law (*Mark* 8: 35; *Matthew* 16: 25; *Luke* 9: 24; *Matthew* 10: 39; *Luke* 17: 33). We have only to think of what this world would have lost if there had been no men who were not prepared to forget their personal safety, to forget security, to forget selfish gain and selfish advancement. The world owes everything to people who recklessly spent their strength and gave themselves to God and to others. No doubt we will exist longer if we take things easily, if we avoid all strain, if we sit at the fire and husband life, if we look after ourselves as a hypochondriac looks after his health. No doubt we will *exist* longer—but we will never *live* at all.

(iii) He was saying that only by service comes greatness. The people whom the world remembers with love are the people who serve others. A certain Mrs. Berwick had been very active in Salvation Army work in Liverpool. She retired to London. There came the war and the air raids. People get queer ideas and the idea got about that somehow Mrs. Berwick's poor house and her shelter were specially safe. She was old now; her Liverpool days of social service were long behind her; but she felt she must do something about it. So she got together a simple first-aid box and she put a notice on her window: " If you need help, knock here." That is the Christian attitude to our fellow men. Once a schoolboy was asked what parts of speech *my* and *mine* are. He answered—more truly than he knew—that they were *aggressive* pronouns. It is all too true that in the modern world the idea of service is in danger of going lost. There are so many people to-day who are in life and in work and in business for nothing else than for that which they can get out of it. They may well become rich, but one thing is certain—they will never be loved, and love is the true wealth of life.

Jesus came to the Jews with a new view of life. They looked on glory as conquest, the acquisition of power, the right to rule. He looked on glory as a cross. He taught men that only by death comes life; that only by spending life do we retain life; that only by service comes greatness. And the extraordinary thing is that when we come to think of it, the paradox of Christ is nothing other than the truth of common sense.

FROM TENSION TO CERTAINTY

John 12: 27-34

" Now my soul is troubled. And what shall I say? ' Father, rescue me from this hour.' But it was for this reason that I came to this hour. Father, glorify your name." A voice came from heaven: " I have both glorified it and I will glorify it again." So the crowd who were standing by, and who heard it, said that there had been thunder. Others said: " An angel spoke to Him." Jesus answered: " It was not for my sake that this voice came, but for yours. Now is the judgment of this world. Now will the ruler of this world be cast out. And I, if I be lifted up from the earth, will draw all men to myself." He said this in indication of what death He was going to die by. The crowd answered Him: " We have heard from the law that God's Anointed One remains for ever. And do you say: ' The Son of Man must be lifted up '? Who is this Son of Man? "

IN this passage John shows us both Jesus' tension and Jesus' triumph, and he shows us that which turned the tension into the triumph.

(i) John does not tell us the story of the agony in Gethsemane at all. It is here that he shows us Jesus fighting His battle with His human longing to avoid the Cross. No one wishes to die; no one wishes to die at thirty-three; and no one wishes to die upon a cross. There would have been no virtue in Jesus' obedience to God at all, if it had come easily and without cost. Real courage does not mean not being afraid. There is no virtue in doing a thing if to do it is an easy thing. Real courage means to be terribly afraid, and yet to do the thing that ought to be done. That was the courage of Jesus. As Bengel put it: " Here there met the horror of death and the ardour of obedience." Here we see the battle that Jesus had to obey the will of God. God's will meant the Cross and Jesus had to nerve Himself to accept it.

(ii) But the end of the story is not tension; the end of the story is triumph and certainty. Jesus was certain that if He went on, something would happen which would break the power of evil once and for all. If He was obedient. and obedient unto death, if He went to the Cross, He was certain that a death-blow would be struck to the Ruler of this world, to Satan, to the Devil. It was to be one last struggle and one last grapple which would break for ever the power of evil. Further, He was certain that if He went to the Cross, the sight of His upraised and crucified figure would in the end draw all men unto Him. Jesus too wanted conquest; Jesus too wanted to subdue men; and Jesus knew that the only way to conquer and to subdue the hearts of men for ever was to show Himself to them on the Cross. He began with the tension; He ended with the triumph.

(iii) What then came between the tension and the triumph? What changed the one into the other? In between them there came the voice of God. Behind this coming of the voice of God there lies something very great and very deep. There was a time when the Jews had really and fully believed that God spoke direct to men. It was directly that God spoke to the child Samuel (*I Samuel* 3: I-I4). It was directly that God spoke to Elijah, when Elijah had fled from the avenging Jezebel (*I Kings* I9: I-I8). It was directly that Eliphaz the Temanite had claimed to hear the voice of God (*Job* 4: I6). But by the time of Jesus the Jews had ceased to believe that God spoke directly to men. The great days were past; God was far too far away now; the voice that had spoken to the prophets was silent. Nowadays they believed in what they called the *Bath qol*; that is a Hebrew phrase which means *the daughter voice* or *the daughter of a voice*. When the *Bath qol* spoke it quoted scripture most often. It was not really the direct voice of God; it was what you might call the echo of God's voice, a distant, faint, whisper instead of a direct, vital communication from God. But it was not so with Jesus. It was not the echo of God's voice that Jesus heard; it was the very voice of God Himself. Here is one great truth. With Jesus there comes to men not some distant whisper of the voice of God, not some faint echo from the heavenly places.

With Jesus there comes to man the unmistakable accents of the direct voice of God.

Further, it is to be noted that the voice of God came to Jesus at all the great moments of His life. It came to Him at His Baptism when He first set out upon the work God had given Him to do (*Mark* I: II). It came to Him on the Mount of Transfiguration when He finally decided to take the way which led to Jerusalem and to the Cross (*Mark* 9: 7). And now it comes to Him when His human flesh and blood had to be strengthened by the divine aid for the ordeal of the Cross. What God did for Jesus, God does for every man. When God sends us out upon a road, He does not send us out without directions and without guidance. When God gives us a task, He does not leave us to do it in the lonely weakness of our own strength. God is not a silent God, and ever and again, when the strain of life is too much for us, when the effort of God's way is beyond our human resources, if we listen we will hear Him speak, and we will go on with His voice ringing in our ears, and His strength surging through our frame. Our trouble is, not that God does not speak, but that we do not listen enough.

FROM TENSION TO CERTAINTY

John I2: 27-34 (*continued*)

IT was Jesus' claim that, when He was lifted up, He would draw all men unto Him. There are some who take this to refer to the Ascension, and who think that it means that when Jesus was exalted in His risen power, He would draw all men unto Him. But that is far from the truth. Jesus was referring to His Cross—and the people knew it. And once again—inevitably—they were moved to incredulous astonishment. How could anyone possibly connect the Son of Man and a Cross? Was not the Son of Man the invincible leader at the head of the irresistible armies of heaven? What had the Son of Man and a Cross to do with each other? Was not the Kingdom of the Son of Man to last for ever? " His dominion is an everlasting dominion, which shall not pass away, and His kingdom that which shall not be destroyed " (*Daniel* 7: 14). Was it not said of the prince of the golden age: " My servant David shall be their prince for ever "? (*Ezekiel* 37: 25). Had Isaiah not said of the ruler of the new world: " Of the increase of his government and peace there shall be no end "? (*Isaiah* 9: 7). Did the Psalmist not sing of this endless kingdom? " Thy seed will I establish for ever, and build up thy throne to all generations " (*Psalm* 89: 4). The Jews connected the Son of Man with an everlasting kingdom, and here was He, who claimed to be the Son of Man, talking about being lifted up upon a Cross. Who was this Son of Man, whose Kingdom was to end before it had begun?

But the whole lesson of history is that Jesus was right. It was on the magnet of the Cross that Jesus pinned His hopes. And Jesus was right because love will live long after might and power and force is dead.

As Kipling had it:

> " Far-called our navies melt away;
> On dune and headland sinks the fire;
> Lo, all our pomp of yesterday
> Is one with Nineveh and Tyre! "

Nineveh and Tyre are but names, but Christ lives on.

One of the great sonnets of the English language is *Ozymandias* by Shelley:

> " I met a traveller from an antique land
> Who said: 'Two vast and trunkless legs of stone
> Stand in the desert . . . Near them, on the sand,
> Half sunk, a shattered visage lies, whose frown
> And wrinkled lip, and sneer of cold command,
> Tell that the sculptor well those passions read
> Which yet survive, stamped on these lifeless things,
> The hand that mocked them, and the heart that fed:
> And on the pedestal these words appear:
> ' My name is Ozymandias, king of kings,
> Look on my works, ye Mighty, and despair! '
> Nothing beside remains. Round the decay
> Of that colossal wreck, boundless and bare
> The lone and level sands stretch far away ."

Ozymandias was king of kings, yet all that he has left is a shattered statue in the desert, and a name that a chance sonnet kept alive.

H. E. Fosdick quotes a poem in one of his books:

" I saw the conquerors riding by
　　With cruel lips and faces wan:
　Musing on kingdoms sacked and burned
　　There rode the Mongol Genghis Khan;

And Alexander, like a god,
　　Who sought to weld the world in one:
And Caesar with his laurel wreath;
　　And like a thing from Hell the Hun;

And, leading like a star, the van,
　　Heedless of upstretched arm and groan,
Inscrutable Napoleon went,
　　Dreaming of Empire, and alone. . . .

Then all they perished from the earth,
　　As fleeting shadows from a glass,
And, conquering down the centuries,
　　Came Christ the swordless on an ass."

It is the fact that the empires founded on force have vanished, leaving only a memory, which with the years becomes ever fainter. But the empire of Christ, founded upon a Cross, each year extends its sway.

When Joan of Arc knows that she had been betrayed to the stake and the flames by the leaders of her own people, as George Bernard Shaw has it in his play, she turns to them and says: " I will go out now to the common people, and let the love in their eyes comfort me for the hate in yours. You will be glad to see me burnt; but if I go through the fire I shall go through it to their hearts for ever and ever." That is a parable of what happened to Jesus. His death upon the Cross made Him go through men's hearts for ever and for ever. The conquering Messiah of the Jews is a figure on whom scholars write their books; but the Prince of Love on the Cross is a king who has His throne for ever in the hearts of men. The only secure foundation for any kingdom is the foundation of sacrificial love.

SONS OF THE LIGHT

John 12: 35, 36

> Jesus said to them: " For a little while yet the light is among you. Walk while you have the light that the darkness may not overtake you. He who walks in the darkness does not know where he is going. While you have the light, believe in the light, that you may become sons of the light."

THERE is in this passage the implicit promise and the implicit threat which are both never very far from the heart of the Christian faith.

(i) There is the promise and the offer of light. The man who walks with Jesus walks in light. The man who walks with Jesus is delivered from the shadows. There are certain shadows which cast their shade sooner or later on every light. There is the shadow of fear. Sometimes we are all afraid to look forward. Sometimes, especially when we see what they can do to others, we are all afraid of the chances and the changes of life. There are the shadows of doubts and uncertainties. Sometimes the way ahead is far from being clear. Sometimes we feel like people groping among the shadows with nothing firm to cling to. There are the shadows of sorrow. Sooner or later the sun sets at midday and the lights go out. But the man who walks with Jesus is delivered from fear; he is liberated from doubt; he has a joy that no man taketh from him. His way is through the light, and not through the dark; and even in the valley of the deep dark shadow the darkness is lit by the presence of Christ.

(ii) But there is the implicit threat. The decision to trust life and all things to Jesus, the decision to take Him as Master and Guide and Saviour, must be made in time. In life all things must be done in time, or they will not be done at all. There is work which we can only do when we have the physical strength to do it. There is study which can only be carried out when our minds are keen enough and our memories retentive enough to cope with it. There are things which have to be said and done or the time for saying and doing them is gone for ever. And it is so with Jesus. At the actual moment Jesus said this, He was appealing to the Jews to accept Him and to believe in Him before the Cross came and He was taken from them. But this is an eternal truth. It is a statistical fact that there is a steep rise in the number of conversions up to the age of seventeen and an equally steep fall afterwards. The more a man lets himself become fixed in his own ways the harder it is for him to jerk himself out of it. In Christ the supreme blessedness is offered to men; in one sense it is never too late to grasp it; but nonetheless it remains true that it must be grasped in time.

BLIND UNBELIEF

John 12: 37-41

> When Jesus had said these things, He went away and hid Himself from them. Although He had done such great signs in their presence they did not believe in Him. It happened thus that the word which Isaiah the prophet spoke should be fulfilled: " Lord, who has believed what he heard from us? And to whom has the arm of the Lord been revealed?" It was for this reason that they could not believe, because Isaiah said again: " He has blinded their eyes, He has hardened their heart, so that they may not see with their eyes and understand with their heart and turn, and I will heal them." Isaiah said these things because he saw His glory and spoke about Him.

THIS is a passage which is bound to trouble many minds. John quotes two passages from *Isaiah*. The first is from *Isaiah* 53: 1, 2. In it the prophet asks if there is anyone who has believed what he has been saying, and if there is anyone who recognizes the power of God when it is revealed to him. But it is the second passage which is the passage which troubles the mind. The original of the passage is in *Isaiah* 6: 9, 10. It runs: " And God said, Go and tell this people, Hear ye indeed, but understand not; and see ye indeed, but perceive not. Make the heart of this people fat, and make their ears heavy, and shut their eyes; lest they see with their eyes, and hear with their ears, and understand with their heart, and convert, and be healed." That is a passage which runs all through the New Testament. It is quoted or echoed in *Matthew* 13: 14, 15; *Mark* 4: 12; *Luke* 4: 10; *Romans* 11: 8; *2 Corinthians* 3: 14. The terrible and the troubling thing about it is that it seems to say that man's unbelief is due to God's action, that when a man fails to believe it is because God has shut his ears and closed his mind and hardened his heart. It seems to say that God has ordained that certain people must not and will not believe. Now in whatever way we are going to explain this passage, we cannot believe that. We cannot believe that the God whom Jesus told us about would make it impossible for His children to believe.

There are two things to be said about this passage.

(1) We must try to understand what Isaiah was saying; we must try to think ourselves back into his heart and his mind. He had preached and he had proclaimed the word of God. He had put everything he had into his message. He had given it to men with all the power and all the persuasion which he possessed. And men had refused to listen. In the end Isaiah was forced to say: " For all the good I have done I might as well never have spoken. Instead of making men better my message seems to have made them worse. They might as well never have heard it, for they are simply confirmed in their lethargy and their disobedience and their unbelief. You would think that God had meant them not to believe." Isaiah's words spring from a broken heart. They are the words of a man bewildered by the fact that his message seemed to make men worse instead of better. To read them with cold literalness is completely to misunderstand the broken heart with which they were uttered. They are the words of a preacher whose heart is broken by the unresponsiveness of his people.

(ii) But there is something else. It was a basic belief of
the Jews that God is behind *everything*. The Jews believed
that *nothing* could happen outside the purpose of God.
Now if that is so they were bound to believe that when
men did not believe God's message that unbelief was still
within the purpose of God. Even unbelief somehow fell
within God's control and within God's purpose. If we put
that into modern terms, and into our way of thought, we
would put it this way—we would not say that unbelief is
God's purpose, but we *would* say that God in His con-
trolling wisdom and power can use *even* men's unbelief for
His divine purposes. That indeed is the way in which
Paul saw it. Paul saw that God used the unbelief of the
Jews for the conversion of the Gentiles. Because the Jews
did not accept God's truth it went out to the world at large.

When we read a passage like this we must understand it
to mean, not that God predestined and pre-ordained certain
people to unbelief, but that even man's unbelief can be used
to further the eternal purposes of God. These Jews did not
believe in Jesus; that was not God's fault; it was their
fault; but even that has somehow its place in the scheme
of God. " Ill that He blesses is our good." God is so great
that He can use even the sin of man for His purposes. There
is nothing in this world, not even sin, which is outside the
power of God.

THE COWARD'S FAITH

John 12: 42, 43

> Nevertheless many of the rulers believed in Him, but
> they did not publicly confess their faith for they did
> not wish to be excommunicated; for they loved the
> glory of men rather than the glory of God.

Jesus did not speak entirely to deaf ears; there were those,
even of the Jewish authorities, who in their heart of hearts
believed. But they were afraid to confess their faith, because they did not wish to run the risk of being excom-

municated from the Synagogue. These people were seeking
to carry out an impossible policy; they were trying to be
secret disciples. It has been said and said truly that secret
discipleship is a contradiction in terms for, " either the
secrecy kills the discipleship, or the discipleship kills the
secrecy." It is never possible in the Christian faith to make
the best of both worlds, and that is what these people were
trying to do.

They feared to become Christian, because they thought
that by becoming confessed Christians they would lose so
much. It is a strange thing how often men have got their
values mixed up. Again and again men have failed to
support some great cause because it interfered with some
lesser interest. When Joan of Arc realised that she stood
forsaken and alone, she said: " Yes: I am alone on earth:
I have always been alone. My father told my brothers to
drown me if I would not stay to mind his sheep while
France was bleeding to death; France might perish if only
our lambs were safe." The French farmer preferred the
safety of his sheep to the safety of his country. These
Jewish rulers were a little like that. They knew that Jesus
was right; they knew that their fellow-rulers were out to
destroy Jesus and all that Jesus was seeking to do for God;
but they were not prepared to take the risk of openly
declaring for Him. It would have meant an end of their
place, their profit, and their prestige. They would have
been ostracised from society, and banished from orthodox
religion. It was too high a price to pay. So they lived a lie
because they were not big enough to stand up for the truth.
In one vivid phrase John diagnoses their position. They
preferred to stand well with men rather than with God.
They thought far more of what men thought of them than
of what God thought of them. Now no doubt these rulers
thought themselves wise and prudent men; no doubt they
thought that they were playing safe. But their wisdom did
not extend to remembering that the opinion of men might

matter for the few years in which they lived upon this earth; but the judgment of God matters for all eternity. For the rewards of the moment they flung away the reward of eternity. It is only wisdom and prudence to prefer the good opinion of God to the good opinion of men. It is always better to be right for eternity than to be right for time.

THE INESCAPABLE JUDGMENT

John 12: 44-50

> Jesus cried and said: " He who believes in me does not believe in me, but in Him who sent me. And He who looks upon me, looks upon Him who sent me. It was as light that I came into the world, that every one who believes in me should not remain in darkness. And, if anyone hears my words and does not keep them, it is not I who judge him. I did not come to judge the world but to save the world. He who completely disregards me as of no account, and who does not receive my words, has one who judges him. The word which I spoke, that will judge him on the last day. That is so because it was not out of my own self that I spoke. But the Father who sent me, it was He who gave me the commandment which laid down what I should speak and what I should say. And I know that His commandment is eternal life. The things that I speak, I speak as the Father spoke to me."

THESE, according to John, are Jesus' last words of public teaching. Hereafter He will teach His disciples, and hereafter He will stand before Pilate, but these are the last words that He will address to people at large.

In these words Jesus makes the claim which is the basis and the essence of His whole life. His claim is that in Him men are confronted with God. To listen to Jesus is to listen to God; to see Jesus is to see God. That is the supreme importance of Jesus. In Him God meets man, and man meets God. Now that confrontation has two results, and both these results have in them the core of judgment as the Christian sees it.

(i) Here once again Jesus returns to a thought that is never far from us in the Fourth Gospel. Jesus did not come into the world to condemn men; He came to save men. It was not the wrath of God which sent Jesus to men; it was the love of God. And yet the fact remains that the coming of Jesus inevitably involves judgment. Why should that be? It is so because by his attitude to Jesus a man shows what he is and therefore judges himself. If a man finds in Jesus an infinite magnetism and attraction, even if he never succeeds in making his life what he knows he ought to make it, that man has felt the tug of God upon his heart; and therefore that man is safe. If on the other hand a man sees in Jesus nothing lovely, if his heart remains completely untouched in the presence of Jesus, then it means that that man is impervious to God; and he has therefore judged himself. Always in the Fourth Gospel there is this essential paradox. Jesus came in love, yet His coming is a judgment. As we have said before, we can in perfect, unmixed love offer a person some great experience, and we may find that confronted with that experience that person sees nothing in it. The result is that we now know that there is something wonderful which that person has not got it in him to appreciate. We confronted the person with that experience in love; but the very confrontation has showed the thing wherein that person is lacking. The experience offered in love has become a judgment. Jesus is God's touch-stone. By a man's attitude to Jesus a man himself stands revealed. By his reaction to Jesus he has passed judgment on himself.

(ii) Jesus said that at the last day the words which these people had heard would be their judges. That is one of the great truths of life. A man cannot be blamed for not knowing, and for not doing a truth which he never heard, or had the chance of hearing. But if a man knows the right and does the wrong, then his condemnation is all the more serious. Therefore every wise thing that we have heard, every opportunity that we have received to know the truth, will in the end be a witness against us.

An old 18th century divine wrote a kind of catechism of the Christian faith for ordinary people. At the end there was a question which asked what would happen to a person if he disregarded the Christian truths and the Christian message. The answer was that, if he did disregard the Christian message, then condemnation would follow, " and so much the more because thou hast read this book."

It is a warning and sobering thing to remember that all that we have known and did not do will be a witness against us at the last.

THE ROYALTY OF SERVICE

John 13: 1-17

Before the Festival of the Passover, Jesus, in the knowledge that His hour had come to leave this world and to go to the Father, although He had always loved His own people in the world, decided to show them what His love was like in a way which went to the ultimate limit. The meal was in progress; and the devil had already put it into his heart that Judas Iscariot, the son of Simon, should betray Him. Well knowing that the Father had given all things into His hands, and that He had come forth from God, and that He was going back to God, Jesus rose from the meal and laid aside His outer robe, and took a towel and put it round Himself. Then He poured water into a ewer and began to wash the feet of His disciples and to wipe them with the towel which He had put round Himself. He came to Simon Peter. Peter said to Him: " Lord, are you going to wash my feet? " Jesus answered him: " You do not know now what I am doing, but you will understand afterwards." Peter said to Him: " You will never wash my feet." Jesus answered Him: " If I do not wash you, you have no part with me." Simon Peter said to Him: " Lord, if that is so, do not wash my feet only, but my hands and my head too." Jesus said to him: " He who has been bathed has need only to have his feet washed. After that is done, he is altogether clean. And you are clean—but not all of you." He knew the one who was engineering His betrayal. That is why He said: "You are not all clean." So when He had washed their feet, and when He had taken His outer robe again, and when He had taken His place at table, He said to them: "Do you understand what I have done to you? You call me ' Teacher,' and you call me ' Lord.' And you are quite right to do so, for so I am. If then I, the Teacher and Lord, have washed your feet, so you ought to wash each other's feet, for I have given you an example, that, as I have done to you, you too should do to each other. This is the truth I tell you—the servant is not greater than his master, nor he who is sent greater than he who sent him. If you know these things you are blessed if you do them."

WE shall have to look at this passage in far more aspects than one, but first of all we must read it as a whole.

There are few incidents in the gospel story which so reveal the character of Jesus, and which so perfectly show His love. It is when we think of what Jesus might have been and of what He might have done that the supreme wonder of what He was and did comes home to us.

(i) Jesus knew that all things had been given into His hands. He knew that His hour of humiliation was near, but He knew also that His hour of glory was near. He knew that it was not long now until He took His place upon the very throne of God. Such a thought and such a consciousness might well have filled Him with pride; and yet, with the knowledge of the power and the glory that were His, He washed His disciples' feet. Just at that moment when He might have had the supreme pride, He had the supreme humility. Love is always like that. When, for example, someone falls ill, the person who loves him will perform the most menial services and will delight to do them, because love is like that. Sometimes men feel that they are too distinguished to do the humble things; they feel they are too important to have to do some menial task. Jesus was not so. He knew that He was Lord of all, and yet He took a towel and girded Himself and washed His disciples' feet.

(ii) Jesus knew that He had come from God and that He was going to God. He might well have had a certain contempt for men and for the things of this world. He might well have thought that He was finished with the world now, for He was on the way to God. It was just at that time when God was nearest to Him that Jesus went to the depths and the limits of His service of men. To wash the feet of the guests at a feast was the office of a slave. The disciples of the Rabbis were supposed to render their masters personal service, but a service like this would never have been dreamed of. The wonderful thing about Jesus was that His nearness to God, so far from separating Him from men, brought Him nearer than ever to men. It is always true that there is no one closer to men than the man who is close to God. T. R. Glover said of certain clever intellectuals: " They thought they were being religious when they were merely being fastidious." There is a legend of St. Francis of Assisi. In his early days he was very wealthy; nothing but the best was good enough for him; he was an aristocrat of the aristocrats. But he was ill at ease and there was no peace in his soul. One day he was riding alone outside the city; and as he rode he saw a leper, a mass of sores, a horrible and a repulsive sight. Ordinarily the fastidious Francis would have recoiled in horror from this hideous wreck of humanity. But something moved within him; he dismounted from his horse and on an impulse flung his arms around the leper; and, behold, the leper turned to the figure of Jesus as he embraced him. It is not as we separate ourselves from men that we come near to God. The nearer we are to suffering humanity, the nearer we are to God.

(iii) Jesus knew one other thing. Jesus was well aware that He was about to be betrayed. Such a knowledge might so easily have turned Him to bitterness and to resentment and to hatred of men; but it made His heart run out in greater love than ever. The astounding thing about Jesus was that the more men hurt Him, the more He loved them. And it is so easy and so natural to resent wrong, and to grow bitter under insult and injury. But Jesus met the greatest injury, the supreme disloyalty, with the greatest humility and the supreme love.

THE ROYALTY OF SERVICE

John 13: 1-17 (*continued*)

BUT there is more in the background of this passage than even John himself tells us. If we turn to Luke's account of the last meal together, we find the tragic sentence: " And there was a strife amongst them which of them should be accounted greatest " (*Luke* 22: 24). Even at the last meal together, within sight of the Cross, the disciples were still arguing about matters of precedence and prestige.

It may well be that this very argument produced the very situation which made Jesus act as He did. The roads of Palestine were quite unsurfaced and uncleaned. In dry weather they were inches deep in dust, and in wet weather they were liquid mud. The shoes the ordinary people wore were sandals; and these sandals were simply soles held on to the foot by a few straps. They gave little protection against the dust or the mud of the roads. For that reason there were always great waterpots at the door of the house; and a servant was there with a ewer and a towel to wash the soiled feet of the guests as they came in. Now Jesus' little company of friends had no servants. The duties which servants would carry out in wealthier circles they must have shared among each other. And it may well be that on the night of this last meal together they had got themselves into such a state of competitive pride that not one of them would accept the duty of being responsible for seeing that the water and the towels were there to wash the feet of the company as they came in. Jesus saw it; and Jesus mended that omission in the most vivid and dramatic way.

He Himself did what none of them was prepared to do. And then He said to them: " You see what I have done. You call me your master and your Lord; and you are quite right; for so I am; and yet I am prepared to do this for you; and surely you don't think that a pupil deserves more honour than a teacher, or a servant than a master. Surely if I do this, you ought to be prepared to do it. I am giving you this example of how you ought to behave towards each other."

A thing like this ought to make us think. So often, even in churches, there is trouble because someone does not get his or her place. So often it can happen that even ecclesiastical dignitaries will be offended because they did not receive the precedence to which their office entitles them. Here is the lesson and the proof that there is only one kind of greatness, and that is the greatness of service. The world is full of people who are standing on their dignity when they ought to be kneeling at the feet of their brethren. In every sphere of life this desire for prominence and this unwillingness to take a subordinate place wrecks the scheme of things. A player in a team is for one day omitted from the team and he will not play any more. An aspirant for political office is passed over for some office to which he thought he had a right and he refuses to accept any subordinate office. A singer in a choir is not given a solo to sing and he or she will not sing any more. In any society it may happen that someone is given a quite unintentional slight and he either explodes in anger or broods in sulkiness for days afterwards. When we are tempted to think of our dignity, our prestige, our place, our rights, let us see again the picture of the Son of God, girt with a towel, and kneeling at His disciples' feet.

It is the man who is truly great and truly beloved who has this regal humility, which makes him both servant and king among men. In *The Beloved Captain* by Donald Hankey, there is a passage which describes how the beloved captain cared for his men after a route march. " We all knew instinctively that he was our superior—a man of finer fibre than ourselves, a ' toff ' in his own right. I suppose that was why he could be so humble without loss of dignity. For he was humble, too, if that is the right word, and I think it is. No trouble of ours was too small for him to attend to. When we started route marches, for instance, and our feet were blistered and sore, as they often were at first, you would have thought that they were his own feet from the trouble he took. Of course after the march there was always an inspection of feet. That is the routine. But with him it was no mere routine. He came into our room, and, if any one had a sore foot, he would kneel down on the floor and look at it as carefully as if he had been a doctor. Then he would prescribe, and the remedies were ready at hand, being borne by a sergeant. If a blister had to be lanced, he would very likely lance it himself there and then, so as to make sure it was done with a clean needle and that no dirt was allowed to get in. There was no affectation about this, no striving after effect. It was simply that he felt that our feet were pretty important, and that he knew that we were pretty careless. So he thought it best at the start to see to the matter himself. Nevertheless, there was in our eyes something almost religious about this care for our feet. It seemed to have a touch of the Christ about it, and we loved and honoured him the more." The strange thing is that it is the man who stoops like that—like Christ—whom men in the end honour as a king, and the memory of whom they will not willingly let die.

THE ESSENTIAL WASHING

John 13: 1-17 (*continued*)

WE have already seen that in John we have always to be looking for two meanings. There is the meaning which lies on the surface, and there is the meaning which is beneath the surface. In this passage there is undoubtedly a second meaning. On the surface it is a great and dramatic and unforgettable lesson in humility. But there is more to it than that.

In it there is one very difficult passage. At first Peter wishes to refuse to allow Jesus to wash his feet. Jesus then tells him that unless he accepts this washing, he will have no part with Him. Peter then begs that not only his feet, but his hands and his head should also be washed. But Jesus tells him that it is enough that his feet should be washed. The difficult sentence and the important sentence, the sentence with an inner meaning, is: " He who has been bathed has only need to have his feet washed."

Beyond a doubt there is a reference to Christian baptism here. " Unless you are washed," said Jesus, " you can have no part in me." That is a way of saying: " Unless you pass through the gate of baptism, you have no part in the Church."

The point about the washing of the feet is this. It was the custom in Palestine that before people went to a feast they bathed themselves. When they came to the house of their host, they did not need to be bathed again; all that they needed was to have their feet washed. The washing of the feet was the ceremony which preceded entry into the house where they were to be guests. It was characteristically and universally what we might call *the washing of entry into the house*. So Jesus says to Peter: " It is not the bathing of your body that you require That you can do for yourself. What you need is the washing which marks entry into the household of the faith." Now this explains still another thing. Peter at first is going to refuse to allow Jesus to wash his feet. Jesus says that if he does, he will have no part in Him. It is as if Jesus said: " Peter, are you going to be too proud to let me do this for you? If you are, you will lose everything."

In the early Church, and still to-day, the way into the Church is the way of baptism; baptism is what we might call the washing of entry. This is not to say that a man cannot be saved unless he is baptized. It may not be possible for him to be so. But it does mean that if a man is able to be baptized and is too proud to enter by that gate, then his pride shuts him out from the family of the faith.

Things are different now. In the early days it was grown men and women who came to be baptized because they were coming direct from heathenism into the faith. Now we bring our children too in many of our churches. But in this passage Jesus was drawing a picture of the washing which is the entry to the Church, and He was telling men that they must not be too proud to submit to it.

THE SHAME OF DISLOYALTY AND THE GLORY OF FIDELITY

John 13: 18-20

> " It is not about you all that I am speaking. I know the kind of men whom I have chosen. It is all happening that the Scripture should be fulfilled: ' He who eats my bread has lifted up his heel against me.' I am telling you this now, before it happens, so that, when it does happen, you may believe that I am who I claim to be. This is the truth I tell you—he who receives whomsoever I will send, receives me; and he who receives me, receives Him who sent me."

THERE are three things stressed in this passage.

(i) The sheer cruelty of the disloyalty of Judas is vividly pictured, and it is pictured in a way which would be specially poignant to an eastern mind. To picture it Jesus used a quotation from *Psalm* 41: 9. In full the quotation runs: " Yea, mine own familiar friend, in whom I trusted, which did eat of my bread, hath lifted up his heel against me." In the east to eat bread with a person was a sign of friendship and an act of loyalty. 2 *Samuel* 9: 7, 13 tell how David granted it to Mephibosheth to eat bread at his table, when he might well have eliminated him as a descendant of Saul. I *Kings* 18: 19 tells how the prophets of Baal ate bread at the table of Jezebel. For one who had eaten bread at someone's table to turn against the person to whom, by that very act, he had pledged his friendship, was a bitter thing. This disloyalty of friends is for the Psalmist the sorest of all hurts. " For it was not an enemy that reproached me; then I could have borne it; neither was it he that hated me that did magnify himself against me; then I would have hid myself from him: but it was thou, a man mine equal, my guide, and mine acquaintance. We took sweet counsel together, and walked unto the house of God in company " (*Psalm* 55: 12-14). There is all the poignant sorrow in the world when a friend is guilty of this heart-breaking and heart-wounding disloyalty. Further, the very phrase that is used is full of cruelty. " He lifted up his heel against me." Literally in the Hebrew it is, " He made great the heel," and it is a phrase which describes " brutal violence." In this passage there is no hint of anger, only of sorrow. In this passage Jesus, with a last appeal, is revealing the wound upon His heart to Judas.

(ii) But this passage also stresses the fact that all this tragedy which is happening is somehow within the purpose of God, and that it is fully and unquestioningly accepted by Jesus. It was as Scripture said it would be. There was never any doubt that the winning of the world, and the redeeming of the world, would cost the broken heart of God. Jesus knew what was happening. He was not the victim but the master of circumstances. He knew the cost and He was ready to pay the cost. He did not want the disciples to think that He was caught up in a blind web of circumstances from which He could not escape. He was not going to be killed; He was going to choose to die. At the moment they did not, and they could not see that, but He wanted to be sure that a day would come when they would look back, and remember and understand.

(iii) But, if this passage stresses the bitterness of disloyalty, it also stresses the glory of fidelity. Some day these same disciples would take the message of Jesus out to the world. When they did so, they would be nothing less than the representatives of God Himself. When an ambassador goes out from this land to some other land, he does not go out as a private individual; he does not go out with only his own personal qualities and qualifications. He goes out with all the honour and all the glory of his country upon him. It may well happen that in a foreign land people do not even know his name; all that they know is that he stands for Britain. To listen to him is to listen to his country; to honour him is to honour the country he represents; to welcome him is to welcome the king or the queen who sent him out. The great honour and the great responsibility of being a pledged Christian is that we stand in the world for Jesus Christ. We speak for Him; we act for Him. The honour of the Eternal is in the hands of men.

LOVE'S LAST APPEAL

John 13: 21-30

When Jesus had said these things, He was troubled in spirit. Solemnly He declared: " This is the truth I tell you, one of you will betray me." The disciples began to look at each other, because they were at a loss to know about whom He was speaking. One of His disciples, the disciple whom Jesus loved, was reclining with his head on Jesus' breast. So Simon Peter made a sign to him and said to him: " Ask who it is that He is speaking about." The disciple who was reclining with his head on Jesus' breast said to Him: " Lord, who is it? " Jesus said: " It is he for whom I will dip the morsel in the dish and give it to him." So He took the morsel and dipped it in the dish and gave it to Judas Iscariot, the son of Simon. And after that man had received the morsel, Satan entered into him. So Jesus said to him: " Hurry on what you are going to do." None of those who were reclining at table understood why He said this to him. Some of them thought that, since Judas had the money-box, Jesus was saying to him: " Buy the things we need for the Feast "; or that He was telling him to give something to the poor. So that man took the morsel and went out at once—and it was night.

WHEN we visualise this scene certain most dramatic things emerge.

The treachery of Judas is seen at its worst. Judas must have been the perfect actor and the perfect hypocrite. One thing is quite clear—if the other disciples had known what Judas was doing, if they had known his scheme of betrayal, Judas would never have left that room alive that night. They would have killed him rather than let him go on his dreadful business. Judas must have had the behaviour of a saint and the heart of a devil. All the time he must have been putting on an act of love and loyalty and piety and devotion which deceived everyone except Jesus. Judas was not only a bare-faced villain; he was a suave hypocrite. There is warning here. By our outward actions we can deceive men; but there is no hiding things from the eye of Christ.

But there is more here. When we understand aright what was happening we can see that here there was appeal after appeal to Judas. First, there were the seating arrangements at the meal. The Jews did not sit at table; they reclined at table. The table was a low solid block, with couches round about it. It was shaped like a U and the place of honour, the place of the host, was in the centre of the single side. They reclined on the left side, resting on the left elbow, thus leaving the right hand free to deal with the food. Sitting in such a way a man's head was literally in the breast of the person who was reclining on his left. Jesus would be sitting in the place of the host, at the centre of the single side of the low table. The disciple whom Jesus loved must have been sitting on Jesus' *right*, for as he lent on his elbow at the table, his head was in Jesus' breast. The disciple whom Jesus loved is never

168

named. Some people have thought that he was Lazarus, for it is said that Jesus loved Lazarus (*John* 11: 36). Some people have thought that he was the rich young ruler. It is said that Jesus loved him (*Mark* 10: 21); and it has been imagined that in the end that young man did decide to stake everything on Jesus. Some people have thought that he was some otherwise unknown young disciple who was specially near and dear to Jesus, like a son. Some people have thought that he was not a real flesh and blood person at all, but only an ideal picture of what the perfect disciple ought to be. But throughout the years the general opinion has always been that the beloved disciple was none other than John himself; and we may well believe that that is so.

But it is the place of Judas that is of special interest It is quite clear that Judas was in a position in which Jesus could speak to him privately without the others overhearing it. There is a kind of private conversation here going on between Jesus and Judas. Now if that be so there is only one place in which Judas could be sitting. He must have been sitting on Jesus' *left*, so that, just as John's head was in Jesus' breast, Jesus' head was in Judas' breast. And the revealing thing about that is that *the place on the left of the host was the place of highest honour, kept for the most intimate friend*. When that meal began, Jesus must have said to Judas: " Judas, come and sit beside me to-night; I want specially to talk to you." The very inviting of Judas to that seat was an appeal.

But there is more than that. For the host to offer the guest a special tit-bit, a special morsel from the dish, was again a sign of special friendship. When Boaz wished to show how much he honoured Ruth, he invited her to come and dip her morsel in the wine (*Ruth* 2: 14). T. E. Lawrence told how when he sat with the Arabs in their tents, sometimes the Arab chief would tear a choice piece of fat mutton from the whole sheep which was before them and hand it to him, often a most embarrassing favour to a western palate, for it had to be eaten! So when Jesus handed the morsel to Judas, again it was a mark of special affection. And we note that even when Jesus did this the disciples did not gather the import of His words. That surely shows that Jesus was so much in the habit of doing this that to His disciples it seemed nothing unusual. Judas had always been picked out for special affection.

There is tragedy here. Again and again Jesus appealed to that dark heart, and again and again Judas remained unmoved. God save us from being thus completely impervious to the appeal of love.

LOVE'S LAST APPEAL

John 13: 21-30 (*continued*)

So this tragic drama plays itself out to the end. Again and again Jesus had showed His affection to Judas. Again and again Jesus had tried to save, not His own life, but Judas from what he was planning to do.

Then quite suddenly the crucial moment came. Here is the most terrible defeat in history, the moment when the love of Jesus admitted defeat. " Judas," He said, " hurry on what you propose to do." There was no point in delay now. Why waste time? Why carry on the useless appeal in this mounting tension? If it was to be done, it would be well to be done quickly.

Still the disciples did not see it. They thought that Judas was being despatched to make the arrangements for the Feast. It was always the custom at the Passover that those who had shared with those who had not. It was the time of all times when people gave to the poor. To this day it is the custom in many churches to take a special offering for those in need at our Communion services. So some of the disciples thought that Jesus was sending Judas out to give the usual present to the poor, that they too might be enabled to celebrate the Passover.

When Judas received the morsel, the devil entered into him. It is a terrible thing that that which was meant to be love's last appeal became hate's dynamic. That is what the devil can do. He can take the loveliest things and warp and twist them until they become the agents of hell. He can take love and turn it into lust; he can take holiness and turn it into pride; he can take discipline and turn it into sadistic cruelty; he can take affection and turn it into spineless complacence. We must be on the watch that in our lives the devil never warps the lovely things until he can use them for his own purposes.

So Judas went out—and it was night. John has a way of using words in the most pregnant way. It was night for the day was late; but there was another night there. It is always night when a man goes out from Christ to follow his own purposes. It is always night when a man listens to the call of evil rather than the summons of good It is always night when hate puts out the light of love. It is always night when a man turns his back on Jesus Christ.

If we submit ourselves to Christ we walk in the light; if we turn our backs on Him we go out into the dark. The way of light and the way of dark are set before us. God give us wisdom to choose aright—for in the dark a man always goes lost.

THE FOURFOLD GLORY

John 13: 31, 32

> When Judas had gone out, Jesus said: " Now the Son of Man has been glorified, and God has been glorified in Him; and now God will glorify Himself in Him; and He will glorify Him immediately."

THIS passage tells us of the fourfold glory.

(i) The glory of Jesus has come; and that glory is the Cross. Now the tension is gone; now any doubts that remained have been finally removed. Judas has gone out, and the Cross is a certainty. The glory of Jesus was the Cross. Here we are face to face with something which is of the very warp and woof of life. The greatest glory in life is the glory which comes from sacrifice. In any warfare the supreme glory belongs, not to those who survive and return, but to those who lay down their lives and never come back. As Binyon wrote:

> " They shall grow not old as we that are left grow old;
> Age shall not weary them, nor the years condemn,
> At the going down of the sun and in the morning
> We will remember them."

In medicine it is not the physicians who have made a fortune who are remembered; it is those who gave their lives that healing and ease from pain might come to men. It is the simple lesson of history that those who have made the great sacrifices have entered into the great glory. Mankind forgets the successful man, but mankind never forgets the sacrificial man.

(ii) In Jesus God has been glorified. It was the obedience of Jesus which brought glory to God. There is only one way in which anyone can show that he loves and admires and trusts a leader; and that is by obeying that leader, if need be to the bitter end. The only way in which an army can really honour a leader, is by unquestioningly following his leadership. The only way in which a child can honour a parent is by obeying that parent. Jesus gave the supreme honour and the supreme glory to God, because He gave to God the supreme obedience, the obedience which obeyed even unto a Cross.

(iii) In Jesus God glorifies Himself. It is a strange thought that the supreme glory of God lies in the Incarnation and the Cross. There is no glory like the glory of being loved. Had God remained aloof and majestic, serene and unmoved, untouched by any sorrow and unhurt by any pain, men might have feared God, and men might have admired God; but men would never have loved God. The law of sacrifice is not only a law of earth; it is a law

172

of heaven and earth. It was in the Incarnation and the Cross that God's supreme glory is displayed.

(iv) God will glorify Jesus. Here is the other side of the matter. At the moment the Cross was the glory of Jesus; but there was more to follow—there was the Resurrection; there was the Ascension; there will be the full and final triumph of Christ, which is what the New Testament means when it talks of the Second Coming of Christ. In the Cross Jesus found His own glory; but the day came, and the day will come, when that glory will be demonstrated to all the world and all the universe. The vindication of Christ must follow the humiliation of Christ; the enthronement of Christ must follow the crucifixion of Christ; the crown of thorns must change into the crown of glory. The campaign is the campaign of the Cross, but the King will yet enter into a triumph which all the world can see.

THE FAREWELL COMMAND

John 13: 33-35

> " Little children, I am still going to be with you for a little while. You will search for me; and, as I said to the Jews, so now I say to you too: ' You cannot go where I am going.' I give you a new commandment, that you love one another; that you too love one another, as I have loved you; it is by this that all will know that you are my disciples—if you have love amongst each other."

HERE Jesus is laying down His farewell commandment to His disciples. The time was short now; if they were ever to hear His voice they must hear it now. He was going on a journey on which none might accompany Him; He was taking a road that He had to walk alone; and before He went, He gave them the commandment that they must love one another as He had loved them. What does this mean for us, and for our relationships with our fellow men? How did Jesus love His disciples?

(i) Jesus loved His disciples *selflessly*. Even in the noblest human love there remains some element of self. We so often think—maybe unconsciously—of what we are to get from love. We think of the happiness, the thrill that we will receive, or the emptiness and the loneliness which we will suffer if love fails or is denied. So often, perhaps always, we are thinking: What will this love do for me? So often at the back of things it is *our* happiness that we are seeking. But Jesus never thought of Himself. His one desire was to give Himself and all He had for those He loved. His one desire was to do something for them, something that He knew that He alone could do.

(ii) Jesus loved His disciples *sacrificially*. There was no limit to what His love would give, and to where His love would go. No demand that could be made upon it was too much. If love meant the Cross, Jesus was prepared to go to that Cross. Sometimes we make a mistake. We think that love is meant to give us happiness. So in the end it does, but it may well be that love brings pain, and that love demands a cross.

(iii) Jesus loved His disciples *understandingly*. He knew His disciples through and through. He knew all their weaknesses and yet He still loved them. Those who really love us are the people who know us at our worst and who still love us. We never really know a person until we have lived with them. When we are only meeting them occasionally, we see them at their best. It is when we live with people that we find out their moods and their irritabilities and their weaknesses. And others have the same experience with us. Now Jesus had lived with His disciples day in and day out for many months. He knew all that was to be known about them and He still loved them. Sometimes we say that love is blind. That is not so, for the love that is blind can end in nothing but bleak and utter disillusionment. Real love is open-eyed. It loves, not what it imagines the person to be, but the person as he or she is. It loves, not a part of the person, but the whole person. It takes the other person, not only for better, but also for worse. The heart of Jesus is big enough to love us as we are.

(iv) Jesus loved His disciples *forgivingly*. The leader of them was to deny Him; they were all to forsake Him and to flee in His hour of need. They never, in the days of His flesh, really understood Him. They were blind and insensitive, and slow to learn, and ununderstanding. In the end they were craven cowards. But Jesus held nothing against them. There was no failure which He could not forgive. The love which has not learned to forgive cannot do anything else but shrivel and die. We are poor creatures, and there is a kind of fate in things which makes us hurt most of all those who love us most of all. And just for that very reason, all enduring love must be built on forgiveness, for without forgiveness it is bound to die.

THE FALTERING LOYALTY

John 13: 36-38

Simon Peter said to Him: " Lord, where are you going? " " Where I am going," Jesus answered, " you cannot now follow; but afterwards you will follow." Peter said to Him: " Lord, why can I not follow you now? I will lay down my life for you." Jesus answered: " Will you lay down your life for me? This is the truth I tell you—the cock will not crow until you will deny me three times."

WHAT was the difference between Peter and Judas? Judas betrayed Jesus, and Peter, in Jesus' hour of need, denied Him even with oaths and curses. And yet, while the name of Judas has become a name of blackest shame, there is something infinitely lovable about Peter. The difference is this. Judas' betrayal of Jesus was absolutely deliberate; it was carried out in cold blood; it must have been the result of careful thought and careful planning; and in the end it deliberately and callously refused the most poignant appeal. But there was never anything in this world less deliberate than Peter's denial of Jesus. Peter never meant to do it. He was swept away by a moment of weakness. For the moment, his will was too weak, but his heart was always right. The difference between Judas and Peter is that the sin of Judas was deliberate; the sin of Peter was the sin of a moment's weakness and a lifetime's regret. There is always a difference between the sin which is coldly and deliberately calculated, and the sin which involuntarily conquers a man in a moment of weakness or of passion. There is always a difference between the sin which knows what it is doing, and the sin that is the result of a moment when a man is so weakened or so inflamed that he does not know what he is doing. God save us from deliberately hurting Himself or those who love us!

There is something very lovely in the relationship between Jesus and Peter. No one ever knew anyone else so well as Jesus knew Peter.

(i) Jesus knew Peter in all his weakness. He knew Peter's impulsiveness; He knew Peter's instability; He knew how Peter had a habit of speaking with his heart before he had thought with his head. He knew well the strength of Peter's loyalty and the weakness of Peter's resolution. Jesus knew Peter as he was.

(ii) Jesus knew Peter in all his love. Jesus knew that whatever Peter did Peter loved Him. If we would only understand that! Sometimes people hurt us, or fail us, or wound us, or disappoint us. If we would only understand that when people act like that, it is not the real person who is acting. The real person is not the person who wounds us or fails us; the real person is the person who loves us. The basic thing is not their failure; the basic thing is their love. Jesus knew that about Peter. It would save us many

a heartbreak and many a tragic breach if we remembered
the basic love and forgave the moment's failure.

(iii) Jesus knew, not only what Peter was, but also what
Peter could become. Jesus knew that at the moment Peter
could not follow Him; but He was sure that the day
would come when Peter too would take the same red road
to martyrdom. It is the greatness of Jesus that He sees
the heroic even in the coward; He sees in us, not only
what we are, but also what He can make us. Jesus has
the love to see what we can be and the power to make us
attain to it.

THE PROMISE OF GLORY

John 14: 1-3

> " Do not let your heart be distressed. Believe in God
> and believe in me. There are many abiding-places in my
> Father's house. If it were not so, would I have told
> you that I am going to prepare a place for you?
> And, if I go and prepare a place for you, I am coming
> again, and I will welcome you to myself, that where
> I am, there you too may be."

In a very short time life for the disciples was going to fall in.
Their sun was going to set at midday and their world was
going to collapse in chaos around them. At such a time
there was only one thing to do—stubbornly to hold on to
trust in God. As the Psalmist had had it: " I had fainted,
unless I had believed to see the goodness of the Lord in
the land of the living " (*Psalm* 27: 13). " But mine eyes
are unto Thee, O God; in Thee is my trust " (*Psalm*
141: 8). There comes a time when we have to believe
where we cannot prove, and to accept where we cannot
understand. If, even in the darkest hour, we believe that
somehow there is a purpose in life, and that somehow that
purpose is love, then even the unbearable becomes bearable,
and even in the darkness there is still a glimmer of light. But
Jesus adds something to that. Jesus says not only:

" Believe in God." He also says: " Believe in me." If
it was possible for the Psalmist to believe in the ultimate
goodness of God, how much more so it is for us. For Jesus
is the proof that God is willing to give to us everything
He has to give. As Paul put it: " He that spared not His
own Son, but delivered Him up for us all, how shall He
not with Him, freely give us all things? " (*Romans* 8: 32).
If we believe that God is as Jesus taught Him to be, if
we believe that in Jesus we see the picture of God, then,
in face of that amazing love, it becomes, not easy, but at
least possible, to accept even what we cannot understand,
and even in the storms of life to retain a faith that is
serene.

Jesus went on to say: " There are many abiding places
in my Father's house." By His Father's house He meant
heaven. But what did He mean when He said that there
are many abiding places in heaven? The word that is used
for *abiding places* is the word *monai*. There are three
suggestions. (i) The Jews held that in heaven there are
different grades or ranks of blessedness which will be given
to men according to their goodness and their fidelity on
earth. In the *Book of the Secrets of Enoch* it is said: " In
the world to come there are many mansions prepared for
men; good for good; evil for evil." In that picture we
might liken heaven to a vast palace in which there are
many rooms, and to each there is assigned a room such
as his life has merited. (ii) In the Greek writer Pausanias
the word *monai* means *stages upon the way*. If that is
the meaning here, then it means that there are many
stages on the way to heaven, that even in heaven there is
progress and development and advance. There were at
least some of the great early Christian thinkers who had
that belief. Origen believed that. He said that when a
man died, his soul went to some place called Paradise,
which is still upon earth. There he received teaching and
training and, when he was worthy of it and fit for it, his
soul ascended into the air. It then passed through various

178

monai, stages, which the Greeks called *spheres* and which the Christians called *heavens*, until finally it reached the heavenly kingdom. In so doing the soul followed Jesus who, as the writer to the Hebrews said, " passed through the heavens " (*Hebrews* 4: 14). Irenaeus speaks of a certain interpretation of the sentence which tells how the seed that is sown produces sometimes a hundredfold, sometimes sixtyfold and sometimes thirtyfold (*Matthew* 13: 8). There was a different yield and therefore a different reward. Some men will be counted worthy to pass all their eternity in the very presence of God; others will rise to Paradise; and others will become citizens of " the city." Clement of Alexandria believed that there were degrees of glory, rewards and stages in proportion to a man's achievement in holiness in this life. There is something very attractive here. There is a sense in which the soul shrinks from what we might call a static heaven. There is something attractive in the idea of a progress, a development which goes on even in the heavenly places. Speaking in purely human and inadequate terms, we sometimes feel that we would be dazzled with too much splendour, if, immediately, we were ushered into the very presence of God, that even in heaven we would need to be cleansed and purified and helped until we can face the greater glory. No man can ever know whether such thoughts are true or not, but no man can say that they are forbidden. (iii) But it may well be that the meaning of this is very simple and very lovely and very precious. " There are many abiding-places in my Father's house." It may simply mean that in heaven there is room for all. An earthly house becomes over-crowded; an earthly inn must turn away the weary traveller because its accommodation is exhausted. It is not so with our Father's house, for heaven is as wide as the heart of God, and in heaven there is room for all. Jesus was saying to His friends: " Don't be afraid. Men may shut their doors upon you. But in heaven you will never be shut out."

THE PROMISE OF GLORY

John 14: 1-3 (*continued*)

THERE are certain other great truths within this passage

(i) It tells us of the honesty of Jesus. " If it were not so," asked Jesus, " would I have told you that I am going to prepare a place for you? " No one could ever claim that he had been inveigled into Christianity by specious promises or under false pretences. Jesus told men bluntly of the farewell to comfort that the Christian must bid (*Luke* 9: 57, 58). He told them of the persecution, the hatred, the penalties they would have to bear (*Matthew* 10: 16-22). He told them of the inevitable cross which they must carry (*Matthew* 16: 24). But He told them also of the glory of the ending of the Christian way. Jesus frankly and honestly told men what they might expect of glory and of pain if they followed Him. He was not a leader who tried to bribe men with promises of an easy way; He tried to challenge them into greatness.

(ii) It tells us of the function of Jesus. He said, " I am going to prepare a place for you." One of the great thoughts of the New Testament is that Jesus goes on in front for us to follow. He opens up a way which we may take and follow in His steps. One of the great words which is used to describe Jesus is the word *prodromos* (*Hebrews* 6: 20). The Authorised Version translates it *forerunner*. There are two uses of this word which light up the picture within it. In the Roman army the *prodromoi* were the reconnaissance troops. They went ahead of the main body of the army to blaze the trail and to ensure that it was safe for the rest of the troops to follow. The harbour of Alexandria was very difficult to approach. When the great corn ships came into it a little pilot boat was sent out to guide them in. It went before them, and they followed it, as it led them along the channel into safe waters. That pilot boat was called the *prodromos*. It went first to make it safe for others to follow. That is what Jesus did. He blazed the way to heaven and to God that we might follow in His steps.

(iii) It tells us of the ultimate triumph of Jesus. He said: " I am coming again." This is a very definite reference to the Second Coming of Jesus. The Second Coming is a doctrine which has to a large extent dropped out of Christian thinking and preaching. The curious thing about the doctrine of the Second Coming is that Christians seem either entirely to disregard it, or to think of nothing else at all. It is quite true that we cannot tell when it will happen; it is quite true that we cannot tell what will happen when it does happen. The very extravagances of the calculation of times and seasons, and of the pictures of the events of the Second Coming have tended to make people place it on one side as the realm of fanatics. But one thing is certain— history is not going nowhere; it is going somewhere. Without an end and a climax history is necessarily incomplete. History must have a consummation, and that consummation must be the triumph of Jesus Christ. And His promise is that in the day of His triumph He will welcome His friends.

(iv) Jesus said: " Where I am, there you will also be." Here is a great truth put in the simplest way. For the Christian, heaven is where Jesus is. We do not need to speculate on what heaven will be like. It is enough to know that we will be for ever with Him. When we love anyone with our whole hearts, life begins when we are with that person; it is only in their company that we are really and truly alive. It is so with Christ. In this world our contact with Him is shadowy, for we can only see through a glass darkly. It is spasmodic, for we are poor creatures and cannot live always on the heights. But the best definition of it is to say that heaven is that state where we will always be with Jesus, and where nothing will separate us from Him any more.

THE WAY, THE TRUTH AND THE LIFE

John 14: 4-6

> " And you know the way to where I go." Thomas
> said to Him: " Lord, we do not know where you are
> going. How do we know the way? " Jesus said to
> him: " I am the Way, the Truth and the Life. No
> one comes to the Father except through me."

AGAIN and again Jesus had told His disciples where He
was going, but somehow they had never yet understood.
" Yet a little while I am with you," He said, " and then
I go unto Him that sent me " (*John* 7: 33). He had told
them that He was going to the Father who had sent Him,
and with whom He was one; but they still did not understand what was going on. Still less did they understand
the way by which Jesus was going, for that way was the
Cross. At this moment the disciples were bewildered and
ununderstanding men. There was one among them who
could never say that he understood what he did not understand, and that one was Thomas. Thomas was the man
who was far too honest and far too much in earnest to be
satisfied with any vague and pious expressions. Thomas
had to be sure. So Thomas expressed his doubts and his
failure to understand, and the wonderful thing is that it
was the question of a doubting man which provoked one
of the greatest things that Jesus ever said. No one need
be ashamed of his doubts; for in this it is amazingly and
blessedly true that he who seeks will in the end find.

Jesus said to Thomas: " I am the Way, the Truth and
the Life." That is a great saying to us, but it would be a
still greater saying to a Jew who heard it for the first time.
In it Jesus took three of the great basic conceptions of
Jewish religion, and made the tremendous claim that in
Him all three found their full realization, and their full
expression.

The Jews talked much about the *way* in which men must
walk and the *ways* of God. God said to Moses: " Ye shall

not turn aside to the right hand or to the left; ye shall walk in all the *ways* which the Lord your God hath commanded you " (*Deuteronomy* 5: 32, 33). Moses said to the people: " I know that after my death ye will utterly corrupt yourselves, and turn aside from the *way* which I have commanded you " (*Deuteronomy* 31: 29). Isaiah had said: " Thine ears shall hear a word behind thee, This is the *way*, walk ye in it " (*Isaiah* 30: 21). In the brave new world there would be a highway which was called *the Way of Holiness*, and in it the wayfaring man, even though a simple soul, would not go lost (*Isaiah* 35: 8). It was the Psalmist's prayer: " Teach me Thy *way*, O Lord " (*Psalm* 27: 11). The Jews knew much about the Way of God in which a man must walk. And Jesus said: " I am the Way." What did Jesus mean? Suppose we are in a strange town and we ask for directions. Suppose the person says: " Take the first to the right, and the second to the left. Cross the square and go past the church and take the third on the right and the road you want is the fourth road on the left." If that happens the chances are that we will be lost before we get half way. But suppose the person we ask says: " Come. I'll take you there." In that case the person to us *is* the way, and we cannot miss it. That is what Jesus does for us. He does not only give us advice and directions and counsel. He takes us by the hand and leads us; He walks with us; He strengthens us and guides us and directs us personally every day. He does not tell us about the way; He is the Way.

Jesus said: " I am the Truth." The Psalmist said: " Teach me Thy way; I will walk in Thy *truth* " (*Psalm* 86: 11). " Thy loving kindness is before mine eyes," he said, " and I have walked in Thy *truth* " (*Psalm* 26: 3). " I have chosen the way of *truth*," he said (*Psalm* 119: 30). Now many men have told us the truth, but no man ever embodied the truth. There is one all-important thing about moral truth. The character of the man who teaches academic or scientific truth does not much affect his message. A man's character does not really affect his teaching of geometry or astronomy or Latin verbs. But if a man proposes to teach moral truth, his character makes all the difference in the world. An adulterer who teaches the necessity of purity, a grasping person who teaches the value of generosity, a domineering person who teaches the beauty of humility, an irascible creature who teaches the beauty of serenity, an embittered person who teaches the beauty of love, is bound to be ineffective. Moral truth cannot be conveyed solely in words; it must be conveyed in example. And that is precisely where the greatest human teacher falls down. No teacher has ever embodied the truth he taught—except Jesus. Many a man could say: " I have taught you the truth." Only Jesus could say: " I am the Truth." The tremendous thing about Jesus is not that the *statement* of moral perfection finds its peak in Him, although that is true; it is that the *fact* of moral perfection finds its realization in Him.

Jesus said: " I am the Life." The writer of the Proverbs said: " The commandment is a lamp, and the law is light; and the reproofs of instruction are the way of *life* " (*Proverbs* 6: 23). " He is in the way of *life* that keepeth instruction " (*Proverbs* 10: 17). " Thou wilt show me the path of *life*," said the Psalmist (*Psalm* 16: 11). In the last analysis what man is always seeking for is life. His search is not for knowledge for its own sake. What men want is that which will make life worth living. A novelist makes one of his characters who has fallen in love say: " I never knew what life was until I saw it in your eyes." Love had brought life. That is what Jesus does. Life with Jesus is life worth living; it is life indeed.

And there is one way of putting all this. " No one," said Jesus, " comes to the Father except through me." Jesus alone is the way to God. In Him alone we see what God is like; in Him alone we have access to God. He alone can show men God; and He alone can lead men into the presence of God without fear and without shame.

THE VISION OF GOD

John 14: 7-11

" If you had known me, you would have known my Father too. From now on you are beginning to know Him, and you have seen Him." Philip said to Him: " Lord, show us the Father, and that is enough for us." Jesus said to him: " Have I been with you for so long, and you did not know me, Philip? He who has seen me has seen the Father. How can you say: ' Show us the Father '? Do you not believe that I am in the Father and that the Father is in me? I am not the source of the words that I speak to you. It is the Father who dwells in me who is doing His own work. Believe me that I am in the Father and that the Father is in me. If you cannot believe it because I say it, believe it because of the very works I do."

IT may well be that to the ancient world this was the most staggering thing that Jesus ever said. To the Greeks God was characteristically *The Invisible*. The Jew would count it as an article of faith that no man has seen God at any time. To people who thought like that Jesus said: " If you had known me, you would have known my Father too." Then Philip asked what he must have believed to be the impossible. Maybe he was thinking back to that tremendous day when God revealed His glory to Moses (*Exodus* 33: 12-32). But even in that great day, God had said to Moses: " Thou shalt see my back parts: but my face shall not be seen." In the time of Jesus men were oppressed and fascinated by what is called the transcendence of God. They were oppressed with the thought of the difference and the distance between God and man. They would never have dared to think that they could see God. Then Jesus says with utter simplicity: " He who has seen me has seen the Father." To see Jesus is to see what God is like. A recent writer said that Luke in his gospel " domesticated God." He meant that Luke shows us God in Jesus taking a part and a share in the most intimate and homely things. When we see Jesus we can say: "This is God taking upon Himself and living our life." If that be so—and it is so—we can say the most precious things about God.

(i) God entered into an ordinary home and into an ordinary family. As Francis Thompson wrote so beautifully in *Ex Ore Infantum*:

> "Little Jesus, wast Thou shy
> Once, and just so small as I?
> And what did it feel to be
> Out of Heaven and just like me?"

Anyone in the ancient world would have thought that if God did come into this world, He would have come as some King into some royal palace with the might and majesty and power which the world calls greatness. As George Macdonald wrote:

> "They all were looking for a king
> To slay their foes, and lift them high;
> Thou cam'st, a little baby thing,
> That made a woman cry."

As the child's verse says:

> "There was a knight of Bethlehem
> Whose wealth was tears and sorrows;
> His men at arms were little lambs,
> His trumpeters were sparrows."

In Jesus God once and for all sanctified human birth, sanctified the humble home of ordinary folk, and sanctified all childhood for ever.

(ii) God was not ashamed to do a man's work. It was as a working man that God entered into the world. Jesus was the carpenter of Nazareth. We can never sufficiently realize the wonder of the fact that God understands our day's work. He knows the difficulty of making ends meet; He knows the difficulty of the ill-mannered customer and the client who will not pay his bills. He knew all the difficulty of living together in an ordinary home and in a big family, and He knew every problem which besets us in the work of every day. According to the Old Testament work is a curse. According to the old story, the curse on man for the sin of Eden was: " In the sweat of thy face shalt thou eat bread " (*Genesis* 3: 19); but according to the New Testament common work is tinged with glory for it was touched by the hand of God.

(iii) God knows what it is to be tempted. The extraordinary thing about the life of Jesus is that it shows us, not the serenity, but the struggle of God. Anyone might conceive of a God who lived in a serenity and peace which were beyond the tensions of this world; but Jesus shows us a God who goes through the eternal struggle through which we must go. God is not like a commander who leads from behind the lines; God too knows the fighting-line of life.

(iv) In Jesus we see God loving. The moment love enters into life pain enters into life. If we could be absolutely detached from human pain and human sorrow, if we could so arrange life that nothing and nobody mattered to us, then there would be no such thing as sorrow and pain of heart and anxiety of mind. But in Jesus we see God caring intensely, yearning over men, feeling poignantly for men and with men, loving men until He bore the wounds of love upon His heart.

(v) In Jesus we see God upon a Cross. There is nothing quite so incredible as this in all the world. It is easy to imagine a God who condemns men; it is still easier to imagine a God who blasts men, and who, if men oppose Him, wipes them out. No one would ever have dreamed of a God who in Jesus Christ chose the Cross for us men and for our salvation.

" He who has seen me has seen the Father." Jesus is the revelation of God, and that revelation leaves the mind of man staggered and amazed into wonder, love and praise.

THE VISION OF GOD

John 14: 7-11 (*continued*)

BUT JESUS goes on to say something else. There was one thing no Jew would ever lose his grip of, and that is the sheer loneliness of God. The Jews were unswerving monotheists. The danger of the Christian faith is that we set up Jesus as a kind of secondary God. But Jesus went on. He insists that the things He said and the things He did did not come from His own initiative or His own power or His own knowledge; they came from God. His words were God's voice speaking to men; His deeds were God's power flowing through Him to men. He was the channel by which God came to men. Let us take a very simple and a very imperfect analogy. There are two which will help us from the relationship which exists between student and teacher. Dr. Lewis Muirhead said of that great Christian and expositor A. B. Bruce, that men " came to see in the man the glory of God." Any teacher has the responsibility of transmitting something of the glory of his subject to those who listen to him; and one who teaches about Jesus Christ can, if he is saint enough, transmit the vision and the presence of Christ to those who listen to him and have fellowship with him. That is what A. B. Bruce did for his students, and in an infinitely greater way that is what Jesus did for God. He transmitted the glory and the love of God to men. But there is another analogy. A great teacher stamps his students with something of himself. W. M. Macgregor was a student of A. B. Bruce. A. J. Gossip tells us in his memoir of W. M. Macgregor that, " when it was rumoured that Macgregor thought of deserting the pulpit for a chair, men, in astonishment, asked, Why? He replied, with modesty, that he had learned some things from Bruce that he would fain pass on." Principal John Cairns wrote to his teacher Sir William Hamilton: " I do not know what life, or lives, may lie before me. But I know this, that, to the end of the last of them, I shall bear your mark upon me." Sometimes if a divinity student has been trained by a great preacher whom he really loves, we can see in the student something of the teacher, and hear something of the teacher's voice. Sometimes people will say of such a disciple and of such a master: " If you shut your eyes you would think it was so-and-so preaching." Jesus did something like that for God, only infinitely and immeasurably more so. He brought God's accent, God's message, God's mind, God's heart to men. We do well every now and then to remember, we *must* every now and then remember, that all is of God. It was not a self-chosen expedition to the world which Jesus made. He did not do it to soften a hard heart in God. He came because God sent Him, because God so loved the world. At the back of Jesus, and in Jesus, there is God.

Then Jesus went on to make a claim and to offer a test, both of which He was always claiming and always offering. Jesus' claim was always based on two things; His *words* and His *works*.

(i) He claimed to be tested by what *He said*. It is as if Jesus said: " When you listen to me, can you not realize at once that what I am saying is God's own truth?" The words of any genius are always self-evidencing. When we read great poetry we cannot for the most part say why it is great and why it grips our heart. It is true that we may analyse the vowel sounds and so on, but in the end there is something which defies analysis, but something which is easily and immediately recognizable. It is so with the words of Jesus. When we hear them we cannot help saying: " If only the world would live on these principles, how different the world would be! If only I would live on these principles, how different I would be! "

(ii) He claimed to be tested by His *deeds*. He said to Philip: " If you cannot believe in me because of what I say, surely you are bound to allow what I can do to convince you." That was the same answer that Jesus sent back to John. John had sent his messengers to ask whether Jesus was the Messiah, or if they must look for another. The answer of Jesus was quite simple: " Go back," He said, " and tell John what is happening—and that will convince him " (*Matthew* 11: 1-6). The proof that Jesus is who He is, is His ability to heal the sick body and to cure the sick mind. No one else ever succeeded in making bad men good.

Jesus said in effect to Philip: " Listen to me! Look at me! And believe! " That is still the way to Christian belief. The way to Christian belief is not to argue about Jesus but to listen to Him and to look at Him. If we do that, the sheer personal impact upon us will compel us to believe.

THE TREMENDOUS PROMISES

John 14: 12-14

> " This is the truth I tell you—he that believes on me will do the works that I do, and he will do greater works than these, because I go to my Father. And I will do whatever you shall ask in my name, that the Father may be glorified in the Son. If you ask me anything in my name, I will do it."

THERE could scarcely be any greater promises than the two promises which are contained in this passage. But they are promises of such a nature that we must try to understand what they mean and what they promise. Unless we grasp what they mean, the experience of life is bound to disappoint us.

(i) First of all Jesus said that one day His disciples would do what He did, and that they would do even greater works than these. What did Jesus mean when He said that?

(*a*) It is quite certain that in the early days the early Church possessed the power of working healing cures. Paul enumerates among the gifts which different people had the gift of healing (1 *Corinthians* 12: 9, 28, 30). James

190

urged that when any Christian was sick, the elders should pray over him and anoint him with oil (*James* 5: 14). But it is clear that that is by no means all that Jesus meant; for though it could be said that the early Church did the things which Jesus did, it surely could not be said that they did greater things than He did, for that would be an impossibility.

(*b*) It is the fact that as time has gone on man has more and more learned to conquer disease. The physician and the surgeon nowadays have powers which to the ancient world would have seemed miraculous and even godlike. The surgeon with his new techniques, the physician with his new treatments and his miracle drugs, can now effect the most amazing cures. There is a long way to go yet but one by one the citadels of pain and disease have been stormed, and the physical enemies of man have capitulated. Now the salient thing about all this is that it was the power and the influence of Jesus Christ which brought it about. Why should men strive to save the weak and the sick and the dying, those whose bodies are broken and whose minds are darkened? Under the Hitler regime such people were eliminated; and yet in this country we find so eminent a doctor as the late Lord Horder adamantly opposed to euthanasia. Why is it that men of skill and science have felt moved, and even compelled, to spend their time and their strength, to ruin their health, and sometimes to sacrifice their lives, to find cures for disease and relief from pain? The answer is that, whether they knew it or not, Jesus was saying to them through His Spirit: " These people must be helped and healed. You must do it. You cannot see pain and suffering unchecked and unhelped. It is your duty and your task and your responsibility and your privilege to do all that you can for them." It is the Spirit of Jesus who has been behind the conquest of disease. It is true that men can do things nowadays which in the time of Jesus no one would ever have dreamed of as possible.

(c) But we are still not at the meaning of this. Think of what Jesus in the days of His flesh had *actually done*. He had never preached outside Palestine. His voice had never gone out to the whole world of men. Within His lifetime Europe had never heard the gospel. Whatever Palestine was like, Jesus had never personally to meet the situation of the moral degradation of a city like Rome. Even Jesus' opponents in Palestine were religious men. The Pharisees and the Scribes had given their lives to religion, as they saw it, and there was never any doubt that they revered and practised purity of life. It was not in Jesus' lifetime that Christianity went out to a world where the marriage bond was set at nought, where adultery was not even a conventional sin, which was riddled with homosexuality, and where vice flourished like a tropical forest. It was into that world the early Christians went; and it was that world which was won for Christ. When it came to a matter of numbers and extent and changing power, the triumphs of the message of the Cross were even greater than the triumphs of Jesus in the days of His flesh. It is of moral recreation, of spiritual victory that Jesus is speaking. And He says that this will happen because He is going to His Father. What does He mean by that? He means this—in the days of His flesh He was limited to Palestine. When He had died and risen again, He was liberated from the limitations of the flesh, and His Spirit could work mightily anywhere. It was precisely because He went to His Father that His Spirit was set free to operate with power throughout the whole world.

In His second promise Jesus says that any prayer offered in His name will be granted. Now it is here of all places that we must understand. Let us note carefully what Jesus said. He did *not* say that all our prayers would be granted. He said that our prayers *made in His name* would be granted. The test of any prayer is: Can I make this prayer in the name of Jesus? No man, for instance, could pray a prayer of personal revenge, of personal ambition, of desire to surpass someone else, someone unworthy and unchristian and unchristlike object *in the name of Jesus*. When we pray, we must always ask: Can I honestly pray this *in the name of Jesus*? or, Am I praying this out of my own personal desires and aims and ambitions? The prayer which can stand the test of that consideration, and the prayer which, in the end says: Thy will be done, is always answered. But the prayer which is based on self cannot expect to be heard, because it is prayed in the name of self and not in the name of Jesus.

THE PROMISED HELPER

John 14: 15-17

> " If you love me, keep my commandments; and I will ask the Father and He will give you another Helper to be with you for ever, I mean the Spirit of Truth. The world cannot receive Him, because it does not see Him or know Him. But you know Him because He remains among you and will be within you."

To John there is only one test of love, and that test is obedience. It was by His obedience that Jesus showed His love of God; and it is by our obedience that we must show our love to Jesus. C. K. Barrett says: " John never allowed love to devolve into a sentiment or emotion. Its expression is always moral and is revealed in obedience." We know all too well how in life there are those who protest their love in words, and who use the outward actions of love, but who, at the same time, bring pain and heartbreak to those whom they claim to love. There are children and young people who would say that they love their parents, and who yet cause grief and anxiety to them. There are husbands who say that they love their wives, and wives who say that they love their husbands, and who yet, by their inconsiderateness and their irritability and their thoughtless unkindness bring pain the one to the other. To Jesus real love is not an easy thing. Real love is shown only in true obedience. And the result is that what men call love is not love at all, for real love is the rarest thing in the world.

Obviously this love which issues in obedience is not an easy thing. But Jesus does not leave us to struggle with the Christian life alone. He would send us another *Helper*. Here we have an untranslatable word. The Greek word is the word *paraklētos*. The Authorised Version translates it *Comforter*, which, although it is hallowed by time and usage, is not a good translation. Moffatt translates it *Helper*. It is only when we examine this word *paraklētos* in detail that we catch something of the riches of the doctrine of the Holy Spirit. The word *paraklētos* really means *someone who is called in*; but it is the reason *why* the person is called in which gives the word its distinctive associations. The Greeks used the word in a wide variety of ways. A *paraklētos* might be a person *called in* to give witness in a law court in someone's favour; he might be an advocate *called in* to plead someone's cause when someone was under a charge which would issue in serious penalty; he might be an expert *called in* to give advice in some difficult situation. He might be a person *called in* when, for example, a company of soldiers were depressed and dispirited to put new courage into their minds and hearts. Always a *paraklētos* is *someone called in to help* when the person who calls him in is in trouble or distress or doubt or bewilderment. Now the word *Comforter* was once a perfectly good translation. It actually goes back to Wicliffe; he was the first person to use it. But in his day it meant much more than it means now. The word *comforter* comes from the Latin word *fortis* which means *brave*; and a comforter was someone who enabled some dispirited creature to be brave. Nowadays the word *comfort* has to do almost solely with sorrow; and a comforter is someone who sympathizes with us when we are sad. Beyond a doubt the Holy Spirit does that, but to limit the work of the Holy Spirit to that function is sadly to belittle Him. We have a modern phrase which we often use. We talk of being able *to cope* with things. That is precisely the work of the Holy Spirit. The Holy Spirit comes to us and takes away our inadequacies and enables us to cope with life. The Holy Spirit substitutes victorious for defeated living.

So what Jesus is saying is: " I am setting you a hard task, and I am sending you out on an engagement very difficult. But I am going to send you someone, the *paraklētos*, who will guide you what to do and who will make you able to do it. The Holy Spirit will bring you truth and will make you able to cope with the battle for the truth."

But Jesus went on to say that the world cannot recognize the Spirit. By the world John meant that section of men who live as if there was no God, those people who, when they organize their lives, leave God out of the reckoning altogether as irrelevant. Now the point of this saying of Jesus is this : we can only see what we are fitted to see. An astronomer will see far more in the sky than an ordinary man. A botanist will see far more in a hedgerow than someone who knows no botany. A doctor will find out far more about a person by looking at him than an unskilled person will. Someone who knows about art will see far more in a picture than someone who is quite ignorant will. Someone who understands a little about music will get far more out of a symphony than someone who knows nothing. Always what we see and what we experience depends on what we bring to the sight and to the experience. Now a person who has eliminated God never has any time of the day or the week when he waits upon God and listens for God. He would think such a time a waste of time. And we cannot receive the Holy Spirit unless we wait in silence and in expectation and in prayer for the Holy Spirit to come to us. The simple fact is that the world is too busy to give the Holy Spirit a chance to enter in. For the Holy Spirit gate-crashes no man's heart; He waits to be received.

So when we think of the wonderful things which the Holy Spirit does and brings to life, surely we will set apart some time amidst the bustle and the rush of life to wait in silence for His coming and His power.

THE WAY TO FELLOWSHIP AND TO REVELATION

John 14: 18-24

> " I will not leave you forlorn. I am coming to you. In a little while the world will no longer see me; but you will see me because I will be alive and you too will be alive. In that day you will know that I am in the Father, and that you are in me, even as I am in you. It is he who grasps my commandments and keeps them who loves me. He who loves me will be loved by my Father, and I will love him and reveal myself to him." Judas, not Iscariot, said to Him: " Why has it happened that you are going to reveal yourself to us, and not to the world? " Jesus answered: " If any man loves me, he will keep my word; and the Father will love him, and we will come to him, and we will make our abode with him. He who does not love me does not keep my words. And the word which you hear is not mine, but it belongs to the Father who sent me."

BY this time it must have been that a sense of foreboding must have enveloped the disciples. Even they must have seen by this time that there was tragedy ahead. But Jesus says: " I will not leave you all forlorn." The word He uses is *orphanos*. *Orphanos* means *without a father*. But it was also used of disciples and students bereft of the presence and the teaching of a beloved master. Plato says that, when Socrates died, his disciples " thought that they would have to spend the rest of their lives forlorn, as children bereft of a father, and they did not know what to do about it." But Jesus told His disciples that would not be the case with Him and them. " I am coming back," He said. This time He is talking of His Resurrection and His risen presence. They will see Him because *He* will be alive, because death could never conquer Him; and they will see Him because *they* will be alive. What Jesus means is that they will be spiritually alive. At the moment they are bewildered and numbed with the sense of impending tragedy; but the day will come when their eyes will be opened, when their minds will understand, when their hearts will be kindled—and then they will really see Him. That in fact is precisely what happened when Jesus rose from the dead. His rising changed despair to hope, and it was then they realized beyond a doubt that He was the Son of God.

In this passage John is playing on certain ideas which are never far from his mind.

(i) First and foremost there is love. For John love is the basis of everything. God loves Jesus; Jesus loves God; God loves men; Jesus loves men; men love God through Jesus; and men love each other; heaven and earth, man and God, man and man are all bound together by this bond of love.

(ii) Once again John stresses the necessity of obedience. Obedience is the only proof of love. It was to those who loved Him that Jesus appeared when He rose from the dead, not to the Scribes and the Pharisees and the hostile Jews.

(iii) This obedient, trusting love leads to two things. First, it leads to ultimate safety. On the day of the triumph of Christ those who have been obedient lovers of Christ will be safe in a crashing world. Second, this obedient, trusting love leads to a fuller and a fuller revelation. It is to the man who loves Him that Jesus reveals Himself ever more fully. The knowledge of God, the revelation of God is a costly thing. There is always a moral basis for revelation. It is to the man who keeps His commandments that Christ reveals Himself. No evil man can ever receive the revelation of God. He can be used by God, but he can have no fellowship with God. It is only to the man who is looking for Him that God reveals Himself; and it is only to the man who, in spite of failure, is reaching up that God reaches down. Fellowship with God, the revelation of God are dependent on love; and love is dependent on obedience. The more we obey God, the more we understand God; and the man who walks in God's way inevitably walks with God.

THE BEQUESTS OF CHRIST

John 14: 25-31

> " I have spoken these things to you while I am still with you. The Helper, the Holy Spirit, whom the Father will send in my name, will teach you all things, and will remind you of all that I have said. I am leaving you peace: I am giving you my peace. I do not give it to you as the world gives peace. Let not your heart be distressed or fear-stricken. You have heard that I said to you: ' I am going away and I am coming to you.' If you loved me, you would be glad that I am going to my Father, because the Father is greater than I. And now I have told you about it before it happens, so that whenever it does happen, you will believe. I shall not say much more to you, because the prince of this world is coming. He has no hold over me. His coming will only make the world know that I love the Father, and that I do as the Father has commanded me. Rise, let us be going.'

THIS is a passage close-packed with truth. In it Jesus speaks of five things.

(i) He speaks of His *ally*, the Holy Spirit. Here Jesus says two basic things about the Holy Spirit. (*a*) The Holy Spirit will teach us all things. To the end of the day the Christian must be a learner, for to the end of the day the Holy Spirit will be leading him deeper and deeper into the truth of God. There is never any time in life when the Christian can say that he knows the whole truth. There is never any excuse in the Christian faith for the shut mind. The Christian who feels that he has nothing more to learn is the Christian who had not even begun

to understand what the doctrine of the Holy Spirit means.
(b) The Holy Spirit will remind us of what Jesus has said.
This means two things. In the matters of belief, the Holy
Spirit is constantly bringing back to us the things which
Jesus said. It is an obligation to think, but all our conclusions must be tested against the things which Jesus
said. It is not so much the truth that we have to discover;
Jesus told us the truth. What we have to discover is the
meaning of the truth, the meaning of the things which
Jesus said. The Holy Spirit saves us from arrogance and
error of thought. (c) The Holy Spirit will keep us right
in matters of conduct. Nearly all of us have a repeated
experience in life. When we are tempted to do something
wrong, when we are on the very brink of doing it, back
into our mind comes a saying of Jesus, the verse of a psalm,
the picture of Jesus, the saying of someone whom we love
and admire, the teaching we received when we were very
young. In the moment of danger unbidden these things
flash into our minds. That is the work of the Holy Spirit.
In the moment of our testing, the Holy Spirit brings to us
the memory of the things we never should forget.

(ii) He speaks of His *gift*, and His gift is *peace*. In the
Bible the word *peace*, *shalōm*, never simply means the
absence of trouble. Peace means everything which makes
for our highest good. The peace which the world offers
us is the peace of escape, the peace which comes from the
avoidance of trouble, the peace which comes from refusing
to face things. The peace which Jesus offers us is the peace
of conquest. It is the peace which no experience in life
can ever take from us. It is the peace which no sorrow,
no danger, no suffering can make less. It is the peace which
is independent of outward circumstances.

(iii) He speaks to us of His *destination*. Jesus is going
back to His Father. And Jesus says that if His disciples
really loved Him, they would be glad that it was so. He
was being released from the limitations of this world;
He was being restored to His glory. If we really grasped

199

the truth of the Christian faith, we would always be glad when those whom we love go to be with God. That is not to say that we would not feel the sting of sorrow and the sharpness of loss; but it is to say that, even in our sorrow and our loneliness, we would be glad that after the troubles and the trials of earth those whom we loved have gone to be with God. We would never grudge them their rest and their release. We would remember that they have entered, not into death, but into blessedness.

(iv) He speaks to them of His *struggle*. The Cross was the final battle of Jesus with the powers of evil. But Jesus was not afraid of the Cross, for He knew that evil had no ultimate power over Him. He went to the Cross in the certainty, not of defeat, but of conquest.

(v) He speaks to us of His *vindication*. At the moment men saw in the Cross only His humiliation and His shame; but the time would come when men would see in the Cross His obedience to God and His love to men. The very things which were the keynotes of Jesus' life found their highest expression in the Cross. There, in a way which there was no surpassing, there was demonstrated Jesus' obedience to God, and Jesus' love for men.

THE VINE AND THE BRANCHES

John 15: 1-10

" I am the real vine and my Father is the vine-dresser. He destroys every branch in me which does not bear fruit; and He cleanses every branch which does bear fruit, so that it may bear more fruit. You are already clean through the word which I have spoken to you. Abide in me even as I abide in you. As the branch cannot bear fruit in its own strength, unless it abides in the vine, so neither can you, unless you abide in me. I am the vine; you are the branches. The man who abides in me, and in whom I abide, bears much fruit, because without me you can do nothing. If anyone does not abide in me he will be cast out like a withered branch. And they gather such branches and throw them into the fire and they are burned. If you abide in me, and my words abide in you, ask what you will, and it will be given to you. It is by the fact that you bear such fruit, and that you show yourselves to be my disciples, that my Father is glorified. As the Father has loved me, so I have loved you. Abide in my love. As I have kept my Father's commandments, so I abide in His love."

JESUS, as He so often did, is working in this passage with pictures and ideas which were part of the religious heritage of the Jewish nation. Over and over again in the Old Testament, Israel is pictured as the vine or the vineyard of God. Isaiah has the great picture of Israel as the vineyard of God. " The vineyard of the Lord is the house of Israel " (*Isaiah* 5: 1-7). " I had planted thee a noble vine " comes God's message to Israel through Jeremiah (*Jeremiah* 2: 21). *Ezekiel* 15 likens Israel to the vine, as does *Ezekiel* 19: 10. " Israel is an empty vine," said Hosea (*Hosea* 10: 1). " Thou hast brought a vine out of Egypt," sang the Psalmist, thinking of God's deliverance of His people from bondage (*Psalm* 80: 8). So much so was this the case that the vine had actually become the symbol of the nation of Israel. The emblem on the coins of the Maccabees was the vine. One of the glories of the Temple was the great golden vine upon the front of the Holy Place. Many a great man had counted it an honour to give gold to mould a new bunch of grapes, or even a new grape on to that vine. The vine was part and parcel of Jewish imagery; it was the very symbol of the nation of Israel.

But Jesus calls Himself the *true* vine, the real, the genuine vine. What is the point of that word *alēthinos*, true, real, genuine? The point is this. It is a curious fact that the symbol of the vine is never used in the Old Testament apart from the idea of *degeneration*. The point of Isaiah's picture is that the vineyard has run wild. It is Jeremiah's complaint that the nation has turned into " a degenerate plant of a strange vine." It is Hosea's cry that Israel is an *empty* vine. It is as if Jesus said: " You think that because

you belong to the nation of Israel you are a branch in the
true vine of God.   You think that just because you are
a Jew, and a member, as you think, of the chosen people,
you are because of your race and birth and nationality
a branch in the vine of God.   But it is not the nation who
is the true vine.   The nation is a degenerate vine, as all
your prophets saw.   It is I who am the true vine.   It is
not the fact that you are a Jew which will save you.   The
only thing that can save you is to have an intimate living
fellowship and belief with *me*, for I am the vine of God,
and you must be branches joined to me."   Jesus was laying
it down that not Jewish blood but faith in Him was the
way to God's salvation.   No external qualification can
set a man right with God; only the friendship of Jesus
Christ can do that.

THE VINE AND THE BRANCHES

John 15: 1-10 (*continued*)

WHEN Jesus drew His picture of the vine He knew what
He was talking about.   The vine was grown all over
Palestine.   It is a plant which needs a great deal of attention
if the best fruit is to be got out of it.   It is grown commonly
on terraces.   The ground has to be perfectly clean.   It is
sometimes trained on trellisses; it is sometimes allowed
to creep over the ground upheld by low forked sticks;
it sometimes even grew round the doors of the cottages; but
wherever it grew careful preparation of the soil was essential.
The vine grows luxuriantly, and drastic pruning is necessary.
So luxuriant is it that the slips are set in the ground at
least twelve feet apart, for the vine will creep over the
ground at speed.   A young vine was not allowed to fruit
for the first three years.   Each year it was cut drastically
back that it might develop and conserve its life and energy.
When it is mature, it is pruned in December and January.
It bears two kinds of branches, one fruit-bearing, and

one non-fruit-bearing; and the non-fruit-bearing branches are drastically and mercilessly pruned back, so that they will drain away none of the strength of the plant. The vine will never produce the crop of which it is capable without this drastic pruning—and Jesus knew that.

Further, the wood of the vine has the curious characteristic that it is good for nothing. It is too soft to use for any purpose. At certain times of the year it was laid down by the law that the people must bring offerings of wood to the Temple for the altar fires for the sacrifices. And it was definitely laid down that the wood of the vine must not be brought. It was useless for that purpose. The only thing that could be done with the wood pruned out of a vine was to make a bonfire of it and to destroy it. Jesus knew that, and it adds to the picture He draws.

Jesus says that His followers are like that. Some of them are lovely fruit-bearing branches of Himself; others are useless because they bear no fruit. Who was Jesus thinking of when He spoke of the fruitless branches? There are two answers to that. First, He was thinking of the Jews. They were branches of God's vine. Was not that the picture that prophet after prophet had drawn of them? But they refused to listen to Him; they refused to accept Him; and therefore they were withered and useless branches. Second, He was thinking of something more general than that. He was thinking of Christians whose Christianity consisted of profession without practice, of words without deeds. He was thinking of Christians who were useless branches, all leaves and no fruit. And He was thinking of Christians who became apostates, who heard the message and who accepted it and who fell away, who abandoned their faith, and who became traitors to the Master whom they had once pledged themselves to serve.

So then there are three ways in which we can be useless branches. We can refuse to listen to Jesus Christ at all. We can listen to Him, and then render Him a lip service unsupported by any deeds. We can accept Him as Master, and then, in face of the difficulties of the way, or moved by the desire to do as we like and not as He likes, we can abandon Him. But there is one thing we must remember. It is a first principle of the New Testament that *uselessness invites disaster*. And the fruitless branch is on the way to destruction.

THE VINE AND THE BRANCHES

John 15: 1-10 (continued)

IN this passage there is much about abiding in Christ. What is meant by that? It is true this phrase has a mystical meaning, that there is a mystical sense in which the Christian is in Christ and Christ is in the Christian. But there are many—maybe they are in the majority—who are not mystics and who never have this mystical experience If we are like that, we must not blame ourselves. There is a much simpler way of looking at this and of understanding it and experiencing it, a way which is open to anyone.

Let us take a human analogy. All analogies are imperfect but we must work with the ideas which we possess. Suppose a person is by himself a weak person. Suppose he has actually fallen to temptation; suppose he has made a mess of things; suppose he is on the way down to degeneracy of mind and heart and mental fibre. Now suppose that this person has a friend of a strong and lovely and loving nature; and suppose this strong friend rescues this person from his degraded situation. There is only one way in which the weaker person can retain his reformation and keep himself on the right way. *He must keep contact with his friend.* If he loses that contact, all the chances are that his weakness will overcome him; the old temptations will rear their heads again; and he will fall. His salvation lies in continual contact with the strength of his friend. Many a time a down-and-out has been taken to live with someone fine. So long as he continued in that fine home and that fine presence he was safe. But if he kicked over the traces, if he wished to become independent again, if he went off on his own, he fell. We must keep contact with the fine thing in order to defeat the evil and the lower thing. Robertson of Brighton was one of the great preachers There was a tradesman who had a little shop; in the back room he kept a photograph of Robertson, for Robertson was his hero and his inspiration. Whenever he was tempted to carry out a bit of sharp practice, he would rush into the back room and look at the photograph and he could not do the evil thing. When Kingsley was asked the secret of his own life, referring to F. D. Maurice he said: " I had a friend." The contact with loveliness made him lovely.

Abiding in Christ means something like that. The secret of the life of Jesus was His contact with God. Again and again He withdrew into a solitary place to meet God. Jesus was always abiding in God. It must be so with us and Jesus. We must keep contact with Him. We cannot do that unless we deliberately take steps to do it. There must be no day when we never think of Jesus and feel His presence. To take but one example—to pray in the morning time, if it be for only a few moments, is to have an antiseptic for the whole day; for we cannot come out of the presence of Christ to touch the evil things. For some few of us abiding in Christ will be a mystical experience which is beyond words to express. For most of us, it will mean a constant contact with Jesus Christ. It will mean arranging life, arranging prayer, arranging silence in such a way that there is never a day when we give ourselves a chance to forget Him.

Finally, in this passage we must note that here there are two things laid down about the good disciple. First, he enriches his own life. His contact makes him a fruitful branch. Second, he brings glory to God. The sight of his life turns men's thoughts to the God who made him like that. God is glorified, as Jesus put it, when we bear much fruit and when we show ourselves to be disciples of Jesus. Surely the greatest glory of the Christian life is that we by our life and conduct can bring glory to God.

THE LIFE OF JESUS' CHOSEN PEOPLE

John 15: 11-17

> " I have spoken these things to you that my joy
> might be in you, and that your joy might be complete.
> This is my commandment, that you love one another,
> as I have loved you. No one has greater love than this,
> that a man should lay down his life for his friend.
> You are my friends, if you do what I command you.
> I no longer call you slaves, because the slave does
> not know what his master is doing. I have called
> you friends because I had made known to you every-
> thing that I heard from my Father. You have not
> chosen me, but I have chosen you, and I have appointed
> you to go out and to bear fruit, of such a kind that it
> will remain. I have done so, so that the Father will
> give you whatever you ask Him in my name. These
> are my orders to you, that you love one another."

THE central words of this passage are the words in which Jesus says that His disciples have not chosen Him, but He has chosen them. It is not we who have chosen God, but God who, in His grace, approached us with a call and an offer made out of His love.

The great interest of this passage lies in the fact that out of it we can compile a list of the things for which we are chosen and to which we are called.

(i) We are chosen for *joy*. However hard the Christian way is, it is, both in the travelling and in the goal, the way of joy. There is always a joy in doing the right thing. When we have evaded some duty or some task, when at last we set our hand to it, joy comes to us. The Christian is the man of joy; the Christian is the laughing cavalier of Christ. A gloomy Christian is a contradiction in terms, and nothing in all religious history has done Christianity more harm than its connection with black clothes and long faces. It is true that the Christian is a sinner, but he is a *redeemed* sinner; and therein lies his joy. How can any man fail to be happy when he walks the ways of life with Jesus?

(ii) We are chosen for *love*. We are sent out into the world to love one another. Sometimes we live as if we were sent into the world to compete with one another, or to dispute with one another, or even to quarrel with one another. But the Christian is sent into the world to live in such a way that he shows what is meant by loving his fellow men. Now it is here that Jesus makes another of His great claims. One of the things that we always instinctively ask of anyone who makes a great demand of us is: What right have you to make that demand? So then if we ask Jesus: What right have you to demand that we love one another? His answer is: " No man can show greater love than to lay down his life for his friends— and I did that." There is many a man who from a pulpit tells others to love each other, when his whole life is a demonstration that that is the last thing that he does himself. But Jesus gave men a commandment which He had Himself first fulfilled.

(iii) Jesus called us to be *His friends*. He tells His men that He does not call them slaves, *douloi*, any more; He calls them friends. Now that is a saying which would be even greater to those who heard it for the first time than it is to us. The title *doulos*, the slave, the servant of God was no title of shame; it was indeed a title of the highest honour. Moses was the *doulos*, the servant, the slave of God (*Deuteronomy* 34: 5); so was Joshua (*Joshua* 24: 29); so was David (*Psalm* 89: 20). It is a title which Paul counted it an honour to use (*Titus* 1: 1); and so did James (*James* 1: 1). The greatest men in the past had been proud to be called the *douloi* of God. And Jesus says: " I have something greater for you yet; you are no longer *slaves*; you are *friends*." The offer of Christ is a blessedness which not even the greatest men knew before He came into the world; He offers an intimacy with God which was impossible before His coming.

But the idea of being the friend of God has also a background. Abraham was the *friend* of God (*Isaiah* 41: 8). In *Wisdom* 7: 27 Wisdom is said to make men the friends of God. But this phrase is lit up by a custom which obtained both at the courts of the Roman Emperors and the eastern kings. At these courts there was a very select group of men who were called *the friends of the king*, or *the friends of the Emperor*. At all times they had access to the king; they had even the right to come to his bedchamber at the beginning of the day. He talked to them before he talked to his generals, his rulers, and his statesmen. The friends of the king were those who had the closest and the most intimate connection with him, and who had the right to come to him at any time.

Jesus called us to be His friends and the friends of God. That is a tremendous offer. It means that no longer do we need to gaze longingly at God from afar off; we are not like slaves who have no right whatever to enter into the presence of the master; we are not like a crowd whose only glimpse of the king is in the passing on some state occasion when, if we tried to come nearer, we would promptly be arrested. Jesus did the amazing thing—He gave us this intimacy with God, so that God is no longer a distant stranger, but our intimate friend.

THE LIFE OF JESUS' CHOSEN PEOPLE

John 15: 11-17 (*continued*)

(iv) But Jesus did not only call us and choose us for a series of tremendous privileges. He called us to be His *partners*. The slave could never be a partner. The slave was defined in Greek law as *a living tool*. His master never opened his mind to him; the slave had to do what he was told without reason and without explanation. But Jesus said to us: " You are not my slaves; you are my partners. I have told you everything; I have told you what I am trying to do, and why I am trying to do it. I have told you everything which God told me." Jesus has given us the honour of making us His partners in His task. He has shared His mind with us, and opened His heart to us, and told us of His plans, His aims and His ambitions. It is the tremendous choice that is laid before us that we can accept or refuse partnership with Christ in the work of leading the world to God.

(v) Jesus chose us to be *ambassadors*. " I have chosen you," He said, " *to send you out.*" He did not choose us to live a life retired from the world; He chose us to represent Him in the world. When a knight came to the court of King Arthur, he did not come to spend the rest of his days in knightly feasting and in knightly fellowship there. He came to the king saying: " Send me out on some great task which I can do for chivalry and for you." Jesus chose us, first to come into Him, and then to go out to the world And that must be the daily pattern and rhythm of our lives.

(vi) Jesus chose us to be *advertisements*. He chose us to go out *to bear fruit*, and to bear fruit which will remain, which will stand the test of time. The only way to spread Christianity is to be Christian. The only way to bring others into the Christian faith is to show them the fruit of the Christian life. Jesus sends us out, not to argue men into Christianity, still less to threaten them into it, not to talk about Christianity, but to attract men into Christianity, so to live it that the fruits of it may be so wonderful that others may desire them for themselves.

(vii) Jesus chose us to be *privileged members of the family of God*. He chose us so that whatever we ask in His name the Father will give to us. Here again we are face to face with one of these great sayings about prayer which we must understand. If we come to this saying thoughtlessly, it sounds as if the Christian, the chosen one of Christ, will receive everything for which he prays. We have already thought about this, but we may well think about it again. The New Testament lays down certain perfectly definite laws about prayer. (*a*) Prayer must be *the prayer of faith* (*James* 5: 15). When prayer is a formality, when prayer is merely the routine and conventional repetition of a form of words, it cannot be answered. When prayer is hopeless it cannot be effective. There is little use in a man praying to be changed, if he does not believe it possible that he can be changed. To pray with power a man must have an invincible belief in the all-sufficient love of God. (*b*) Prayer must be *in the name of Christ*. We cannot pray for things of which we know that Jesus would disapprove. We cannot pray that we should be given possession of some forbidden person or some forbidden thing; we cannot pray that some personal ambition should be realized, if that ambition means that someone else must be hurt and wounded in the fulfilling of it. We cannot pray in the name of Him who is love for vengeance on our enemies. Whenever we try to turn prayer into something to enable us to realize our own ambitions and to satisfy our own desires, prayer must be ineffective, for it is not real prayer at all. (*c*) Prayer must say: " *Thy will be done.*" When we pray we must first realize that we never know better than God. The essence of prayer is not that we say to God: " Thy will be changed," but that we say to Him: " Thy will be done." So often real prayer must be, not that God would send us the things we wish, but that He would make us able to accept the things He wills. (*d*) Prayer must never be *selfish*. Almost in the passing Jesus said a very illuminating thing. He said that, *if two people agreed* in asking anything in His name, then it would be granted (*Matthew* 18: 19). Now we are not to take that with a crude literalism, because it would simply mean that if you can mobilise enough people to pray for a thing, that thing will happen. What it does mean is this—no man when he prays should think entirely of his own needs. To take the simplest example, the holiday-maker might be praying for sunshine while the farmer was praying for rain. When we pray, we must ask, not: " Is this for my good? " but: " Is this for the good of all men? " The greatest temptation of all in prayer is to pray as if nobody but ourselves mattered; such a prayer cannot be effective.

Jesus chose us to be privileged members of the family of God. We can and must take everything to God in prayer; but when we have done so we can and must take, not the answer which our limited knowledge and our imperfect goodness desire, but the answer which God in His perfect wisdom and perfect love sends to us. And the more we love God, the easier it will be to do that.

THE WORLD'S HATRED

John 15: 18-21

> " If the world hates you, you know that it hated me before it hated you. If you were of the world, the world would love its own; but the world hates you, because you are not of the world, but I have picked you out of the world. Remember the word which I spoke to you—the servant is not greater than his master. If they persecuted me, they will persecute you. If they kept my word, they will keep yours. But they will do these things to you because of my name, because they do not know Him who sent me."

IT is always John's way to see things in terms of black and white. To John there are two great entities—the Church and the world. And there is no contact and no fellowship between them. To John there is no neutrality, no halfway house, no compromise solution. To John it is,

" Stand thou on that side, for on this am I."

As John saw it, a man is either of the world, or of Christ, and there is no stage between.

Further, we must remember that by this time the

Church was living under the constant possible threat of persecution. It was quite true that Christians were persecuted because of the name of Christ. By this time Christianity was illegal as such. A magistrate did not need to ask what crimes a man had committed. All he had to ask was whether or not he was a Christian, and, no matter what kind of man he was, no matter what he had done or had not done, if he was a Christian he was liable to death. John is not threatening a situation which did not exist. It existed in the most clear-cut and agonising way.

One thing is certain—no Christian who was involved in persecution could say that he had not been warned. On this matter Jesus was quite explicit. He had told His people beforehand what they might expect. " They shall deliver you up to councils; and in the synagogues ye shall be beaten; and ye shall be brought before rulers and kings for my sake, for a testimony against them. . . . Now the brother shall betray the brother to death, and the father the son; and children shall rise up against their parents, and shall cause them to be put to death. And ye shall be hated of all men for my name's sake " (*Mark* 13: 9-13; cp. *Matthew* 10: 17-22; 23-29; *Luke* 12: 2-9; 51-53). Jesus had forewarned His people of what awaited them in the days ahead.

When John wrote this hatred had long since begun. Tacitus spoke of the people " hated for their crimes, whom the mob call Christians." Suetonius had spoken of " a race of men who belong to a new and evil superstition." Why was this hatred so virulent?

The Roman government hated the Christians because it regarded them as disloyal citizens. The position of the government was quite simple and quite understandable. The Empire was vast; it stretched from the Euphrates to Britain, from Germany to North Africa. It included all kinds of peoples and all kinds of countries within it. Some unifying idea and force had to be found to weld this varied mass into one; and that unifying force was found in Caesar worship. Now it must be clearly understood that Caesar worship was not imposed on the world; it actually arose from the people themselves. The government did not think it up; the people produced it. Away back in the old days there had been the goddess Roma—the spirit of Rome. It is easy to see how men could think of that spirit of Rome incarnated, symbolised in the Emperor. He stood for Rome; he embodied Rome; the Spirit of Rome found its home and resting place in him. It is a great mistake to think that the subject peoples resented Roman government; for the most part they were profoundly grateful for it. Rome brought justice, and freed them from capricious kings. Rome brought peace and prosperity. The land was cleared of brigands and the sea of pirates. The *pax Romana*, the Roman peace, stretched over all the world. It was in Asia Minor that men began to think of Caesar, the Emperor, as the god who embodied Rome, and they did so in sheer gratitude for the blessings Rome had brought. At first the Emperors discouraged and deprecated this worship; they insisted that they were men and must not be worshipped as gods. But they saw that they could not stop this movement. At first they confined it to the excitable Asiatics of Asia Minor, but it spread everywhere. Then the government saw that they could use it. Here was the unifying principle which was needed. So there came slowly the day when once a year every inhabitant of the Empire had to burn his pinch of incense to the godhead of Caesar. By so doing, he showed that he was a loyal citizen of Rome. When he had done so, he received a certificate to say that he had done so. Here was the practice and the custom and the convention which made all men feel that they were part of Rome, and which guaranteed their loyalty to Rome. Now Rome was the essence of toleration. After he had burned his pinch of incense and had said, " Caesar is Lord," a man could go away and worship any god he liked, so long as the worship did not affect public decency and public order.

But that is precisely what the Christians would not do They would call no man " Lord." Jesus Christ was Lord and Jesus Christ alone was Lord. They refused to conform, and therefore the Roman government regarded them as dangerous and disloyal.

The government persecuted the Christians because the Christian insisted he had no king but Christ. Persecution came to the Christians because they put Christ first. Persecution always comes to the man who does that.

THE WORLD'S HATRED

John 15: 18-21 (*continued*)

BUT not only the government persecuted the Christians; the mob hated them. Whence came that hatred? It came because the mob believed certain slanderous things about the Christians. There is no doubt that the Jews were at least to some extent responsible for these slanders. It so happened that the Jews had the ear of the government. To take but two examples, Nero's favourite actor Aliturus, and his harlot empress Poppaea, were both adherents of the Jewish faith. The Jews whispered their slanders to the government, slanders which they must have well known to be untrue. There were four slanderous reports which were spread about the Christians.

(i) They were said to be insurrectionaries. We have already seen the reason for that. It was useless and futile for the Christians to point out that in fact they were the best citizens in the country, that they lived good and useful lives. The fact remained they would not burn their pinch of incense and say, " Caesar is Lord," and thus they were branded as dangerous and disloyal men.

(ii) They were said to be cannibals. This charge came from the words of the sacrament. " This is my body broken for you." " This cup is the new testament in my blood." On the basis of these words, it was not difficult to disseminate amongst ignorant people, who were prepared to believe the worst, the slanderous rumour that the Christians' private meal was based on cannibalism. The charge stuck, and it is little wonder that the mob looked on the Christians with loathing.

(iii) They were said to practice the most flagrant and promiscuous immorality. The weekly meal of the Christians was called the *Agapē*, the Love Feast. When the Christians met each other in the early days they greeted each other with the kiss of peace. It was not difficult to spread abroad the report that the Love Feast was an orgy of sexual indulgence, of which the kiss of peace was the symbol and the sign. It was easy to twist a title and a practice like that into a charge of indiscriminate immorality.

(iv) They were said to be incendiaries. They looked to the Second Coming of Christ. To the Second Coming of Christ they had attached all the Old Testament pictures of the Day of the Lord, these pictures which foretold of the flaming disintegration and destruction of the world. " The elements shall melt with fervent heat; the earth also and the works that are therein shall be burned up " (2 *Peter* 3: 10). In the day of Nero there did happen the disastrous fire which devastated Rome. It was easy to connect the fire with people who preached of the consuming fire which would destroy the world. Here was another ready-made slander to level against the Christians.

(v) There was still a fifth charge, and for the fifth charge there was an understandable cause. The charge was that the Christians " tampered with family relationships," that they divided families and split up homes and broke up marriages. In a way that was true. Christianity did come to bring not peace but a sword (*Matthew* 10: 34). Often a wife became a Christian and a husband did not. Often children became Christians and parents did not. Then the home was split in two, the family was divided. In those days it was necessary for a Christian to love Christ more than he loved the nearest and the dearest ties.

Christianity did in fact divide homes and split families with a divided loyalty.

These were the charges which were spread about the Christians; the Jews helped them to spread; it is little wonder that the name of Christian was a hated name.

THE WORLD'S HATRED

John 15: 18-21 (*continued*)

SUCH were the causes of hatred in the early days. But it is still true that the world will hate the Christian. As we have already said, by the *world* John meant *human society organising itself without God.* There is bound to be a cleavage between the man who regards God as the only reality in life and the man who regards God as totally irrelevant for life. In any event the word has certain characteristics, which are always part of the human situation.

(i) The world suspects people who are different. That comes out in the simplest things. One of the commonest things in the world nowadays is an umbrella; but when Jonas Hanway tried to introduce the umbrella into England and walked down the street beneath one he was pelted with stones and dirt. He was in fact persecuted. In the early days of the Boys' Brigade, the boys who marched down the street in uniform were often attacked and pelted with stones and garbage. Anyone who is different, who wears different clothes, who has different ideas is automatically suspect. He may be regarded as an eccentric or as a madman or a danger; but life will not be comfortable for him.

(ii) The world acutely dislikes people whose lives are a condemnation of it. It is in fact dangerous to be good. The classic instance of that is the fate which befell Aristides in Athens. He was called Aristides the Just; and yet he was banished. When one of the citizens was asked why he had voted for the banishment of Aristides, he answered: " Because I am tired of hearing him always called the Just." That was why men killed Socrates; they called him the human gadfly. He was always compelling men to think and to examine themselves, and men hated that and hated him and killed him. It is dangerous to have and to practise a higher standard than the standard of the world. Nowadays a man can be persecuted even for working too hard or too long.

(iii) To put it at its widest—the world always suspects nonconformity. The world likes a pattern; it likes to be able to label a person and to classify him and to put him in a pigeon-hole. And anyone who does not conform to the pattern will certainly meet trouble. It is even said that if a hen with different markings is put into a hen run where all the hens are the same, the other hens will peck her to death.

The basic demand on the Christian is the demand that the Christian should have the courage to be different. To be different is dangerous, but no man can be a Christian unless he accepts that risk, for there will be a difference between the man of the world and the man of Christ.

KNOWLEDGE AND RESPONSIBILITY

John 15: 22-25

> " If I had not come and spoken to them, they would not be guilty of sin. As it is, they have no excuse for their sins. He who hates me hates the Father too. If I had not done deeds among them which no one else had ever done, they would not be guilty of sin. As it is, they have seen and they have heard both me and my Father. But it has all happened that the word which stands written in their law might be fulfilled— ' They have hated me without a cause.' "

HERE Jesus has returned to a thought which in the Fourth Gospel is never far from His mind. It is the conviction that knowledge and privilege bring with them responsibility.

Until Jesus had come men had never had the opportunity really and fully to know God; they had never fully heard the voice of God, and they had never seen fully demonstrated the kind of life which God wished them to live. They could not be blamed for being such as they were. There are things which are allowable in a child which are not allowable in an adult, because the child does not know any better. There are things which are allowable in someone whose upbringing and home surroundings have been bad or inadequate which are not allowable in someone who has been brought up in all the benefits of a Christian home, because such a person never really had a chance. No one expects the same kind of conduct from a savage as he expects from a civilized man. The more knowledge a man has, and the more privileges he enjoys, the greater the responsibility which is laid upon him.

Now Jesus did two things. First, He exposed sin. He told men of the things which grieved God, and He told men of the way in which God wished men to walk. He set the true way before men. Secondly, He provided the remedy for sin; and He did that in a double sense. He opened the way to forgiveness for past sin, and He provided the dynamic and the power which would enable a man to overcome sin and to do the right. These were the privileges and the knowledge which He brought to men. Suppose a man to be ill; suppose he consults a doctor, and the doctor diagnoses what is wrong and prescribes a cure. If that man disregards the diagnosis and refuses to use the cure, then he has no one to blame but himself if he dies, or if he survives in a condition which makes life wretched for himself. That is what the Jews had done. As John saw it, they had only done what it was foretold they would do. Twice the Psalmist had said: " They hated me without a cause " (*Psalm* 35: 19; 69: 5).

It is still possible for us to do the same. There are not many who are actively hostile to Christ, but there are still many who live their lives as if Christ had never come, and who simply disregard Him. But no man can know life in this world or in the world to come if he disregards the Lord of all good life.

WITNESS DIVINE AND HUMAN

John 15: 26, 27

> "When the Helper comes, the Helper whom I will send to you from my Father, I mean the Spirit of Truth who comes forth from the Father, He will be a witness about me. And you will be witnesses about me because you have been with me from the beginning."

HERE John uses two ideas which lie very closely to his heart, and which are constantly entwined in his thought.

The first is the witness of the Holy Spirit. What does John mean by the witness of the Holy Spirit? We shall have occasion to think of this again very soon. But for the moment, think of it this way : when the story of Jesus is told to us, when the picture of Jesus is set before us, when the teaching of Jesus is unfolded to us, what makes us feel that this picture is none other than the picture of the Son of God, what makes us feel—as we say, instinctively— that here is wisdom which is divine? That reaction of the human mind, that answer of the human heart is the work of the Holy Spirit. It is the Holy Spirit within us who moves us to respond to Jesus Christ.

The second is the witness which men must bear to Christ. "You," said Jesus to His disciples, "will be witness about me." There are three elements in Christian witness.

(i) Christian witness comes from long fellowship and intimacy with Christ. The disciples are the witnesses of Christ because they have been with Him from the beginning. A witness is a man who says of something: "This is true, *and I know it.*" There can be no witness without personal experience. We can only witness for Christ when we have been with Christ.

(ii) Christian witness comes from inner conviction. The accent of personal inner conviction is one of the most unmistakable accents in the world. A man hardly starts to speak before we know whether or not he really believes what he is saying. There can be no effective Christian witness without this inner conviction which comes from personal intimacy with Christ.

(iii) Christian witness issues in outward testimony. A witness is not only someone who knows that something is true; he is someone who is prepared to say that he knows that it is true. A Christian witness is a man who not only knows Christ but who wants others to know Him too.

It is our privilege and our task to be witnesses for Christ in the world; and we cannot be witnesses without the personal intimacy, the inner conviction and the outward testimony to our faith.

WARNING AND CHALLENGE

John 16: 1-4

" I have spoken these things to you in case you should be caused to stumble in the way. They will excommunicate you from the Synagogue. Yes, a time is coming when anyone who kills you will think that he is rendering a service to God; and they will do these things because they did not recognize the Father or me. But I have spoken these things to you, so that when their time comes, you will remember that I spoke them to you."

By the time John was writing it was inevitable that some Christians should fall away, for persecution had struck the Church. *Revelation* condemns those who are unbelieving and fearful (*Revelation* 21: 8). When in the time of Trajan, Pliny, the governor of Bithynia, was examining people to see whether or not they were Christians, he wrote to Trajan to say that some admitted " that they had been Christians, but they had ceased to be so many years ago, some as much as twenty years ago." Even amidst the heroism of the early Church, there were those whose faith was not great enough to resist persecution and whose endurance was not strong enough to stay the course.

Jesus foresaw this, and He gave warning beforehand. He did not want anyone to be able to say that he had not known what to expect when he became a Christian. When Tyndale was persecuted, and when his enemies were out for his life, because he sought to give the Bible to the people in the English language, he said calmly: " I never expected anything else." Jesus offered men glory, but He offered them a cross as well.

Jesus spoke of two ways in which His followers would be persecuted. They would be excommunicated from the Synagogue. This for a Jew would be a very hard fate. The Synagogue, the House of God, had a very special place in the life of the Jews. Some of the Rabbis went the length of saying that prayer was not effective unless it was offered in the Synagogue. But there was more to it than that. It may be that a great scholar or a great theologian does not need human company; he may be able to live alone and solitary, keeping company with the great thoughts and adventures of his mind. But the disciples were simple folk; they needed the fellowship of their fellow men. They needed the Synagogue and its worship. It would be hard for them to be alone, sent to coventry, ostracized, with all doors shut against them. Men have sometimes to learn, as Joan of Arc said, that: " It is better to be alone with God." Sometimes loneliness among men is the price of fellowship with God. Jesus said that men would think they were rendering a service to God when they killed His followers. The word Jesus uses for service is *latreia*, and that is the normal word for the service that a priest rendered at the very altar and in the very Temple of God. It is the standard word for religious service, for the holy service of God. One of the tragedies of religion has so often been that men thought that they were serving God by persecuting those whom they believed to be heretics. No man ever more truly thought that he was serving God than Paul did, when he was trying to eliminate the name of Jesus and to wipe out the Church (*Acts* 26: 9-11). The torturers and judges of the Spanish Inquisition have left a name which is loathed and hated; yet they were quite sure that they were serving God by torturing heretics into accepting what they considered to be the true faith. As they saw it, they were doing nothing less than save men from hell. " Liberty," said Madame Roland, " what crimes have been committed in thy name!" And that also is true of religion. It happens, as Jesus said, because they do not recognize God and do not recognize Him. The tragedy of the Church is that men have so often laboured to propagate *their* idea of religion; they have so often believed that *they* have a monopoly of and corner in God's truth and grace. The staggering fact is that it still happens; it is nothing less than that which is the barrier to union and unity between the Churches. There will always be persecution—not necessarily killing and torture and death—but exclusion and banishment from the house of God so long as men believe that there is only one way to God.

There is no doubt that Jesus knew how to deal with men. He was in effect saying: " I am offering you the hardest task in the world. I am offering you something which will lacerate your body and tear your heart out. Are you big enough to accept it?" All the world knows Garibaldi's proclamation to his soldiers after the siege of Rome in 1849. " Soldiers, all our efforts against superior forces have been unavailing. I have nothing to offer you, but hunger and thirst, hardship and death; but I call on all who love their country to join with me." And join they did in their hundreds. When the Spaniards were conquering South America Pizarro presented his men with a choice. They might have the wealth of Peru with its dangers, or the comparative poverty of Panama with its safety. He drew a line in the sand with his sword and he said: " Comrades, on that side are toil, hunger, nakedness, storm, desertion and death; on this side is ease. There lies Peru with its riches; here lies Panama with its poverty. Choose, each man, what best becomes a brave Castilian. For my part, I go to the south." There was a silence and a hesitation; and then an old pilot and twelve soldiers stepped across to Pizarro's side. It was with them that the discovery and the conquest of Peru began.

Jesus offered, and still offers, not the way of ease, but the way of glory. He still wants men who are prepared with open eyes to venture for His name.

THE WORK OF THE HOLY SPIRIT

John 16: 5-11

> " I did not tell you these things at the beginning, because I was with you. But now I am going away to Him who sent me, and none of you asks me: ' Where are you going? ' But grief has filled your hearts because I have spoken these things to you. But it is the truth I am telling you—it is to your interest that I should go away, for if I do not go away the Helper will not come to you. But when He has come, He will convict the world of sin, and convince it of righteousness and judgment; of sin, because they do not believe in me; of righteousness, because I go to my Father, and you no longer see me; of judgment, because the ruler of this world is judged."

THE disciples were bewildered and grief-stricken men. All they knew was that they were going to lose Jesus. But Jesus told them that in the end this was all for the best, because, when He went away, the Holy Spirit, the Helper, would come. When He was in the body they could not take Him everywhere with them; it was always a case of greetings and farewells; when He was in the body, He could not reach the minds and hearts and consciences of men everywhere; He was confined by the human limitations of place and time. But there were no limitations in the Spirit. Everywhere a man goes the Spirit is with him; everywhere throughout the world, the Spirit appeals to men. The coming of the Spirit would be the fulfilment of the promise: " Lo, I am with you always even unto the end of the world " (*Matthew* 28: 29). The Spirit would bring to men an uninterrupted fellowship for ever; and the Spirit would bring to the Christian preacher a power and an effectiveness no matter where he preached.

Here we have an almost perfect summary of the work of the Spirit. The word that John uses of the work of the Spirit is the word *elegchein*. The Authorised Version translates it *reprove*, and in the margin gives the alternative translation *convince*. The trouble is that no one word will translate *elegchein*. It is the word which is used for the cross-examination of a witness, or a man on trial, or an opponent in an argument. It has always this idea of cross-examining a man until he sees and admits his errors, or acknowledges the force of some argument which he had not yet seen. It is, for instance, sometimes used by the Greeks for the action of conscience on a man's mind and heart. Now clearly such cross-examination can do two things—it can *convict* a man of the crime he has committed or the wrong that he has done; or it can *convince* a man of the weakness of his own case, and the strength of the case which, up to this time, he has opposed. In this passage we need *both* the meanings; we need both *convict* and *convince*. Now let us go on to see what Jesus says that the Holy Spirit will do.

(i) The Holy Spirit will *convict men of sin*. When the Jews crucified Jesus, they did not believe that they were sinning; they believed that they were serving God. But when the story of that crucifixion was later preached, they were pricked in their heart (*Acts* 2: 37). When the story was presented to them, they suddenly had the terrible conviction of sin, the conviction that the crucifixion was the greatest crime in history, and that their sin had caused it. What is it that gives a man a sense of sin? What is it that abases a man in face of the Cross? It is told that in an Indian village a missionary was telling the story of Christ by means of lantern slides flung on the white-washed wall of a village house. When the picture of the Cross was shown, an Indian stepped forward, as if he could not help it: " Come down! " he cried. " I should be hanging there—not you." We cannot know our need of a Saviour without a sense of sin. Why should this sight of a man crucified as a criminal in Palestine two thousand years ago tear the hearts of people open throughout the centuries and still to-day? *That is the work of the Holy Spirit.* It is the influence of the Holy Spirit in a man's heart which convicts him of sin.

(ii) The Holy Spirit will *convince men of righteousness.* What does this mean? It becomes clear what it means when we see that it is *Jesus Christ's righteousness* of which men will be convinced. Jesus was crucified as a criminal. He was tried; He was found guilty; He was regarded by the Jews as an evil heretic, and by the Romans as a dangerous character. He was given the punishment that the worst criminals had to suffer, branded as a felon and an enemy of God. What changed that? What made men see in this crucified figure the Son of God as the centurion saw at the Cross (*Matthew* 27: 54) and Paul on the Damascus Road (*Acts* 9: 1-9)? When you think of it, it is an amazing thing that men should put their trust for all eternity in a crucified Jewish criminal. What *convinces* men that this crucified Jew is the Son of God? *That is the work of the Holy Spirit.* It is the Holy Spirit who convinces men of the sheer righteousness of Christ, backed by the fact that Jesus rose again, and went to His Father.

(iii) The Holy Spirit *convinces men of judgment.* There on the Cross evil stands condemned, judged and defeated. What makes us feel what we can only call the danger of God? What confronts a man with the certainty of judgment? Why should a man not do what he likes? What makes him feel certain that judgment lies ahead? *That is the work of the Holy Spirit.* It is the Holy Spirit who gives us the inner and unshakable conviction that we shall all stand before the judgment seat of God.

(iv) But there remains one thing which at the moment John does not go on to mention. When we are convicted of our own sin, when we are convinced of Christ's righteousness, when we are convinced of judgment to come, what gives us the certainty that in the Cross of Christ is our salvation, and that with Christ we are forgiven, and saved from judgment? *That too is the work of the Holy Spirit.* It is the Holy Spirit who convinces us and makes us certain and sure that in this crucified figure we too can find our Saviour and our Lord. The Holy Spirit convicts us of our sin, and convinces us of our Saviour.

THE SPIRIT OF TRUTH

John 16: 12-15

> " I have many things to say to you, but you cannot bear them now. When the Spirit of Truth has come, He will lead you into all the truth. For He will not speak on His own authority and out of His own knowledge, but He will speak all that He will hear, and He will tell you of the things to come. He will glorify me, for He will take of the things which belong to me, and will tell you of them. All things that the Father has are mine. That is why I said that the Spirit will take of the things which belong to me, and tell them to you."

To Jesus the Holy Spirit is the Spirit of Truth, and the great work of the Spirit is to bring God's truth to men. We have a special name for this bringing of God's truth to men; we call it *revelation*, and there is no passage in the New Testament which shows us what we might call the principles of revelation better than this passage does.

(i) *Revelation is bound to be a progressive process.* There were many things which Jesus knew, but which He could not at that moment tell His disciples, because they were not at that time able to receive them. It is only possible to tell a man as much as he can understand. All teaching, all revelation must be fitted to the capacity of a man to receive it. We do not start with the binomial theorem when we wish to teach a boy algebra; we work up to it. We do not start with advanced theorems when we wish to teach a child geometry; we approach them gradually. We do not start with difficult passages to translate when we teach a lad Latin or Greek; we start with the easy and the simple things. God's revelation to men is like that. It is a developing revelation. God can teach men what they are able and fit to learn. This most important fact has certain consequences. (a) It is the explanation of the parts of the Old Testament which sometimes worry and distress us. At that stage that was all of God's truth that men could grasp. Take an actual illustration—in the Old Testament there are many passages which call for the wiping out of enemies and for the destruction of cattle and men and women and children when an enemy city is taken. At the back of these passages there is a great thought, the thought that Israel must not risk the taint of any heathen and lower religion. Rather than risk the taint and infection of it, those who do not worship the true God must be destroyed. That is to say, the Jews had grasped the fact that the purity of religion must be at all costs safeguarded. But at that stage they wished to preserve that purity by destroying the heathen; when Jesus came, men came to see that the way to preserve that purity is to convert the heathen, and to lead them to God. The people of the Old Testament times had grasped a great truth, but they had only grasped one side, one bit of it. Revelation has to be that way; God can only reveal as much as a man can understand. (b) It is the proof that there is no end to God's revelation. One of the mistakes which men sometimes make is to identify God's revelation solely with the Bible. That would be to say that since about A.D. 120, when the

227

latest book in the New Testament was written, God has ceased to speak, that since then there has been no more revelation from God. God's Spirit is *always* active; God is *always* revealing Himself. It is true that God's supreme and unsurpassable revelation came in Jesus Christ; but Jesus is not a figure in a book, He is a living person, and in Him God's revelation goes on. God is still leading us into a greater and greater realization of what Jesus means. God is not a God who spoke up to A.D. 120 and who is now silent. God is still revealing His truth to men.

(ii) We shall see that very clearly if we think of the next principle of revelation which this passage contains. God's revelation to men is a revelation of *all* truth, of the *whole* truth. It is quite wrong to think of God's revelation as being confined to what we might call theological truth. The theologians and the preachers are not the only persons who are inspired. When a great poet delivers to men a great message in words which defy time, he is inspired. When H. F. Lyte wrote the words of *Abide with me* he had no feeling of composing them; he wrote them as to dictation. A great musician is inspired. Handel, telling of how he wrote *The Hallelujah Chorus* in his *Messiah*, said: " I saw the heavens opened, and the Great White God sitting on the Throne." When a scientist discovers something which will help the world's toil and make life better for men, when a surgeon discovers a new technique which will save men's lives and ease their pain, when someone discovers a new treatment, a new drug, which will bring life and hope to suffering humanity, that is a revelation from God. It actually happens in a way that we can see. Often what happens is that a man thinks and thinks, searches and searches, experiments and experiments. Then he reaches a dead end. Human thought can go no farther. He has come up against a shut door. And just then the solution to his problem flashes into his mind. He did not think it out; it was *given* to him. When his thinking mind had reached its limit, God came in. It would be an odd thing to think of God's revelation solely in terms of theology. All truth is God's truth, and the revelation of all truth is the work of the Holy Spirit.

(iii) Here again we are led on to another principle of revelation. That which is revealed comes from God. God is alike the possessor and the giver of all truth. Truth is not men's discovery; it is God's gift. It is the truth of God that the Holy Spirit brings to us. Truth is not something which we create by the processes of our mind; it is something already waiting to be discovered, something which we appropriate, but do not create. At the back of all truth there is God.

(iv) Revelation is the taking of the things of Jesus, and the revealing of their significance to us. The greatness of Jesus is His inexhaustibleness. No man has ever grasped all that Jesus came to say. No man has fully worked out all the significance of the teaching of Jesus. No man knows all that it means for life and for belief, for the individual and for the world, for society and for the nation. Revelation is a continual opening out of the meaning and the significance of Jesus Christ.

There we have the crux of the whole matter. Revelation comes to us, not from any book, or creed, or printed word. Revelation comes to us from a living person. The nearer we live to Jesus, the better we will know Him. The more we become like Him, the more He will be able to tell us. To enjoy His revelation we must accept His mastery. Submission to Christ and knowledge of Christ go hand in hand. It is only to the man of God that God can reveal His truth, although it sometimes happens that a man is a chosen vessel of God without knowing that it is so.

SORROW TURNED TO JOY

John 16: 16-24

" In a little while you will not see me any more; and again in a little while you will see me." Some of His

229

disciples said to each other: " What is the meaning
of this that He is saying to us—' In a little while
you will not see me, and again in a little while you
will see me '? And what does He mean when He says:
' I am going to my Father '? What does He mean
when He talks about ' A little '? We do not know
what He means." Jesus knew that they wished to
ask Him their questions, and He said to them: " You
are discussing among yourselves what I meant when
I said: ' In a little while you will not see me, and
again in a little while you will see me.' This is the
truth I tell you—you will weep and you will lament,
but the world will rejoice. You will be grieved, but
your grief will turn into joy. When a woman bears
a child she has grief, because her hour has come.
But, when the child is born, she does not remember
her pain because of her joy that a man is born into
the world. So you too for the present have grief.
But I will see you again, and your heart will rejoice,
and no one will take your joy from you. In that day
you will not have any questions to ask me. This is
the truth I tell you—the Father will give you in my
name whatever you will ask Him. Up till now you
have asked nothing in my name. Ask, and you will
receive, that your joy may stand complete."

HERE Jesus is looking beyond the present to the new age
which is to come. When He does so, He uses a conception
which was deeply rooted in Jewish thought. The Jews
believed that all time was divided into two ages—the
present age, and the age which is to come. The present
age was wholly bad, and wholly under condemnation;
the age to come was the golden age of God. In between the
two ages, preceding the coming of the Messiah, who would
bring in the new age, there lay the Day of the Lord; and
the Day of the Lord was to be a terrible day, when the
world would be shattered and disintegrated into fragments,
when all things would be convulsed, and then after that
the golden age would dawn. The Jews were in the habit
of calling that terrible between-time " the birth travail
of the days of the Messiah." They actually used this
picture of the pain of birth which precedes the entry of

new life into the world. The Old Testament and the literature which was written between the Testaments are both full of pictures of this terrible between-time. " Behold the Day of the Lord cometh, cruel both with wrath and fierce anger, to lay the land desolate; and He shall destroy the sinners thereof out of it " (*Isaiah* 13: 9). " Let all the inhabitants of the land tremble; for the Day of the Lord cometh, for it is nigh at hand; a day of darkness and of gloominess, a day of clouds and of thick darkness, as the morning spread upon the mountains " (*Joel* 2: 1, 2). " And honour shall be turned into shame, and strength humiliated into contempt, and probity destroyed, and beauty shall become ugliness " (2 *Baruch* 27). " The Day of the Lord will come as a thief in the night, in which the heavens shall pass away with a great noise, and the elements shall melt with fervent heat, the earth also and the works that are therein shall be burnt up " (2 *Peter* 3: 10). Such was the picture of the travail, the birthpangs of the coming of the Messiah.

Jesus knew the Scriptures; He knew these pictures ; they were in His mind and in His memory. And now He was saying to His disciples: " I am leaving you; but I am coming back; the day will come when my reign will begin and my Kingdom will come; but before that you will have to go through terrible things, with pain like birth-pangs upon you. But, if you faithfully endure, and go through that terrible time, the blessings will be very precious." Then Jesus went on to outline the life of the Christian who endures.

(i) Sorrow will turn to joy. There may be a time when it looks as if to be a Christian brings nothing but sorrow, and to be of the world brings nothing but joy. But the day comes when the roles are reversed. The world's careless joy will turn to sorrow; and the Christian's apparent sorrow will turn to joy. The Christian must always remember, when his faith costs him dear, that this is not the end of things, that after the sorrow there comes the joy.

(ii) There will be two precious things about this Christian joy. (*a*) It will never be taken away. It will be independent of the chances and the changes of the world. It will be untouchable by any of the activities and assaults of men. It is the simple fact that in every generation people who were suffering terribly have spoken of sweet times with Christ. The joy the world gives is at the mercy of the world. The joy which Christ gives is independent of anything the world can do. It does not depend on what the world gives and takes away, because it is dependent only on the presence of Christ, and it is grounded only in God. (*b*) It will be complete. It is characteristic of life that in life's greatest joy there is always some element of incompleteness. There is always something lacking. It may be that somehow there lingers in it some regret; that there is the feeling that there may be a cloud no bigger than a man's hand to mar it; that the memory that it cannot last is always at the back of our minds. In the Christian joy, the joy of the presence of Christ and of life lived with Him, there is no alloy, no tinge of imperfection. It is perfect and complete.

(iii) In the Christian joy the pain which went before is forgotten. The mother forgets the pain in the wonder of the child. The martyr forgets the agony in the glory of heaven. As Browning wrote of the martyr's tablet on the wall:

> " I was some time in being burned.
> At last a hand came through
> The flames and drew
> My soul to Christ whom now I see;
> Sergius a brother writes for me
> This testimony on the wall.
> For me—I have forgot it all."

If a man's fidelity costs him much, he will forget the cost in the joy of being for ever with Christ, and in the simple joy of having proved himself true.

(iv) There will be fulness of knowledge. " In that day,"

said Jesus, " you will not need to ask me any questions any more." In this life there are always some unanswered questions and some unsolved problems. In the last analysis in this life we must always walk by faith and not by sight; we must always be accepting what we cannot understand. It is only fragments of the truth which we can grasp and glimpses of God that we may see; but in the age to come with Christ there will be fulness of knowledge. As Browning had it in *Abt Vogler:*

> " The evil is null, is nought, is silence implying sound;
>> What was good, shall be good, with, for evil, so much good more;
> On earth the broken arcs; in the heaven, a perfect round.
>
> All we have willed or hoped or dreamed of good shall exist;
>> Not its semblance, but itself; no beauty, nor good, nor power
> Whose voice has gone forth, but each survives for the melodist
>> When eternity affirms the conception of an hour.
> The high that proved too high, the heroic for earth too hard,
>> The passion that left the ground to lose itself in the sky,
> Are music sent up to God by the lover and the bard;
>> Enough that He heard it once: we shall hear it by and by."

When we are fully with Christ the time of questions will be gone and the time of answers will have come.

(iv) There will be a new relationship with God. When we really and truly know God we are able to go to God and to ask Him for anything. We know that the door is open; we know that His name is Father; we know that His heart is love. We are like children who never doubt that their father delights to see them, and that they can talk to him as they wish. In that relationship Jesus says we will ask for anything. But let us think of it in human terms—the only terms we have. When a child loves and trusts his father, he knows quite well that sometimes his father will say no because his father's knowledge and his father's love know best. We can become so intimate with God that we can take everything with us to Him, but always we end by saying: " Thy will be done."

(v) That new relationship is made possible by Jesus. It exists *in His name*. It is because of who Jesus is and what Jesus did that our joy is indestructible and perfect, that our knowledge is complete, that the new way to the heart of God is open to us. All that we have came to us through Jesus Christ. It is in His name that we ask and receive, that we approach and are welcomed.

THE DIRECT ACCESS

John 16: 25-28

" I have spoken these things to you in sayings that are hard to understand; but the hour is coming when I will no longer speak to you in sayings that are hard to understand, but I will tell you plainly about the Father. In that day you will ask in my name. I do not say that I will ask the Father for you, because the Father Himself loves you, because you have loved me and have believed that I came forth from the Father. I came forth from the Father, and I came into the world; I am leaving the world again, and I am going to the Father."

THE Authorised Version has it that up till now Jesus has been speaking to His disciples in *proverbs*, or, as the margin has it, in *parables*. The word is *paroimia*; it is the word which is used for Jesus' parables; but basically the word means a saying that is hard to understand, a saying the meaning of which is veiled to the casual listener, a saying which demands thought before its meaning can become clear. It can, for instance, be used for the pithy sayings of wise men which are so brief that the mind must grapple with their pregnant brevity; it can be used for a riddle, the meaning of which a man must guess as best he can. What Jesus is saying is: " So far I have been giving you hints and indications; I have been giving you the truth with a veil on it; I have been saying things which you had to think your way through; but now I am going to speak the truth in all its stark clarity to you." It is then that He tells them plainly that He came from God, and that He is going back to God. Here is the tremendous claim— the claim that He is none other than the Son of God, and the claim that the Cross is not for Him a criminal's death, but the way back to God.

But then Jesus says something which we must for ever and for ever remember. He says that His men can approach God direct, because God loves them; He says that He does not need to take their requests to God; they can take their own. Here is the final proof of something which must never be forgotten. So often we tend to think in terms of an angry God and a gentle Jesus; so often what Jesus did is presented in a way which seems to mean that something that Jesus did changed the attitude of God to men, and made God a God of love instead of a God of judgment. But here Jesus is saying: " You can go to God, because God loves you," and He is saying that *before the Cross*. Jesus did not die to change God into love; He died to tell us that God is love. He came, not because God so hated the world, but because God so *loved* the world. At the back of everything there is the love of God, and we never could have known that if Jesus had not told us so. Jesus brought to men the love of God.

He tells them that His work is done. He came from the Father, and now, by way of the Cross, He goes back. And the way for every man is open to God. Their privilege is so tremendous that He does not need to take their prayers to God; they can take their own. The lover of Christ is the beloved of God.

CHRIST AND HIS GIFTS

John 16: 29-33

> His disciples said: " See! now you are speaking clearly,
> and you are not speaking in hard sayings. Now we
> know that you know all things, and that you do not
> need that anyone should ask you anything. Because
> of this we believe that you came forth from God."
> Jesus answered them: " So you believe at this
> moment? See! the hour is coming—it has come—
> when each of you will be scattered to your own homes,
> and you will leave me alone. And yet I am not alone,
> because the Father is with me. I have spoken these
> things to you that you might have peace in me. In
> the world you will have tribulation. But courage!
> I have conquered the world."

THERE is a strange light here on how the disciples finally
surrendered to Jesus. They suddenly leapt into full belief
because, as they said, they realized that Jesus did not
need to ask any man anything. What did they mean?
Back in verses 17 and 18 we find them discussing what
Jesus had said and puzzled about it. Beginning in verse 19
Jesus begins to answer their questions *without asking them
what their questions were.* In other words—Jesus could
read their hearts like an open book. That is why they
believed in Him; they felt they were confronted by one
who knew all about them before ever they had told Him.
To Jesus the human heart was wide open; and He could
answer the unasked question and deal with the unexpressed
problem. A traveller in Scotland in the old days described
two preachers whom he had heard. Of one he said: " He
showed me the glory of God." Of the other he said: " He
showed me my whole heart." Jesus could do *both* of these
things. It was His knowledge of God and His knowledge
of the human heart which convinced the disciples that
He was the Son of God. No one ever knew God and knew
men as Jesus knew them.

But Jesus was a realist. He told them that, in spite of
their belief, the hour was coming when they would desert

Him. Here is perhaps the most extraordinary thing about Jesus. He knew the weakness of His men; He knew their failure; He knew that they would let Him down in the moment of His direst need; *and yet He still loved them*; and what is more wonderful still—*and yet He still trusted them*. He knew men at their worst and yet He still loved and trusted them. It is quite possible for a man to forgive someone and yet, at the same time, to make it clear that he is never prepared to trust that person again. But Jesus said: " I know that in your weakness you will desert me; nevertheless I know that you will still be conquerors." Never in all the world were forgiveness and trust so combined. What a lesson is there! Jesus teaches us how to forgive, and how to trust the man who made the mistake.

There are four things about Jesus which this passage makes very clear.

(i) *There is the loneliness of Jesus.* He was to be left alone by men. And yet He was never alone, because He still had God. No man ever stands alone for the right; he always stands with God. No good man is ever completely forsaken, for He is never forsaken by God. It is in just such a situation that we realize the preciousness of God, for we never realize the value of a friend until we need him as we needed nothing and no one on earth.

(ii) *There is the forgiveness of Jesus.* Of that we have already thought. He knew that His friends would abandon Him, yet at the moment He did not upbraid them, and afterwards He did not hold it against them. He loved men in all their weakness; He saw men and loved them as they are. Love must be clear-sighted. If we idolize a person, if we think him or her faultless, we are doomed to disappointment. We must love, not the ideal, but the real person, as he or she is.

(iii) *There is the sympathy of Jesus.* There is one verse here which at first sight seems out of place: " I have spoken these things to you that you might have peace in me." The point is this—if Jesus had not foretold the weakness of the disciples, when they realized afterwards how they had failed Him and forsaken Him and abandoned Him, it might well have driven them to utter and absolute despair. But He warned them before it happened. It is as if He said: " I know what's going to happen; I am telling you about it now; you must not think that your disloyalty came as a shock to me; I knew it was coming; and it does not make any difference to my love. When you think about it afterwards, don't despair." Here is divine pity and divine forgiveness. Jesus was thinking, not of how men's sin would hurt Him, but of how it would hurt them. Sometimes it would make all the difference if we thought, not of how much someone has hurt us, but of how much the fact that they hurt us has driven them to remorse, regret and the sorrow of an aching heart.

(iv) *There is the gift of Jesus.* And the gift of Jesus is courage and conquest. Very soon something was going to be unanswerably proved to the disciples. They were going to see that the world could do its worst to Jesus and still not defeat Him. They were going to see the world doing its worst when it crucified Him; they were going to see His invincibility when He rose again. And He says: " The victory which I will win can be your victory too. The world did its worst to me, and I emerged victorious. Life can do its worst to you, and you too can emerge victorious. You too can possess the courage and the conquest of the Cross."

THE GLORY OF THE CROSS

John 17: 1-5

When Jesus had spoken these words, He lifted up His eyes to heaven, and said: " Father, the hour has come. Glorify the Son that the Son may glorify you. Glorify Him, just as you gave Him authority over mankind, that He may give eternal life to every one whom you have given to Him. It is eternal

life to know you, who are the only true God, and to
know Jesus Christ, whom you sent. I have glorified
you upon earth, because I have finished the work
which you gave me to do; and now, Father, glorify
me in your own presence with the glory which I
had with you before the world began."

FOR Jesus life was life with a climax, and that climax
was the Cross. To Jesus the Cross was the glory of life
and the way to the glory of eternity. " The hour is come,"
He said, " that the Son of Man should be glorified " (*John*
12: 23). Wherein lay the glory of the Cross? What did
Jesus mean when He repeatedly spoke of the Cross as
His glory and His glorification? There is more than one
answer to that question.

(i) It is one of the great facts of history that again and
again it was in death that the great ones found their
glory. It was when they died, and how they died, which
showed people what and who they really were. They
may have been misunderstood, undervalued, condemned
as criminals in their lives, but their deaths showed their
true nobility and their true place in the scheme of things.
Abraham Lincoln had his enemies during his life-time;
but even those who had criticized and undervalued him
saw his greatness when he died. Someone came out of the
room where Lincoln died, after the assassin's shot had
killed him, saying: " Now he belongs to the ages." Stanton,
Lincoln's war minister, who had always regarded Lincoln
as a crude and uncouth creature, and who had taken no
pains to conceal his contempt, looked down at Lincoln's
dead body with tears in his eyes. " There lies," he said,
" the greatest ruler of men the world has ever seen."
Joan of Arc was burned as a witch and a heretic by the
English. Amidst the crowd there was an Englishman who
had sworn to add a faggot to the fire. " Would that my
soul," he said, " were where the soul of that woman is! "
One of the secretaries of the King of England left the scene
of Joan's burning saying: " We are all lost because we
have burned a saint." When Montrose was executed by

his enemies, he was taken down the High Street to the Mercat Cross to be executed. His enemies had actually encouraged the crowd to revile him, and had provided them with ammunition to fling at him, but not one voice was raised to curse, and not one hand was lifted to fling anything. He had on his finest clothes, with ribbons on his shoes and fine white gloves on his hands. James Fraser, an eye-witness, said of him: "He stept along the street with so great state, and there appeared in his countenance so much beauty, majesty and gravity as amazed the beholder, and many of his enemies did acknowledge him to be the bravest subject in the world, and in him a gallantry that braced all that crowd." John Nicoll, the notary public, thought him more like a bridegroom than a criminal. An Englishman in the crowd, a government agent, wrote back to his superiors: "It is absolutely certain that he hath overcome more men by his death, in Scotland, than he would have done if he had lived. For I never saw a more sweeter carriage in a man in all my life." Again and again a martyr's majesty has appeared in death. It was so with Jesus, for even the centurion at the foot of the Cross was left saying: "Truly this was the Son of God" (*Matthew* 27: 54). The Cross was the glory of Jesus because Jesus was never more majestic than in His death. The Cross was His glory because the magnet of the Cross drew men to Jesus in a way that even His life had never done— and it is so yet.

THE GLORY OF THE CROSS

John 17: 1-5 (*continued*)

(ii) Further, the Cross was the glory of Jesus because it was the completion of His work. "I have finished the work," He said, "which you gave me to do." For Jesus to have stopped short of the Cross would have been to stop short with His task uncompleted. Why should that be so? Jesus had come into this world to tell men about, and to show men, the love of God. If Jesus had stopped short of the Cross, it would have been the proof that there is some length to which the love of God is not prepared to go for men. It would have been to say that God's love said: "Thus far and no farther." But, by going to the Cross, Jesus showed that there was nothing that the love of God was not prepared to do and suffer for men, that there was literally no limit to the love of God. H. L. Gee tells of a war incident from Bristol. Attached to one of the A.R.P. Stations there was a boy messenger called Derek Bellfall. He was sent with a message to another station on his bicycle. On his way back a bomb came down and mortally wounded him. When they found him, he was still conscious. His last whispered words were: "Messenger Bellfall reporting—I have delivered my message." To deliver the message had cost his death, but the message was delivered. There was a famous painting from the First World War. It showed an engineer fixing a field telephone line which was essential. He had just completed the line so that the essential messages might come through when he was shot. The picture shows him in the moment of death, and beneath it there is the one word, "Through!" He had died, he had given his life, that the message might get through. That is exactly what Jesus did. He had completed His task; He had brought God's love to men. For Him that meant the Cross; and the Cross was His glory because He had finished the work God gave Him to do; He had made men for ever certain of the love of God.

(iii) But there is another question—how did the Cross of Jesus glorify God? There is only one way to glorify God, and that is to obey God. A child brings honour to his parents when he brings obedience to his parents. A citizen brings honour to his country when he obeys his country. A scholar brings honour to his teacher when he obeys and follows his master's teaching. Jesus brought glory and honour to God by His perfect obedience to God. The gospel story makes it quite clear that Jesus could have escaped the Cross. Humanly speaking, He could have turned back, and He need never have gone to Jerusalem. As we look at Jesus in the last days, at His trial, on His Cross, we are bound to say: " See how He loved God! See to what lengths His obedience would go!" Jesus glorified God on the Cross by rendering the perfect obedience in the perfect love.

(iv) But there is still more than that. Jesus prayed to God to glorify Him and to glorify Himself. *The Cross was not the end.* There was the Resurrection to follow. The Resurrection was the vindication of Jesus. It was the proof that men could do their worst, and that Jesus could triumph over it. It was as if God pointed at the Cross and said: " That is what *men* think of my Son," and then pointed at the Resurrection and said: " That is what *I* think of my Son." The Cross was the worst that men could do to Jesus; but not all men's worst could eliminate Him or conquer Him or break Him. The glory of the Resurrection obliterated the shame of the Cross.

(v) For Jesus the Cross was the way back. " Glorify me," He prayed, " with the glory which I had before the world began." Jesus was like a knight who left the king's court to perform some perilous and terrible deed, and who, having performed it, came home in triumph to enjoy the victor's glory. Jesus came from God, and returned to God. The exploit between His coming forth and His going back was the Cross. For Him, therefore, the Cross was the gateway to glory; and, if He had refused to pass through that gateway, there would have been no glory for Him to enter into. For Jesus the Cross was His return to God.

ETERNAL LIFE

John 17: 1-5 (*continued*)

THERE is another most important thought in this passage,

for this passage has the great New Testament definition of eternal life. It is eternal life to know God, and to know Jesus Christ whom God has sent. Let us remind ourselves of what the word *eternal* means. In Greek it is the word *aiōnios*. This word has got to do, not so much with duration of life, for *duration* of life need not necessarily be a boon. A life which went on for ever would not necessarily be a good or desirable thing. The main meaning of this word is *quality* of life. There is only one person to whom the word *aiōnios*, *eternal*, can properly be applied, and that one person is God. Eternal life is therefore nothing other than the life of God. To possess eternal life, to enter into eternal life, is to experience here and now something of the splendour, and the majesty, and the joy, and the peace, and the holiness which are characteristic of the life of God.

To know God is a characteristic thought of the Old Testament. Wisdom is " a tree of life to them that lay hold on her " (*Proverbs* 3: 18). " To know thy power," said the writer of *Wisdom*, " is the root of immortality " (*Wisdom* 5: 3). " Through knowledge shall the righteous be delivered " (*Proverbs* 11: 9). It is Habbakuk's dream of the golden age that "the earth shall be filled with the knowledge of God " (*Habbakuk* 2: 14). Hosea hears God's voice saying to him: " My people are destroyed for lack of knowledge " (*Hosea* 4: 6). A Rabbinic exposition asks what is the smallest section of scripture on which all the essentials of the Law hang? It answers, *Proverbs* 3: 6, which literally means: " Know Him, and He shall direct thy paths." Again there was a Rabbinic exposition which said that Amos had reduced all the many commandments of the Law to one, when he said: " Seek ye me, and ye shall live " (*Amos* 5: 4), for *seeking* God means seeking to *know* God. The Jewish teachers had long insisted that to know God is necessary to true life. What then does it mean to know God?

(i) Undoubtedly there is an element of intellectual knowledge here. It means, at least in part, to know what

God is like. To know what God is like does make the most tremendous difference to life. Take but two examples. Heathen peoples, especially in primitive countries, believe in a horde of gods. Every tree, brook, hill, mountain, river, stone has its god and its spirit; all these spirits are hostile and grudging to man; and primitive people are haunted by the gods; they live in perpetual fear of offending one of these many gods. Missionaries tell us that it is almost impossible for us to understand the sheer wave of relief which comes to these people when they discover that *there is only one God*. This new knowledge makes all the difference in the world to life. Further, it obviously makes a tremendous difference to know that God is not stern and harsh and cruel, but that God is love. We know these things; but we could never have known them unless Jesus had come to tell us them. We enter into a new life, we share something of the life of God Himself, when, through the work of Jesus, we discover what God is like. It is eternal life, God's life, to know what God is like.

(ii) But there is something else here. The Old Testament regularly uses the word *know* for sexual knowledge. " Adam knew Eve his wife, and she conceived, and bare Cain " (*Genesis* 4: 1). Now the knowledge of husband and wife is the most intimate knowledge that there can be. Husband and wife are no longer two; they are one flesh. The sexual act itself is not the important thing; the important thing is the intimacy of heart and mind and soul which ought to precede that act in true love. To *know* God is therefore not merely to have intellectual knowledge of God; it is to have an intimate personal relationship with God, which is like the nearest and dearest and most intimate relationship in life. Knowledge of God is not merely intellectual knowledge of God; it is a personal relationship with God. And, once again, without Jesus such intimacy with God would have been unthinkable and impossible. It is Jesus who taught men that God is not distant and remote and unapproachable; but that He is the Father whose name and nature are love.

To know God is to know what God is like, and to be on the most intimate terms of friendship with God; and neither of these things is possible without Jesus Christ. Through Jesus we know what God is like; and through Jesus we enter into the friendship of God.

THE WORK OF JESUS

John 17: 6-8

> " I have shown forth your name to the men whom you gave me out of the world. They were yours and you gave them to me, and they have kept your word. Now they realize that everything you gave me comes from you, because I gave to them the words you gave to me, and they received them, and they truly know that I came forth from you, and they believe that you sent me."

HERE Jesus gives us a definition of the work that He did. Jesus said to God: " I have showed forth your name." There are two great ideas here, both of which would be quite clear to those who heard this saying for the first time.

(i) There is an idea which is an essential and characteristic idea of the Old Testament. In the Old Testament the expression the *name* is used in a very special way. It does not mean simply the name by which a person is addressed or called; it means the whole nature and character of the person in so far as it can be known. The Psalmist says: " They that know thy name will put their trust in thee " (*Psalm* 9: 10). Now clearly that does not mean that those who know what God *is called* will trust Him; it means that those who know what God *is like*, those who know the character and the nature of God will be willing and glad to put their trust in Him. The Psalmist says: " Some trust in chariots, and some in horses; but we will remember the name of the Lord our God " (*Psalm* 20: 7).

This means that the Psalmist puts his trust in the nature and the character of God. He knows that he can trust God because he knows what God is like. The Psalmist says: " I will declare thy name unto my brethren " (*Psalm* 22: 22). This was a psalm which the Jews believed to be a prophecy of the Messiah, and of the work that the Messiah would do; and this means that the Messiah's work would be to declare to His fellow-men what God is like. It is the vision of Isaiah that in the new age, " My people shall know my name " (*Isaiah* 52: 6). That is to say that in the golden days men will know fully and truly what God is like. So when Jesus says: " I have shown forth your name," Jesus is saying: " I have enabled men to see what the real character and nature of God is like." It is in fact another way of saying: " He who hath seen me hath seen the Father " (*John* 14: 9). It is Jesus' supreme claim that in Him men see the mind, the character, the heart of God.

(ii) But there is another idea here. In later times when the Jews spoke of *the name of God* they meant the sacred four-letter symbol, the tetragrammaton as it is called, IHWH. That name was held to be so sacred that it was never pronounced, except by the High Priest when he went into the Holy of Holies on the Day of Atonement. It was so sacred that it might not even be taken on the lips of men. These four letters stand for the name Jahweh. We usually speak about Jehovah; the change in the vowels is due to the fact that the vowels of Jehovah are the vowels of the word *Adonai*, which means *Lord*. In the Hebrew alphabet there are no vowels at all. Later the vowel sounds were shown by little signs put above and below the consonants. The four letters IHWH were so sacred that the vowels of Adonai were put below them, so that when the reader came to IHWH he read, not Jahweh, but Adonai. So then in the time of Jesus the name of God was so sacred that ordinary people were not even supposed to know it, and were certainly not supposed to speak it. God was the remote, invisible king, whose name was not for ordinary men to speak. So Jesus is saying: " I have told you God's name; that name which is so sacred that it may not be spoken, can be spoken now because of what I have done. I have brought the remote, invisible God so close that even the simplest people can speak to Him and take His name upon their lips."

It is Jesus' great claim that He showed to men the true nature and the true character of God; and that He brought God so near and so close to men that the humblest Christian can take the unutterable name of God upon his lips.

THE MEANING OF DISCIPLESHIP

John 17: 6-8 (continued)

THIS passage also sheds an illuminating light on the meaning of discipleship.

(i) Discipleship is based on the realization that Jesus came forth from God. The disciple is essentially a person who has realized that Jesus is God's ambassador, and that in Jesus' words we hear the voice of God, and that in Jesus' deeds we see the action of God. The disciple is one who sees God in Jesus, and who knows that there is no one in all the universe who is one with God as Jesus is.

(ii) Discipleship issues in obedience. A disciple is one who keeps God's word as he hears that word in Jesus. There can be no discipleship without obedience. The disciple is the person who has accepted the mastery of Jesus Christ, and who has made the words of Jesus the law of his life. So long as we desire independence, so long as we wish to do what we like, we cannot be disciples. Discipleship involves submission, and is based on obedience.

(iii) Discipleship is something which is destined. Jesus' men were given to Him by God. In the plan of God these men were destined for discipleship. That does not mean that God destined some men to be disciples and some men to refuse discipleship. It does not involve a kind of predestination to discipleship and an equal predestination to refusal of discipleship. Think of it this way. A parent dreams great dreams for his son; he works out and builds up in his mind a future for his son; but the son can refuse that future and go his own way. A teacher thinks out a great future for a scholar or student; he sees that that scholar or student has it in him to do great work for God and man; but the student can lazily or selfishly refuse the offered task. If we love anyone we are always dreaming of that person's future and planning for greatness; but the dream and the plan can be frustrated. The Pharisees believed in fate, but they also believed in free-will. One of the great sayings of the Pharisees was: " Everything is decreed except the fear of God." God has His plan, His dream, His destiny for every man; and the tremendous responsibility of being a man is that we can accept or reject God's destiny for us. We are in the hands not of Fate but of God; and as someone has said: " Fate is what we are compelled to do; destiny is what we are meant to do." No one could avoid doing what he is compelled to do; any man can refuse to do what he is meant to do.

There is throughout this whole passage, and indeed throughout this whole chapter, a ringing confidence about the future in the voice of Jesus. He was with His men; He was with the men God had given Him; He thanked God for them; and He never doubted that they would carry on the work He had given them to do. Let us remember who and what they were. A great commentator said this about Jesus' men: " Eleven Galilaean peasants after three years' labour! But it is enough for Jesus, for in these eleven He beholds the pledge of the continuance of God's work upon earth." When Jesus left this world, He did not seem to have great grounds for hope. He seemed to have achieved so little and to have won so few, and it was the great and the orthodox and the religious of the day who had turned against Him. But Jesus had that divine confidence which springs from God. He was not afraid of small beginnings. He was not pessimistic about the future. He seemed to say: " I have only won eleven very ordinary men; but give me eleven ordinary men and I will change the world."

Jesus had two things—He had belief in God and belief in men. He trusted God and He trusted men. It is one of the most uplifting things in the world to think that Jesus put His trust and confidence in men like ourselves. We too must never be daunted by human weakness or by the small beginning. We too must go forward with Jesus' confident belief in God and in men. If we believe in God and in men we will never be pessimists, because with these two beliefs the possibilities of life are infinite.

JESUS' PRAYER FOR HIS DISCIPLES

John 17: 9-19

" It is for them that I pray. It is not for the world that I pray, but for those whom you have given me because they are yours. All that I have is yours, and all that you have is mine. And through them glory has been given to me. I am no longer in the world and they are no longer in the world, and I go to you. Holy Father, keep them in your name, which you gave to me, that they may be one, as we are one. When I was with them I kept them in your name, which you gave to me. I guarded them and none of them went lost, except the one who was destined to be lost— and this happened that the scriptures might be fulfilled. And now I come to you. I am saying these things while I am still in the world that they may have my joy completed in themselves. I gave them your word, and the world hated them, because they are not of the world. I do not ask that you should take them out of the world, but that you should preserve them from the evil one. They are not of the

world, just as I am not of the world. Consecrate
them by the truth; your word is truth. As you send
me into the world, I send them into the world. And
for their sakes I consecrate myself, that they too may
be consecrated by the truth."

HERE is a passage which is close-packed with truths so
great that we can only grasp fragments of them.

First of all, it tells us something about the disciple
of Jesus.

(i) The disciple is given to Jesus by God. What does
that mean? It means that the Spirit of God moves our
hearts to respond to the appeal of Jesus. When our hearts
go out in love and devotion to Jesus, that is the Spirit
of God working in them.

(ii) Through the disciple glory has come to Jesus. It is
the patient whom he has cured who brings honour to a
doctor; it is the scholar whom he has taught who brings
honour to the teacher; it is the athlete whom he has trained
who brings honour to his trainer. It is the men whom
Jesus has rescued and redeemed and made good who bring
honour to him. The bad man who has been made good,
the man who has been strengthened to live the Christian
life, is the honour of Jesus.

(iii) The disciple is the man who is commissioned to a
task. As God sent out Jesus, so Jesus sends out His disciples
Here indeed is the explanation of a puzzling thing in this
passage. Jesus begins by saying that He does not pray
for the world; and yet He came into the world because
God so loved the world. But, as we have seen, in John's
gospel the term *the world* stands for " human society
organizing itself without God." What Jesus does for the
world is to send out His disciples into it, in order to lead
the world back to God, and to make the world aware of
God. He prays for His men in order that His men may be
such that they will win the world for Him.

Further, this passage tells us that Jesus offered His men
two things.

(i) He offered them His *joy*. All that He was saying to them was designed to bring them joy.

(ii) But He also offered them *warning*. He told them that they were different from the world, and that they could not expect anything else but hatred from the world. Their values were different from the world's values; their standards were different from the world's standards. But there is a joy in battling against the storm and struggling against the tide. It is by facing the hostility of the world that we enter into the Christian joy.

Still further, in this passage Jesus makes the greatest claim He ever made. He prays to God, and He says: " All that I have is yours, and all that you have is mine." The first part of that sentence is natural and easy to understand, for all things belong to God, and again and again Jesus had said so. But the second part of this sentence is an astonishing claim—" All that you have is mine." Luther said: " This no creature can say with reference to God." Never did Jesus so vividly lay down His kinship, His unity, His oneness with God. Jesus is so one with God that He exercises the very power and prerogatives of God.

JESUS' PRAYER FOR HIS DISCIPLES

John 17: 9-19 (*continued*)

THE great and sacred interest of this passage is that it tells us of the things for which Jesus prayed for His disciples.

(i) The first essential is to note that Jesus did not pray that His disciples should be taken out of this world. Jesus never prayed that His disciples might find escape; He prayed that they might find victory. The kind of Christianity which buries itself in a monastery or a convent would not have seemed Christianity to Jesus at all. The kind of Christianity which finds the essence of the Christian life in prayer and meditation, and in a life withdrawn from the world, would have seemed to Jesus a sadly truncated version of the faith He died to bring to men. It was Jesus' insistence that it was in the hurly-burly and the rough and tumble of life that a man must live out his Christianity. Of course there is need of prayer and meditation and quiet times, times when we shut the door upon the world to be alone with God, but all these things are not the end of life; they are the means to the end; and the end of life is to demonstrate the Christian life in the ordinary work of the world. Christianity was never meant to withdraw a man from life; it was meant to equip him better for life. Christianity does not offer us release from problems; it offers us a way to solve our problems. Christianity does not offer us an easy peace; it offers us a triumphant warfare. Christianity does not offer us a life in which troubles are escaped and evaded; it offers us a life in which troubles are faced and conquered. However much it may be true that the Christian is not of the world, it still remains true that it is within the world that his Christianity must be lived out. The Christian must never desire to abandon the world; he must always desire to win the world.

(ii) Jesus prayed for the unity of His disciples. His prayer was that they might be one as He and His Father are one. As it has been put, He prayed that they might live, " not as units, but as a unity." Where there are divisions, where there is exclusiveness, where there is competition between the Churches, where there is disunity and dispeace, the cause of Christianity is harmed and hindered, and the prayer of Jesus is frustrated. The gospel cannot truly be preached in any congregation which is not one united band of brothers. The world cannot be evangelized by competing Churches. Jesus prayed that His disciples might be as fully one as He and the Father are one; and there is no prayer of Jesus which has been so hindered from being answered by individual Christians and by all the Churches than this prayer.

(iii) Jesus prayed that God would keep and protect His disciples from the attacks of the Evil One. The Bible is not a speculative book; it does not discuss the origin of evil; but it is quite certain that in this world there is a power of evil which is in opposition to the power of God, a power which seeks to lure men out of the right way and into the wrong way. It is an uplifting thing to feel that God is the sentinel who stands over our lives to protect us and guard us from the assaults of evil. The fact that we fall so often is due to the fact that we try to meet life in our own strength, and we forget to seek the help and to remember the presence of our protecting God.

(iv) Jesus prayed that His disciples might be consecrated by the truth. The word for to *consecrate* is the word *hagiazein* which comes from the adjective *hagios*. In the Authorised Version the word *hagios* is usually translated *holy*. But the basic meaning of *hagios* is *different* or *separate*. A thing which is *hagios* is different from other and from ordinary things. So then this word *hagiazein* has two ideas in it. (a) It means *to set apart for a special task*. When God called Jeremiah, He said to him: " Before I formed thee in the belly I knew thee; and before thou camest forth out of the womb I *sanctified* thee, and I ordained thee a prophet unto the nations " (*Jeremiah* 1: 5). Even before his birth God had set Jeremiah apart for a special task. When God was instituting the priesthood in Israel He told Moses to *consecrate* the sons of Aaron and to *sanctify* them that they might serve in the office of the priests (*Exodus* 28: 41). Aaron's sons were to be set apart for a special office and a special duty. (b) But *hagiazein* means not only to set apart for some special office and task, it also means *to equip a man with the qualities of mind and heart and character which are necessary for that task*. If a man is to serve God, he must have something of God's goodness and God's wisdom in him. He who would serve the holy God must himself be holy too. And so God does not only choose a man for His special service, and set

253

him apart for it, He also equips a man with the qualities
he needs to carry out that service.

We must always remember that God has chosen us
out, He has consecrated and dedicated us for His special
service. That special service is that we ourselves should
love and obey Him, and we should bring others to do the
same. And we must always remember that God has not
left us to carry out that great task and responsibility in
our own strength, but that He, out of His grace, has fitted
and equipped us for our task, if we will place our lives in
His hands.

A GLIMPSE OF THE FUTURE

John 17: 20, 21

> " It is not only for these that I pray, but also for
> those who are going to believe in their word of testi-
> mony to me. And my prayer is that they may all
> be one, even as you, Father, are in me, and I in you,
> so that they may be in us, so that the world may
> believe that you sent me."

GRADUALLY in this section Jesus' prayer has been going
out to the ends of the earth. First, He prayed for Himself
as the Cross faced Him. Second, He prayed for His disciples,
and for God's keeping power for them. But now His
prayers take a sweep into the distant future, and He
prays for those who in distant lands and far-off ages will
also enter the Christian faith.

Here are two great characteristics of Jesus full displayed.
First, we see His complete faith and His radiant certainty.
At the moment His followers were few, but even with the
Cross facing Him, His confidence was unshaken, and He
was praying for those who would believe in His name.
This passage should be specially precious to us, for this
passage is Jesus' prayer for us. Second, we see Jesus'
confidence in His men. He knew that they did not fully
understand Him; He knew that in a very short time they

were going to abandon Him in His hour of sorest need. Yet it was to these very same men that He looked with complete confidence to spread His name abroad throughout the world. It is the great characteristic of Jesus that He never lost His faith in God or His confidence in men.

And what was His prayer for the Church which was to be? His prayer was that all its members would be one as He and His Father are one. What was that unity for which Jesus prayed? It was not a unity of administration or organization. It was not in any sense an ecclesiastical unity. *It was a unity of personal relationship.* We have already seen that the union between Jesus and God was a union of love and obedience. It was a unity of love for which Jesus prayed. It was a unity in which men loved each other because they loved Him. It was a unity based entirely on the relationship between heart and heart. It will never be that Christians will organize their Churches all in the same way. It will never be that they will worship God all in the same way. It will never even be that they will all believe precisely and exactly the same things. But the Christian unity is a unity which transcends all these differences, and joins men together in love. The cause of Christian unity at the present time, and indeed all through history, has been injured and violated and hindered, because men loved their own ecclesiastical organizations, men loved their own creeds, men loved their own ritual, more than they loved each other. If we really loved each other and really loved Christ no man would ever be excluded from any Church, and no Church would exclude any man who was Christ's disciple. Only love implanted in the hearts of men by God can tear down the barriers which men have erected between each other and between their Churches.

Still further, as Jesus saw it and prayed for it, it was to be precisely that unity which convinced the world of the truth of Christianity and of the place of Christ. It is more natural for men to be divided than to be united.

It is more human for men to fly apart than to come together. Real unity between all Christians would be a " supernatural fact which would require a supernatural explanation." It is the tragic fact that it is just that united front that the Church has never shown to men. Faced by the disunity of Christians and Churches, the world cannot see the supreme value of the Christian faith. It is our individual duty to demonstrate that unity of love with our fellow men which is the answer to the prayer of Christ. It may well be that the rank and file of the Churches can do and must do what the leaders of the Church refuse officially to do.

THE GIFT AND THE PROMISE OF GLORY

John 17: 22-26

" And I have given them the glory which you gave me, that they may be one as we are one. I am in them, and you are in me, so that their unity with us and with each other may stand consummated and complete. I pray for this that the world may realize that you sent me, and that you loved them as you loved me. Father, it is my will that those whom you have given me should be with me where I am going, that they may see my glory which you gave me, because you loved me before the foundation of the world. Righteous Father, the world did not know you, but I knew you, and these realized that you sent me. I have told them what you are like, and I will go on telling them, that the love with which you loved me may be in them, and that I may be in them."

BENGEL, the old commentator, exclaimed as he began to comment on this passage: " O how great is the Christians' glory ! " And indeed it is, for here is a passage which is all about the glory which Jesus gave to and prayed for for His disciples.

First, Jesus said that He had given His disciples the glory which His Father had given Him. We must fully understand what that means. What was the glory of Jesus ? There were three ways in which Jesus talked of

His glory. (*a*) The Cross was His glory. Jesus did not speak of being crucified; He spoke of being glorified. Therefore, first and foremost, a Christian's glory is the cross that he must bear. It is an honour and a glory to suffer for Jesus Christ. We must never think of our cross as our penalty; we must think of it as our glory. The harder the task a knight was given, the greater he considered the glory of it. The harder the task we give a student, or a craftsman, or a surgeon, the more we honour him. We, in effect, say that we believe that nobody but him could attempt that task at all. So when it is hard to be a Christian, we must regard it as our glory, as our honour given to us by God. (*b*) Jesus' perfect obedience to the will of God was His glory. We find our glory, our honour, our life, not in doing as we like, but in doing as God wills. When we try to do as we like—and many of us have tried it—we find nothing but sorrow and disaster both for ourselves and for others. We find the real glory of life in doing God's will. The greater the obedience, the greater the glory. (*c*) Jesus' glory lay in the fact that, from His life, His deeds, His words, His powers, men recognized His special relationship with God. They saw and admitted that no one could live like that unless He was specially and uniquely near to God. Our glory is when men see in us the reflection of God. It is our glory when men see in the service we render to others, in the love which we show to others, nothing less than the reflection of the love of God. As with Christ, it is our glory when men see God in us.

Second, Jesus said that it was His will that His disciples should see His glory in the heavenly places. It is the Christian conviction that the Christian will share *all* the experiences of Christ. If he has to share Christ's Cross, he will also share Christ's glory. " It is a faithful saying: For if we be dead with Him, we shall also live with Him: if we suffer with Him, we shall also reign with Him " (2 *Timothy* 2: II, 12). Here in this world at best we see through a glass darkly, but then we shall see face to face (I *Corinthians* 13: 12). The joy we have now is only a faint foretaste of the joy which is to come. It is Christ's promise that if we share His glory and His sufferings on earth, we shall share His glory and His triumph when life on this earth is ended. And what greater promise could there be than that?

From this prayer Jesus was to go straight out to the betrayal, the trial and the Cross. He was not to speak to His disciples again. It is a wonderful and a precious thing to remember that before these terrible hours His last words were not of despair but of glory.

THE ARREST IN THE GARDEN

John 18: 1-11

When Jesus had said these things He went out with His disciples across the Kedron valley to a place where there was a garden, into which He and His disciples entered; and Judas, His betrayer, knew the place for Jesus often met with His disciples there. So Judas took a company of soldiers, together with officers from the chief priests and Pharisees, and went there with lanterns and torches and weapons. Jesus knew the things which were going to happen to Him, so He came out and said: "Who are you looking for?" They answered: "Jesus of Nazareth." Jesus said to them: "I am He." And Judas, His betrayer, stood there with them. When He said to them: "I am He," they stepped back and fell on the ground. So Jesus again asked them: "Who are you looking for?" They said: "Jesus of Nazareth." Jesus said: "I told you that I am He. If it is I for whom you are looking, let these go, so that the word which scripture said may be fulfilled—I have lost none of those whom you gave me." Now Simon Peter had a sword and he drew it; and he struck the high priest's servant and cut off his right ear. The servant's name was Malchus. Jesus said to Peter:

258

" Put your sword in its sheath. Shall I not drink the cup which my Father gave me? "

WHEN the last meal was finished, and when Jesus' talk and prayer with His disciples were ended, He and His friends left the upper room. They were bound for the Garden of Gethsemane. They would leave by the gate, go down the steep valley and cross the channel of the brook Kedron. There a symbolic thing must have happened. All the Passover lambs were killed in the Temple, and the blood of the lambs was poured on the altar as an offering to God. The number of lambs which were slain for the Passover was immense. On one occasion, thirty years later than the time of Jesus, a census was taken and the number was 256,000. We may imagine what the Temple courts were like when the blood of all these lambs was dashed on to the altar. From the altar there was a channel down to the brook Kedron, and through that channel the blood of the Passover lambs drained away. When Jesus crossed the brook Kedron it would still be red with the blood of the lambs which had been sacrificed. And surely as He did so, the thought of Jesus' own sacrifice would be vivid in His mind.

Having crossed the channel of the Kedron, they came to the Mount of Olives; and on the slopes of it there lay the little garden of Gethsemane which means the oil-press, the press where the oil was extracted from the olives which grew on the hill. Many well-to-do people had their private gardens there. Space in Jerusalem was too limited for private gardens, for Jerusalem was built on the top of a hill. Further, there were ceremonial prohibitions which forbade the use of manure on the soil of the sacred city. That was why the wealthy people had their private gardens outside the city on the slopes of the Mount of Olives. They still show pilgrims to this day a little garden on the hillside. It is lovingly tended by the Franciscan friars, and in it there are eight great olive trees of such girth that they seem, as H. V. Morton says, more like rocks than trees.

They are very old; it is known that they go back to a time before the Moslem conquest of Palestine. It is scarcely possible that they go back to the time of Jesus Himself; but certainly the little paths which criss-cross the Mount of Olives were trodden by the feet of Jesus Himself. So to this garden Jesus went. Some wealthy citizen—an anonymous friend of Jesus whose name will never be known—must have given Him the key of the gate and the right to use it when He was in Jerusalem. Often Jesus and His disciples had gone to that garden for peace and quiet. Judas knew it. Judas knew that he would find Jesus there and it was there that Judas had decided that it would be easiest to engineer the arrest of Jesus.

There is something astonishing about the force which came out to arrest Jesus. John said that there was a company of soldiers, together with officers from the chief priests and Pharisees. The *officers* would be the Temple police. The Temple authorities had a kind of private police force to keep good order, and the Sanhedrin had its police and officers to carry out its decrees. The officers were the Jewish police force. But there was a band of soldiers there too. The word is *speira*. Now that word, if it is correctly used, can have three meanings. It is the Greek word for a Roman cohort and a cohort had six hundred men. If it was a cohort of auxiliary soldiers, a *speira* had one thousand men, two hundred and forty cavalry and seven hundred and sixty infantry. Sometimes, much more rarely, the word is used for the detachment of men called a maniple which was made up of two hundred men. Even if we take this word to mean the smallest force, the maniple, what an expedition to send out against an unarmed Galilaean carpenter! At the Passover time there were always extra soldiers in Jerusalem, quartered in the Tower of Antonia which overlooked the Temple, and men would be available. But what a compliment to the power of Jesus! When the authorities decided to arrest Jesus, they sent what was almost an army to do it. There was such a power in this one single man that His enemies felt that they needed an army to reduce Him to submission and to ensure His capture.

THE ARREST IN THE GARDEN

John 18: 1-11 (*continued*)

THERE are few scenes in scripture which so show us the qualities of Jesus as does the arrest in the garden.

(i) It shows us His courage. At the Passover time it was full moon, and the night was almost daylight. Yet the enemies of Jesus had come with lamps and torches. Why? They did not need them to see the way in the silver light of the moon. They must have thought that they would have to search among the trees and in the hillside nooks and crannies to find Jesus. They must have assumed that He would hide. So far from hiding, when they arrived, Jesus stepped out. "Who are you looking for?" He demanded. "Jesus of Nazareth," they said. Back came the answer: "I am He." The man they had thought they would have to search for as He skulked in the trees and the caves was standing before them with a glorious, reckless defiance. Here is the courage of the man who will face things out. During the Spanish Civil War a city was besieged. There were some who wished to surrender, but a leader arose. "It is better," he said, "to die on our feet than to live on our knees." If Jesus had to die, He was going to die like a hero.

(ii) It shows us His authority. There He was, one single, lonely, unarmed figure. There they were, hundreds of them, armed and equipped; and yet in face of Him, they step back and fall to the ground. In that moment power radiated from Jesus. There flowed from Him an authority which in all His loneliness made Him stronger than the might of His enemies.

(iii) It shows us that Jesus chose to die. Here again

it is clear that Jesus could have escaped death if He had so wished. He could have walked through them and could have gone His way. But He did not. Jesus even helped His enemies to arrest Himself. He chose to die.

(iv) It shows His protective love. It was not for Himself that He took thought; it was for His friends. " Here I am," He said. " It is I whom you want. Take me, and let them go." He thought more of their peril than of His own. Among the many immortal stories of the Second World War that of Alfred Sadd, the missionary of Tarrawa, stands out. When the Japanese came to his island, he was lined up with twenty other men, mostly New Zealand soldiers who had been part of the garrison. The Japs laid a Union Jack on the ground and ordered Mr. Sadd to walk over it. Mr. Sadd approached the flag and, as he came to it, he turned off to the right. They ordered him again to trample on the flag; this time he turned off to the left. The third time he was compelled to go up to the flag; and he gathered it in his arms and kissed it. When the Japanese took them all out to be shot, many were so young that they were heavy-hearted, but Mr. Sadd cheered them up. They stood in a line, Mr. Sadd in the middle, and presently he went out and stood a little in front of them and spoke words of cheer. When he had finished, he went back and still stood a little in front of them, so that he would be the first to die. Alfred Sadd thought more of others' trouble than his own. Jesus' protecting love was over His disciples even in Gethsemane.

(v) It shows His utter obedience. " Shall I not drink," He said, " the cup that God has given me to drink? " This was God's will, and for Him that was enough. He was Himself faithful unto death.

And there is one figure in this story to whom we must do justice, and that figure is Peter. Peter, one man, drew his sword against hundreds. As Macaulay had it:

> " How can a man die better
> Than facing fearful odds? "

Peter would soon deny his master, but in that moment he was prepared to take on hundreds all alone for the sake of Christ. We may talk of the cowardice and the failure of Peter; but we must never forget the sublime courage of this moment.

JESUS BEFORE ANNAS

John 18: 12-14, 19-24

The company of soldiers and their commander and the officers of the Jews took Jesus, and bound Him, and led Him first of all to Annas. He was the father-in-law of Caiaphas, who was High Priest in that year. It was Caiaphas who had advised the Jews that it was better that one man should die for the people. . . . The High Priest questioned Jesus about His disciples and about His teaching. Jesus answered him: " I spoke openly in the world. I taught at all times in the Synagogue and in the precincts of the Temple, where all the Jews assemble, and I spoke nothing in secret. Why do you ask me questions? Ask those who heard me what I said to them. See! These know what I have said." When He had said these things, one of the officers who was standing by, dealt Jesus a blow. " Do you answer the High Priest like this? " he said. Jesus answered: " If I have spoken ill, produce evidence about the ill; if I have spoken well, why do you strike me? " So Annas sent him bound to Caiaphas the High Priest.

FOR the sake of keeping the narrative continuous we will take the two passages which deal with the trial before Annas together; and we will do the same with the two passages which deal with the tragedy of Peter.

It is only John who tells us that Jesus was brought first of all to Annas. Annas was a notorious character. Edersheim writes of him: " No figure is better known in contemporary Jewish history than that of Annas; no person deemed more fortunate or successful, but none also more generally execrated than the late High Priest." Annas was the power behind the throne in Jerusalem

He himself had been High Priest from A.D. 6 to 15. Four
of his sons had also held the high priesthood and Caiaphas
was his son-in-law. That very fact is itself suggestive and
illuminating. There had been a time, when the Jews were
free, when the High Priest had been High Priest for life;
but when the Roman governors came, the office of High
Priest became a matter for contention and intrigue and
bribery and corruption. The office now went to the greatest
sycophant and to the highest bidder, to the man who
was most willing to toe the line with the Roman governor.
The High Priest was the arch-collaborator, the man who
bought comfort and ease and prestige and power at the
expenditure of money in bribes and at the cost of close
co-operation with his country's masters. The family of
Annas was immensely rich and one by one they had
intrigued and bribed their way into office, while Annas
remained the power behind it all.

Even the way in which Annas made his money was most
probably disgraceful. In the Court of the Gentiles there
were the sellers of victims for the sacrifices, these sellers
whom Jesus had driven from the Temple courts. They
were not traders; they were extortioners. Every victim
which was offered in the Temple had to be without spot
and blemish. There were inspectors to see that it was so.
If a victim was bought outside the Temple it had to be
inspected and examined, and it was certain that a flaw
would be found. The worshipper was then directed to
buy at the Temple booths where the victims had already
been examined and where there was no risk of rejection
That would have been convenient and helpful but for
one thing. Outside the Temple a pair of doves could cost
as little as 9d.; inside it they could cost as much as 15s.
The whole Temple business was sheer exploitation; and
the shops where the Temple victims were sold were called
The Bazaars of Annas. They were the property of the
family of Annas; it was by the exploitation of the worshippers, by trading on the sacred sacrifices that Annas had

amassed a fortune. The Jews themselves hated the household of Annas. There is a passage in the *Talmud* which says: " Woe to the house of Annas! Woe to their serpent's hiss! They are High Priests; their sons are keepers of the treasury; their sons-in-law are guardians of the Temple; and their servants beat the people with staves." Annas and his whole household were notorious.

Now we can see why Annas arranged that Jesus should be brought first to him. Jesus was the man who had attacked Annas' vested interest; Jesus was the man who had cleared the Temple of the sellers of victims, and who had hit Annas where it hurt—in his pocket and his bank account. Annas wanted to be the first to gloat over the capture, the defeat, the discomfiture of this disturbing Galilaean.

The examination before Annas was a mockery of justice. It was an essential regulation of the Jewish law that a prisoner must be asked no question by answering which he would admit any kind of guilt. Maimonides, the great Jewish medieval scholar, lays it down: " Our true law does not inflict the penalty of death upon a sinner by his own confession." Annas violated the principles of Jewish justice when he questioned Jesus. It was precisely of that that Jesus reminded Annas. Jesus said: " Don't ask me questions. Ask those who heard me." Jesus was, in effect, saying: " Take your evidence about me in the proper and the legal way. Examine your witnesses, which you have every right to do; stop examining me, which you have no right to do." When Jesus said that, one of the officers hit Jesus a slap across the face. He said, in effect, " Are you trying to teach the High Priest how to conduct a trial? " Jesus' answer was: " If I have said or taught anything illegal, witnesses should be called. I have only stated the law. Why hit me for that? "

Jesus never had any hope of justice. The self-interest of Annas and his colleagues had been touched; and Jesus was condemned before He was tried. When a man is engaged on an evil way, his only desire is to eliminate anyone who opposes him. He cannot do it by fair means, so he is compelled to do it by foul means. A case which must be supported by injustice and by blows is no case at all.

THE HERO AND THE COWARD

John 18: 15-18, 25-27

> Simon Peter was following Jesus with another disciple. That disciple was known to the High Priest, and he went in with Jesus into the courtyard of the High Priest's house. Peter was standing at the dor outside., The other disciple, who was known to the Hoigh Priest came out and spoke to the door-keeper, and brought Peter in. The maid-servant, who kept the door, said to Peter: " You are not one of this man's disciples, are you? " He said: " I am not." The servants and the officers stood beside a charcoal brazier they had kindled, because it was cold, and they were warming themselves; and Peter too was standing with them warming himself.... Simon Peter was standing warming himself. They said to him: " Surely you too are one of His disciples? " He denied it, and said: " I am not." One of the servants of the High Priest, a relation of the man whose ear Peter had cut off, said: " Did I not see you in the garden with Him? " Again Peter denied it, and immediately cockcrow sounded.

WHEN the other disciples forsook Jesus and fled, Peter refused to do so. He followed Jesus, even after His arrest because he could not tear himself away. So he came to the house of Caiaphas, the High Priest; and he was in the company of another disciple who had the right of entry to the High Priest's house, because he was known to the High Priest. There have been many speculations about who this other disciple was, because he is left unnamed, and there is no real certainty about his identity. Some have thought that he was simply some unknown disciple whose name we can never know. Some people have very naturally connected him with either Nicodemus or Joseph of Arimathaea who were both members of the Sanhedrin, and must both have known the High Priest well. One very interesting suggestion has been made. It has been suggested that the other unnamed disciple was Judas Iscariot. Judas must have had much coming and going to arrange the betrayal, and he would be well known both to the maid-servant who answered the door and to the High Priest himself. The one thing that seems to invalidate that theory is that, after the scene in the garden, when Judas had arrived with the soldiers and the officers, Judas' part in the betrayal must have been quite clear; and it is almost incredible that Peter would have had anything more to do with him. The traditional view has always been that the unnamed disciple was John himself; and the tradition is so strong that it is difficult to set it aside. But the question is, in that case, How could John from Galilee be known, apparently intimately, to the High Priest?

Two suggestions have been made to explain this relationship between John and the High Priest's household. (*a*) In the later days a man called Polycrates was writing about the Fourth Gospel and its writer, and about the beloved disciple. Polycrates never doubted that John wrote the gospel and that John was the beloved disciple, but he says a very curious thing about John. He says that John was by birth a priest, and that he wore the *petalos*, which was the narrow gold band, or *ziz*, inscribed with the words, "Holiness unto the Lord," which the High Priest wore upon his forehead. If that is so, John was actually of the High Priest's family and kinship; but it is difficult to believe that John was of the priestly line, for the gospels so clearly show him to us as a Galilaean fisherman. (*b*) The second explanation is easier to accept. It is clear that John's father must have had a very flourishing fishing business because he could afford to employ hired servants (*Mark* 1: 20). One of the great Galilaean industries was the salt fish industry. In those days fresh fish was a great luxury because there was no way of transporting fish in such a way that it would remain fresh. But on the other hand, salt fish was a staple article of diet. It has been supposed that John's father was in the salt fish trade, and that he actually supplied the household of the High Priest with salt fish. If that were so, then John would be well-known to the High Priest and to his servants and his staff, because often he would bring to the house the supplies the household needed. John, in that case, would be a regular visitor to the High Priest's house. It so happens that there is some kind of support in legend for this theory. H. V. Morton tells us that to this day there is in the back streets of Jerusalem a little building which is now an Arab coffee house. In it there are certain stones and arches which were once part of a very early Christian church. The Franciscans believe that that old Christian church stood on the site of a house which belonged to Zebedee, John's father. The family, so the Franciscans believe, were fish merchants in Galilee with a branch office in Jerusalem, and they supplied the household of Caiaphas the High Priest with salt fish, and that was why John had the entry into the High Priest's house.

However these things may be, Peter was brought into the courtyard of the High Priest's house and there he three times denied his Lord.

There is one very interesting thing about the cockcrow. Jesus had said that Peter would deny Him three times before the cock crew. Now there are difficulties about that. According to Jewish ritual law, it was not lawful to keep cocks in the holy city, although we cannot be sure whether that law was kept or not. Further, it is never possible to be sure that a cock will crow. But the Romans had a certain military practice. The night was divided into four watches—6 p.m. to 9 p.m., 9 p.m. to 12 midnight, 12 midnight to 3 a.m., and 3 a.m. to 6 a.m. After the third watch the guard was changed and to mark the changing of the guard there was a trumpet call at 3 a.m. That trumpet call was called in Latin *gallicinium* and in Greek *alektorophōnia,* which both mean *cockcrow.* It may well be that Jesus said to Peter: " Before the trumpet sounds the cockcrow you will deny me three times." Everyone in Jerusalem must have known that trumpet call at 3 a.m. That night it sounded through the city, and when it sounded Peter remembered.

THE HERO AND THE COWARD

John 18: 15-18, 25-27 (*continued*)

So in the courtyard of the High Priest's house Peter denied his Lord. No man has ever been so unjustly treated as Peter by preachers and commentators. Always what is stressed in this story is Peter's failure and Peter's shame. But there are things we must remember.

(i) We must remember that all the other disciples, except John, if John is the unnamed disciple, had forsaken Jesus and fled. All of them except Peter had run away. Think what Peter had done. He alone drew his sword against fearful odds in the garden; he alone followed out to see the end. He was the one brave man. The first thing to remember about Peter is not his failure, but the courage which kept him near to Jesus when everyone else had run away. The tremendous thing about Peter was that his failure was a failure that could only have happened to a man of superlative courage. True, Peter failed; but he failed in a situation which none of the other disciples even dared to face. He failed, not because he was a coward, but because he was a brave man.

(ii) We must remember how much Peter loved Jesus. Only his love had stood the test. The others had abandoned Jesus; Peter alone stood by Him. Peter loved Jesus so much that he could not leave Him. True, Peter failed; but he failed in a situation into which only a faithful lover of Jesus would ever have come.

(iii) We must remember how Peter redeemed himself. Things could not have been easy for Peter. The story of his denial would soon get about, for people love a malicious story. It may well be, as legend has it, that people imitated the crow of the cock when Peter passed. But Peter had the courage and the tenacity of purpose to redeem himself, to start from his failure and to attain to true greatness.

The whole essence of the matter was that it was the real Peter who protested his loyalty in the upper room; it was the real Peter who drew his lonely sword in the moonlight of the garden; it was the real Peter who followed Jesus, because he could not leave his Lord alone; it was *not* the real Peter who cracked beneath the tension and who denied his Lord. *And that is just what Jesus could see.* The tremendous thing about Jesus is that beneath all our failures He sees the real man. Jesus understands. He loves us in spite of what we do, because He loves us, not for the things we are, but for the things we have it in us to be. The forgiving love of Jesus is so great that He sees our real personality, not in our faithlessness, but in our loyalty, not in our defeat by sin, but in our reaching after goodness, even when we are defeated.

JESUS AND PILATE

John 18: 28—19: 16

They brought Jesus from Caiaphas to the governor's headquarters. It was early in the morning and they themselves did not enter into the headquarters, in case they should be defiled; but they wished to avoid defilement because they wished to eat the Passover. So Pilate came out to them and said: "What charge do you bring against this man?" They answered him: "If He had not been an evil-doer, we would not have handed Him over to you." Pilate said to them: "You take Him, and judge Him according to your laws." The Jews said to Pilate: "It is not permitted to us to put anyone to death." This happened that there might be fulfilled

the word of Jesus, which He spoke in indication of
the kind of death He was going to die. So Pilate
went again into his headquarters, and called Jesus,
and said to Him: "Are you the King of the Jews?"
Jesus answered: "Are you saying this because
you have discovered it yourself? Or did others tell
it to you about me?" Pilate answered: "Am I a
Jew? Your own countrymen and the chief priests
handed you over to me. What have you done?"
Jesus answered: "My kingdom is not of this world.
If my kingdom was of this world, my servants would
have fought to prevent me being handed over to
the Jews. But, as it is, my kingdom does not have
its source here." So Pilate said to Him: "So you
are a king then?" Jesus said: "It is you who are
saying that I am a king. The reason why I was born
and came into the world is that I should bear witness
to the truth. Every one who is of the truth hears
my voice." "What is truth?" Pilate said to Him.

When he had said this, he again went out to the
Jews and said to them: "I find no fault in Him.
You have a custom that I should release one person
to you at the Passover time. Do you wish me to
release the King of the Jews for you?" They shouted:
"Not this man, but Barabbas." And Barabbas was
a brigand.

Then Pilate took Jesus and scourged Him; and
the soldiers plaited a crown of thorns, and put it
on His head. And they put a purple robe on Him;
and they kept coming to Him and saying: "Hail!
King of the Jews!" And they dealt Him repeated
blows. Pilate came out again and said to them:
"See! I bring Him out to you, because I want you
to know that I find no fault in Him." So Jesus came
out, wearing the crown of thorns and the purple
robe. And Pilate said to them: "See! The Man!"
So, when the chief priests and officers saw Him, they
shouted: "Crucify Him! Crucify Him!" Pilate
said to them: "You take Him, and crucify Him!
For I find no fault in Him." The Jews answered
him: "We have a law, and by that law He ought
to die, because He made Himself out to be the Son
of God." When Pilate heard this saying, he was still
more alarmed.

He went into his headquarters again, and said to
Jesus: "Where do you come from?" Jesus gave

271

him no answer. Pilate said to Him: "Do you refuse
to speak to me? Are you not aware that I have
authority to release you, and authority to crucify
you?" Jesus answered him: "You would have
no authority against me whatsoever, unless it had
been given to you from above. That is why he who
betrayed me to you is guilty of the greater sin."
From this moment Pilate tried every way to release
Him; but the Jews kept insistently shouting: "If
you release this man, you are not Caesar's friend.
Every man who makes himself a king is an opponent
of Caesar." So when Pilate heard these words, he
brought Jesus out. He took his seat on his judgment
seat, in the place that is called the Pavement—in
Hebrew, Gabbatha. It was the day of the preparation
for the Passover. It was about twelve o'clock midday. He said to the Jews: "See! Your king!"
They shouted: "Away with Him! Away with Him!
Crucify Him!" Pilate said to them: "Shall I crucify
your king?" The chief priests answered: "We have
no king but Caesar." Then he handed Him over to
them to be crucified.

THIS is the most dramatic account of the trial of Jesus
in the New Testament, and to have cut it into small
sections would have been to lose the drama. This is a
passage which has to be read as one. But now that we
have read it as one, we shall go on to take several days
to study it. The drama of this passage lies in the clash
and interplay of personalities. It will therefore be best to
study this passage, not section by section, but in the light
of the persons who are the actors within it.

We will begin by looking at the *Jews*. In the time of
Jesus the Jews were subject to the Romans. The Romans
allowed them a good deal of self-government, but they
had not the right to carry out the death penalty. The
ius gladii, as it was called, the right of the sword belonged
to the Romans. As the *Talmud* records: "Forty years
before the destruction of the Temple, judgment in matters
of life and death was taken away from Israel." The first
Roman governor of Palestine was named Coponius, and
Josephus, telling of his appointment as governor, says

that Coponius was sent as procurator " having the power of life and death put into his hands by Caesar." (Josephus, *Wars of the Jews*, 2, 8, 1). Josephus tells of a certain priest called Ananus who determined to execute certain of his enemies. Jews of more prudent mind protested against his decision on the grounds that he had no right either to take it or to carry it out. Ananus was not allowed to carry out his decision and was deposed from office for even thinking of doing so. (Josephus, *Antiquities of the Jews*, 20, 9, 1). It is true that sometimes, as, for instance, in the case of Stephen, the Jews did take the law into their own hands; but legally and officially they had no right to inflict the death penalty on anyone. That was why the Jews had to bring Jesus to Pilate before He could be crucified.

If the Jews had themselves been able to carry out the death penalty it would have been by stoning. The Law lays it down: " And he that blasphemeth the name of the Lord, he shall surely be put to death, and all the congregation shall certainly stone him " (*Leviticus* 24: 16). In such a case the witnesses whose word proved the crime had to be the first to fling the stones. " The hands of the witnesses shall be the first upon him to put him to death, and afterwards the hands of all the people (*Deuteronomy* 17: 7). That is the point of verse 32. That verse says that all this was happening that there might be fulfilled the word of Jesus which He spoke in indication of the kind of death by which He was going to die. Jesus had said that if He was *lifted up*, that is, if He was *crucified*, He would draw all men to Him (*John* 12: 32). If that prophecy of Jesus was to be fulfilled, He must be *crucified*, not *stoned*; and therefore, even apart from the fact that Roman law would not allow the Jews to carry out the death penalty, Jesus had to die a Roman death, because He had to be *lifted up*.

The Jews from start to finish were seeking to use Pilate for their purposes. They could not kill Jesus themselves,

273

so they were determined that the Romans would kill Him for them.

JESUS AND PILATE

John 18: 28—19: 16 *(continued)*

BUT there were more things about the Jews than that. As we read this story certain things about the Jews stand out.

(i) They began by hating Jesus; but they finished in a very hysteria of hatred. They finished by becoming a maddened, shrieking crowd, howling like wolves, with faces twisted in bitterness: " Crucify Him! Crucify Him! " In the end the Jews reached such an insanity of hatred that they were impervious to reason and to mercy and even to the claims of common humanity. There is nothing in this world which warps a man's judgment as hatred does. Hatred is a kind of madness. Once a man allows himself to hate, he can neither think nor see straight, nor listen without distortion. Hatred is so terrible a thing just because it takes a man's senses away.

(ii) The hatred of the Jews made them lose all sense of proportion. They were so careful of ceremonial and ritual cleanness that they would not enter Pilate's headquarters, and yet they were busy doing everything possible to crucify the Son of God. To eat the Passover a Jew had to be absolutely ceremonially clean. Now if they had gone into Pilate's headquarters, they would have incurred uncleanness in a double way. First, the scribal law said: " The dwelling-places of Gentiles are unclean." Second, the Passover was the Feast of Unleavened Bread. Part of the preparation for it was a ceremonial search for leaven, and the banishing of every particle of leaven from every house. Leaven was the symbol of evil and it had to be completely banished from every house. To go into Pilate's headquarters would have been to go into a place where leaven might have been found; and to go into such a place when the Passover was being prepared was to render oneself unclean. Even if the Jews had done that, if they had entered a Gentile house and a house with leaven, they would only have been unclean until evening, and then they would have had to undergo a ceremonial bathing, and they would have been clean. Now see what the Jews were doing. They were carrying out the details of the ceremonial law with absolutely meticulous care; and at the same time they were hounding to the Cross the Son of God, who was incarnate love. That is just the kind of thing that men are always liable to do. There is many a church member who fusses about the sheerest trifles, and who breaks God's law of love and of forgiveness and of service every day. There is even many a church in which the details of vestments, furnishings, ritual, ceremonial are attended to with the most detailed care, and where the spirit of love and fellowship are conspicuous only by their absence. One of the most tragic things in the world is how the human mind can lose its sense of proportion, and its ability to put first things first.

(iii) The Jews did not hesitate to twist their charge against Jesus. In their own private examination the charge they had formulated against Jesus was a charge of blasphemy (*Matthew* 26: 65). They knew well that Pilate would not proceed on a charge like that. He would have said that that was their own private religious quarrel and they could settle it as they liked without coming to him. In the end what the Jews produced was a charge of rebellion and political insurrection. They accused Jesus of claiming to be a king, and they knew that their accusation was a lie. Hatred is a terrible thing; it does not hesitate to twist the truth. A man has no case at all when he has to support that case by a lie.

(iv) In order to compass the death of Jesus the Jews denied every principle they had. The most astonishing thing the Jews said that day was: " We have no king

but Caesar." It was Samuel's word to the people that
God and God alone was their king (I *Samuel* 12: 12).
When the crown was offered to Gideon, his answer was:
" I will not rule over you, neither shall my son rule over
you: the Lord shall rule over you " (*Judges* 8: 23). When
the Romans had first come into Palestine, they had taken
a census in order to arrange the normal taxation to which
subject people were liable. And there had been the most
bloody rebellion, because the Jews had insisted that God
alone was their king, and to Him alone they would pay
tribute. When the Jewish leader said: " We have no
king but Caesar," it was the most astonishing *volte-face*
in history. The very statement must have taken Pilate's
breath away, and he must have looked at them in half-
bewildered, half-cynical amusement. The Jews were
prepared to abandon every principle they had in order to
eliminate Jesus.

It is a terrible picture. The hatred of the Jews turned
them nto a maddened mob of shrieking, frenzied fanatics.
In their hatred they forgot all mercy, they forgot all
sense of proportion, they forgot all justice, they forgot
all their principles, they even forgot God. Never in history
was the insanity of hatred so vividly shown.

JESUS AND PILATE

John 18: 28—19: 16 (*continued*)

Now we turn to the second personality in this story—
to *Pilate*. Throughout the whole trial the conduct of
Pilate is well-nigh incomprehensible. It is abundantly
clear, it could not be clearer, that Pilate knew that the
charges of the Jews were a series of lies, that he knew that
Jesus was completely innocent, that he was deeply impressed
with Jesus, and that he did not wish to condemn Him
to death—and yet he did. First, he tried to refuse to
deal with the case; then he tried to release Jesus on the

grounds that at the Passover a criminal was always released; then he tried to compromise by scourging Jesus; then he makes a last appeal. But he refused all through to put his foot down and to tell the Jews that he would have nothing to do with their evil machinations. We will never even begin to understand Pilate unless we understand his history, which is set out for us partly in the writings of Josephus, and partly in the writings of Philo.

To understand the part that Pilate played in this drama we must go back a long way. To begin with, what was a Roman governor doing in Judaea at all?

In 4 B.C. Herod the Great died. Herod had been king of the whole of Palestine. For all his faults he was in many ways a good king, and he had been very friendly with the Romans. In his will he divided up his kingdom between three of his sons. Antipas received Galilee and Peraea; Philip received Batanea, Auranitis and Trachonitis, the wild unpopulated regions of the north-east; and Archelaus, who at the time was only eighteen years old, received Idumaea, Judaea and Samaria. The Romans approved this distribution of the kingdom, and ratified it. Antipas and Philip governed quietly and well; but Archelaus governed with such extortion and tyranny that the Jews themselves requested the Romans to remove him, and to appoint a governor. The likelihood is that they expected to be incorporated into the large province of Syria; and had that been so, the province was so large that they would very probably have been left pretty much to carry on the way they were. All Roman provinces were divided into two classes. Those which required troops stationed in them were in the direct control of the Emperor and were imperial provinces; those which did not require troops, but which were peaceful and trouble-free, were in the direct control of the senate, and were senatorial provinces. Now Palestine was obviously a troubled land; it needed troops and therefore it was in the control of the Emperor. Really great provinces were governed either by a proconsul or a legate; Syria was like that. Smaller provinces, provinces of the second class, were governed by a procurator. The procurator was in full control of the military and judicial administration of the province. He visited every part of the province at least once a year, and heard cases and complaints. He superintended the ingathering of taxes but had no authority to increase them. He was paid a salary from the treasury and was strictly forbidden to accept either presents or bribes; and, if he exceeded his duties, the people of his province had power to report him to the Emperor.

It was a procurator that Augustus appointed to control the affairs of Palestine, and the first procurator took over in A.D. 6. Pilate took over in A.D. 26 and remained in office until A.D. 35. Palestine was a province bristling with problems, a province which required a firm and a strong and a wise hand. We do not know Pilate's previous history, but we do know that he must have had the reputation of being a good administrator or he would never have been given the responsible position of governing Palestine. Palestine had to be kept in order, for, as a glance at the map will show, Palestine was the bridge between Egypt and Syria.

But as a governor Pilate was a failure. He seemed to begin with a complete contempt and a complete lack of sympathy for the Jews. Three famous, or infamous, incidents marked his career. The first occurred on his first visit to Jerusalem. Jerusalem was not the capital of the province. The headquarters of the province were at Caesarea. But the procurator of course paid many visits to Jerusalem, and when he did he stayed in the old palace of the Herods in the west part of the city. When the procurator came to Jerusalem, he always came with a detachment of soldiers. The soldiers had their standards; and on the top of the standard there was a little bust in metal of the reigning Emperor. The Emperor was a god, and to the Jew that little bust on the standards was a

graven image. All previous Roman governors, in deference
to the religious scruples of the Jews, had removed that
image before they entered the city. Pilate refused to do so.
The Jews besought him to do so. Pilate was adamant;
he would not pander to the superstitions of the Jews.
He went back to Caesarea. The Jews followed him. They
dogged his footsteps for five days. They were humble,
but determined in their requests. Finally he told them to
meet him in the amphitheatre. He surrounded them there
with armed soldiers, and informed them that if they did
not stop their requests they would be killed there and
then. The Jews bared their necks and bade the soldiers
strike. Not even Pilate could massacre defenceless men
like that. Pilate was beaten; he had to give in; he was
compelled to agree that the images should thereafter be
removed from the standards. That was how Pilate began,
and it was a bad beginning.

The second incident was this. The Jerusalem water
supply was inadequate. Pilate determined to build a new
aqueduct. Where was the money to come from? Pilate
raided the Temple treasury. There were millions in the
treasury. It is very unlikely that Pilate took money
that was deposited for the sacrifices and the Temple
service. Much more likely, he took money which was
entitled *Korban*, and which came from sources which
made it impossible to use it for sacred purposes. Pilate's
aqueduct was much needed; it was a worthy and a great
undertaking; the water supply would even be of much
benefit to the Temple which needed much cleansing with
its continual sacrifices. But the people resented it; they
rioted and surged through the streets. Pilate mingled
his soldiers with them in plain clothes, with concealed
weapons. At a given signal the soldiers attacked the mob
and many a Jew was clubbed or stabbed to death. Once
again Pilate was rendered unpopular—and he was rendered
liable to report to the Emperor.

The third incident turned out even worse for Pilate. As

we have seen, when he was in Jerusalem, he stayed in the ancient palace of the Herods. He had certain shields made; and on them he had inscribed the name of Tiberius the Emperor. These shields were what is known as votive shields. They were devoted to the honour and the memory of the Emperor. Now the Emperor was a god; here was the name of a strange god inscribed and displayed for reverence in the holy city. The people were enraged; the greatest men, even his closest supporters, besought Pilate to remove them. Pilate refused. The Jews reported the matter to Tiberius, the Emperor, and Tiberius ordered Pilate to remove them.

It is relevant to note how Pilate ended up. This last incident happened after Jesus had been crucified, in the year A.D. 35. There was a revolt in Samaria. It was not very serious. Pilate crushed it with sadistic ferocity and with a plethora of executions. The Samaritans had always been regarded as loyal citizens of Rome. The legate of Syria intervened. Tiberius ordered Pilate back to Rome. When Pilate was on the way, Tiberius died; and, so far as we know, Pilate never came to judgment; and from that moment he vanishes from history.

Now it is clear why Pilate acted as he did. The Jews blackmailed him into crucifying Jesus. They said: " If you let this man go, you are not Caesar's friend." They said, in effect: " Your record is not too good; you were reported once before; if you do not give us our way, we will report you to the Emperor, and you will be dismissed." On that day in Jerusalem Pilate's past rose up and haunted him. Pilate was blackmailed into assenting to the death of Christ, because his previous mistakes had made it impossible for him to defy the Jews and to keep his post. Somehow one cannot help being sorry for Pilate. He wanted to do the right thing; but he had not the courage to defy the Jews and to do it. Pilate crucified Jesus in order to keep his job.

JESUS AND PILATE

John 18: 28—19: 16 (*continued*)

WE have seen Pilate's history; let us now look at his conduct during his trial of Jesus. Pilate did not wish to condemn Jesus, because he knew that Jesus was innocent; and yet Pilate was caught in the mesh of his own past. What then did Pilate try to do, and do?

(i) Pilate began by trying to put the responsibility on to someone else. He said to the Jews: " You take this man and judge Him according to your laws." Pilate tried to evade the responsibility of dealing with Jesus. That is precisely what no one can do. No one can deal with Jesus for us; we must deal with Him ourselves.

(ii) Pilate went on to try to find a way of escape from the entanglement in which he found himself. He tried to use the custom whereby a prisoner was released at the Passover time to engineer the release of Jesus. Pilate tried to evade dealing directly with Jesus himself. Again that is precisely what no one can do. There is no escape from a personal decision in regard to Jesus. We ourselves have to take the decision what we will do with Him, whether we will accept Him or reject Him.

(iii) Pilate went on to see what compromise could do. He ordered Jesus to be scourged. It must have been in Pilate's mind that a scourging might satisfy, or at least blunt the edge of Jewish hostility. He felt that he might possibly avoid having to give the verdict of the cross by giving the verdict of scourging. Once again, that is what no man can do. No man can compromise with Jesus; no man can serve two masters. We are either for or against Jesus, and there is no half-way house of compromise.

(iv) Pilate went on to try what appeal could do. He led Jesus out broken by the scourging and showed Him to the people. He asked them: " Shall I crucify your king? " He tried to swing the balance by this appeal to emotion and to pity. But no man can hope that appeal to others can take the place of his own personal decision. It was Pilate's place to make his own decision, and not to attempt to make the crowd make his decision for him. No man can evade that personal verdict and that personal decision in regard to Jesus Christ.

So in the end Pilate admitted defeat. He abandoned Jesus to the mob, because he had not the courage to take the right decision and to do the right thing.

But there are still more side-lights on the character of Pilate here.

(i) There is a hint of Pilate's ingrained attitude of contempt. He asked Jesus if He was a king. Jesus asked whether he asked this on the basis of what he himself had discovered, or on the basis of information indirectly received. Pilate's answer is: " Am I a Jew? How do you expect me to know anything about Jewish affairs? " Pilate was too proud to involve himself in what he regarded as Jewish squabbles and superstitions. And that pride was exactly what made Pilate a bad governor. No one can govern a people if he makes no attempt to understand them and to enter into their thoughts and minds.

(ii) There is a kind of superstitious curiosity about Pilate. He wished to know whence Jesus came—and it was more than Jesus' native place that Pilate was thinking of. When he heard that Jesus had claimed to be the Son of God, Pilate was still more disturbed. Pilate was superstitious rather than religious. His fear was that there might be something in it. He was afraid to come to a decision in Jesus' favour because of the Jews; he was equally afraid to come to a decision against Jesus, because he had the lurking suspicion that God was in this. Pilate had not the courage to defy men or to recognize God.

(iii) But at the heart of Pilate there was a wistful longing. When Jesus said that he had come to witness to the truth, Pilate's answer is: " What is truth? " There are many ways in which a man might ask that question. He might ask it in cynical and sardonic humour. Bacon immortalised Pilate's answer, when he wrote: "What is truth? said jesting Pilate; and would not stay for an answer." It was not in cynical humour that Pilate asked this question; nor was it the question of a man who did not care. Here is the chink in Pilate's armour. He asked the question wistfully and wearily. Pilate by this world's standards was a successful man. He had come almost to the top of the Roman civil service; he was governor-general of a Roman province; but there was something missing. Here in the presence of this simple, disturbing, hated Galilaean, Pilate felt that for him the truth was still a mystery—and that now he had got himself into a situation where there was no chance to learn it. It may be Pilate jested, but it was the jest of despair. Philip Gibbs somewhere tells of listening to a debate between T. S. Eliot, Margaret Irwin, C. Day Lewis and other distinguished people on the subject, "Is this life worth living?" "True, they jested," he said, "but they jested like jesters knocking at the door of death." Pilate was like that. Into his life there came Jesus, and suddenly he saw what he had missed in life. Pilate that day might have found all that he had missed; but Pilate had not the courage to defy the world in spite of his past, and to take his stand with Christ, and a future which was glorious.

JESUS AND PILATE

John 18: 28—19: 16 (*continued*)

WE have thought of the picture of the crowd in this trial of Jesus. We have thought of the picture of Pilate; and now we must come to the central character in the whole drama—to Jesus Himself. Here Jesus is depicted before us with a series of master-strokes.

(i) First and foremost, no one can read this story without seeing the sheer majesty of Jesus. There is no sense that Jesus is upon trial. When a man faces Jesus, it is not

Jesus who is on trial; it is the man. Pilate may have treated many Jewish things with arrogant contempt, but he did not so treat Jesus. As we read the story, we cannot help feeling that it is Jesus who is in control and Pilate who is bewildered and floundering in a situation which he cannot understand. The majesty of Jesus never shone more radiantly than in the hour when He was on trial before men.

(ii) Here Jesus with utter directness speaks to us of His kingdom. His kingdom, He lays it down, is not of this earth. The atmosphere in Jerusalem was always explosive; during the Passover time it was sheer dynamite. The Romans well knew that, and during the Passover time they always drafted extra troops into Jerusalem. But Pilate never at any time had more than three thousand troops under his command. Some of them would be in Caesarea, his headquarters; some of them would be on garrison duty in Samaria; there cannot really have been more than a few hundred on duty in Jerusalem. If Jesus had wished to raise an insurrection, if He had wished to raise the standard of rebellion, if He had wished to summon a corps of would-be servants, and to fight it out, He could have done it easily enough. But Jesus here makes it quite clear that He claims to be a king, and makes it equally clear that His kingdom is not based on force and arms, but that it is a kingdom in the hearts of men. He would never deny that He aimed at conquest, but it was the conquest of love.

(iii) Here Jesus tells us why He came into the world. He came to witness to the truth. He came to tell men the truth about God, the truth about men themselves, and the truth about life. As Emerson had it:

> " When the half-gods go,
> The gods arrive."

The days of guessings and gropings and half-truths were gone. He came to tell men the truth. That is one of the great reasons why we must either accept or refuse Christ.

There is no half-way house about the truth. A man either accepts it, or rejects it. And Christ is the truth.

(iv) Here we see the heroic physical courage of Jesus. Pilate had Jesus scourged. When a man was scourged he was tied to a whipping-post in such a way that his back was fully exposed. The lash was a long leathern thong, studded at intervals with pellets of lead, and sharpened pieces of bone. It literally tore a man's back into strips. Few remained conscious throughout the ordeal; some died; and many went raving mad. Jesus stood that. And after it Pilate led Him out to the crowd and said: " See! The man! " Here is one of John's double meanings. It must have been Pilate's first intention to awaken the pity of the Jews. " Look! " he said. " Look at this poor, bruised, bleeding creature! Look at this wretchedness! Can you possibly wish to hound a creature like this to an utterly unnecessary death? " But even as he said it, we can almost hear the tone of Pilate's voice change and see the wonder dawn in his eyes. And instead of saying it half-contemptuously, to awaken pity, he says it with a dawning wonder and an admiration that will not be repressed. The word that Pilate used is *ho anthrōpos*, which is the normal Greek for a human being; but not so long afterwards the Greek thinkers were using that very term for *the heavenly man*, the ideal man, the perfect man, the pattern of manhood. It is always true that whatever else we say or do not say about Jesus, His sheer heroism is without parallel. Here indeed is a man.

JESUS AND PILATE

John 18: 28—19: 16 (*continued*)

(v) Once again we see here in the trial of Jesus the spontaneousness of Jesus' death, and the supreme control of God. Only once Pilate resorts to a threat, and it is not so much a threat as a warning. Pilate warned Jesus that he had power to release Him, and power to crucify Him.

Jesus' answer was that Pilate had no power at all, except what had been given to him by God. The strange thing about the whole story of the crucifixion of Jesus is that it never, from beginning to end, reads like the story of a man who was caught up in an inexorable web of circumstances over which he had no control; it never reads like the story of a man who was hounded to his death. It never reads like the story of a man who was killed; it is the story of a man whose last days were a triumphant procession towards the goal of the Cross.

(vi) And here also is the terrible picture of the silence of Jesus. There was a time when Jesus had no answer to give to Pilate. There were other times when Jesus was silent. Jesus was silent before the High Priest (*Matthew* 26: 63; *Mark* 14: 61). He was silent before Herod (*Luke* 23: 9). He was silent when the charges against Him were made to Pilate by the Jewish authorities (*Matthew* 27: 14; *Mark* 15: 5). We have sometimes the experience, when we are talking to other people, of finding that argument and debate and discussion are no longer possible, because we and they have no common ground. There is nothing further to be said. We do not understand them; and they do not understand us. It is almost as if we spoke another language. That happens when men do in fact speak another mental and spiritual language. It is a terrible day when Jesus is silent to a man. There can be nothing more terrible for a man's mind to be so shut by his pride and by his determination to take his own way, that there is nothing that Jesus can say to him that will make any difference.

(vii) Finally, it is just possible that in this trial scene there is a strange, dramatic climax, which, if it is really there, is a magnificent example of John's dramatic irony. The scene comes to an end by saying that Pilate brought Jesus out; as we have translated it, and as the Authorised Version translates it, Pilate came out to the place that was called the Pavement or Gabbatha—which may mean the tessellated pavement of marble mosaic—and took his seat upon the judgment seat. The judgment seat was the *bēma* on which the magistrate sat to give his official decisions. Now the verb for *to sit* is *kathizein*, and that verb can be either intransitive or transitive. It can mean either to sit down oneself, or to seat another in a certain place. Just possibly here it means that Pilate with one last mocking gesture brought Jesus out, clad in the terrible finery of the old purple robe and with His forehead girt with the crown of thorns and the drops of blood the thorns had wakened, and set *Him* in the judgment seat, and with a wave of his hand said: " Am I to crucify your king? " The apocryphal Gospel of Peter says that in the mockery, they set Jesus on the seat of judgment and said: " Judge justly, King of Israel." Justin Martyr too says that " they set Jesus on the judgment seat, and said, ' Give judgment for us'. " It may be that Pilate jestingly caricatured Jesus as judge. If that is so, if Pilate really set Jesus in the judgment seat to make a fool of Jesus, what dramatic irony is there. That which was a mockery was the truth. And one day those who had mocked Jesus as judge would meet Him as judge—and would remember.

So in this dramatic trial scene we see the immutable majesty, the undaunted courage, and the serene acceptance of the Cross of Jesus. Never was He so regal as when men did their worst to humiliate Him.

JESUS AND PILATE

John 18: 20—19: 16 (*continued*)

WE have looked at the main personalities at the trial of Jesus. There were the Jews with their hatred; there was Pilate with his haunting past; and there was Jesus in the serenity of His regal majesty. But there were certain other people, as it were, on the outskirts of the scene and of the drama.

(i) There were the soldiers. When Jesus was given into their hands to be scourged, they amused themselves with their crude horse-play. He was a king? Well then, let Him have a robe and crown. So they put an old purple robe on Him, and they put a crown of thorns round His brow; and they slapped Him on the face. They were playing a game that ancient people quite commonly played. Philo in his work entitled *On Flaccus* tells of a very similar thing that the mob at Alexandria did. " There was a madman named Carabas, afflicted not with the savage and beastlike sort of madness—for this form is undisguisable both for sufferers and bystanders—but with the quiet and milder kind. He used to spend his days and nights naked in the streets, sheltering from neither heat nor frost, a plaything of children and idle lads. They joined in driving the wretch to the gymnasium, and, setting him aloft so that he could be seen by everyone, they flattened a strip of bark for a fillet and put it on his head, and wrapped a floor-rug round his body for a mantle, and for sceptre someone catching sight of a small piece of the native papyrus that had been thrown on the road handed it to him. And when he had assumed the insignia of kingship as in theatrical mimes, and had been arrayed in the character of king, young men bearing staffs on their shoulders took their stance on either side in place of spearmen, mimic lancers. Then others approached, some as if to greet him, others as though to plead their causes, others as though to petition him about public matters. Then from the surrounding multitudes rang forth an outlandish shout of ' Marin,' the name by which it is said that kings are called in Syria." It is a poignant thing that the soldiers treated Jesus as a ribald crowd might treat an idiot boy.

And yet of all the people involved in the trial of Jesus, the soldiers were least to blame, for they at least did not know what they were doing. Most likely they had come up from Caesarea and most likely they did not know what it was all about. Jesus to them was only a chance criminal; it was true of them that they knew not what they did.

But here again is another example of the dramatic

irony of John. The soldiers made a caricature of Jesus as king, while the truth of it was that He was indeed the only king. Beneath the jest there was an eternal truth.

JESUS AND PILATE

John 18: 28—19: 16 (*continued*)

(ii) And last of all there was Barabbas. John tells the incident of Barabbas very briefly indeed. Of the custom of freeing a prisoner at the Passover time we know nothing more than the gospels tell us. The other gospels to some extent fill out John's brief picture of Barabbas. When we put all our information together we find that Barabbas was a notable prisoner, that he was a brigand, that he had taken part in a certain insurrection in the city, and that he had committed murder (*Matthew* 27: 15-26; *Mark* 15: 6-15; *Luke* 23: 17-25; *Acts* 3: 14).

The name of Barabbas is interesting. There are two possibilities as to its derivation. It may be compounded of Bar Abba which would mean " son of the father," or it may be compounded of Bar Rabban, which would mean " son of the Rabbi." It is not impossible that Barabbas was the son of some Rabbi, a scion of some noble family who had gone wrong; and it may well be that, criminal though he was, he was popular with the people as a kind of Robin Hood character. It is certainly true that we must not think of Barabbas as a sneak thief, or a petty pilferer, or a burglar. He was a *lēstēs*, which means a *brigand*. Either he was one of these warrior brigands who infested the Jericho road, the kind of man into whose hands the traveller in the parable fell, or, perhaps even more probable, he was one of these Zealots who had sworn to rid Palestine of the Romans, even if it meant a career of murder, and robbery, and assassination, and crime. Barabbas was no petty criminal. A man of violence he might be, but his violence was the kind of violence which

would have a romance and a glamour about it, and which
well might make him the popular hero of the crowd and
the despair of the law at one and the same time.

But there is a still more interesting thing about his
name. *Barabbas* is not a Christian name at all; it is a
second name. Barabbas must have had a second name,
just as Peter was Simon bar-Jonah, Simon the son of
Jonah. Now there are certain ancient Greek manuscripts,
and certain Syrian and Armenian translations of the New
Testament which actually give the name of Barabbas as
Jesus. That is by no means impossible, because in those
days *Jesus* was a common name, for it is the Greek form
of the name *Joshua*. If so, the choice of the crowd would
be even more dramatic, for they would shout: "Not
Jesus the Nazarene, but Jesus Barabbas."

The choice of the mob has been the eternal choice.
Barabbas was the man of force, the man of blood, the man
who chose to reach his end by violent means. Jesus was
the man of love and of gentleness, who would have nothing
to do with force and whose kingdom was in the hearts of
men. It is the tragic fact of history that all through the
ages men have chosen the way of Barabbas and refused
the way of Jesus.

What happened to Barabbas no man knows; but John
Oxenham in one of his books has an imaginary picture
of him. At first Barabbas could think of nothing but his
freedom; but then he began to look at the man who had
died that he might live. Something about Jesus fascinated
him and he followed Him out to see the end. As he saw
Jesus bearing His Cross, one thought burned into his
mind: "I should have been carrying that Cross; not He;
He saved me!" And as he saw Jesus hanging there on
Calvary, the only thing of which Barabbas could think
was: "I should have been hanging there; not He; He
saved me!" It may be so, or it may not be so; but very
certainly Barabbas was one of the sinners whom Jesus
died to save.

THE WAY TO THE CROSS

John 19: 17-22

> So they took Jesus, and He, carrying His Cross for
> Himself, went out to the place that is called the
> Place of a Skull, which is called in Hebrew Golgotha.
> They crucified Him there, and with Him they crucified
> two others, one on either side, and Jesus in the middle.
> Pilate wrote a title, and put it on the Cross. On it
> was written: " Jesus of Nazareth, the King of the
> Jews." Many of the Jews read this title, because the
> place where Jesus was crucified was near the city;
> and it was written in Hebrew, in Latin and in Greek.
> So the chief priests repeatedly said to Pilate: " Do
> not write, ' The King of the Jews.' But write, ' He said
> I am the King of the Jews.' " Pilate answered:
> " What I have written, I have written."

THERE was no more terrible death than death by crucifixion.
Even the Romans themselves regarded it with a shudder
of horror. Cicero declared that it was " the most cruel
and horrifying death." Tacitus said that it was a " despi-
cable death." Cruxifixion was originally a Persian method
of execution. It may have been used because, to the
Persians, the earth was sacred, and they wished to avoid
defiling it with the body of a criminal and an evil-doer;
so they nailed him to a cross and left him to die there,
and then left the vultures and the carrion crows to complete
the work. The Carthaginians took over crucifixion from
the Persians; and the Romans learned it from the Carthaginians. Crucifixion was never used as a method of execution
in Italy; it was only used in the provinces, and there only
in the case of slaves. It was unthinkable that a Roman
citizen should die by such a death. Cicero says: " It is a
crime for a Roman citizen to be bound; it is a worse
crime for him to be beaten; it is well nigh parricide for
him to be killed; what am I to say if he be killed on a
cross? A nefarious action such as that is incapable of
description by any word, for there is none fit to describe
it." It was that death, the most dreaded death in the

ancient world, the death of slaves and criminals, that Jesus died.

The routine of crucifixion was always the same. When the case had been heard, and the criminal had been condemned, the judge uttered the fateful sentence: *" Ibis ad crucem,"* " You will go to the cross." The verdict was carried out there and then. The criminal was placed in the centre of a quaternion, a company of four Roman soldiers. His own cross was placed upon his shoulders. It is to be remembered that scourging always preceded crucifixion, and it is to be remembered how terrible scourging was. Often the criminal had to be lashed and goaded along the road, to keep him on his feet, as he staggered to the place of crucifixion. Before him there walked an officer with a placard on which was written the crime for which he was to die. He was led through as many streets as possible on the way to the place of execution. There was a double reason for that. There was the grim reason that as many as possible should see it, and should realize that crime does not pay, and should take warning from such a fate. But there was a merciful reason. The placard was carried before the condemned man, and the long route was chosen, so that if anyone could still bear witness in his favour, he might come forward and do so. In such a case, the procession was halted and the case was retried.

In Jerusalem the place of execution was called *The Place of a Skull*, in Hebrew, *Golgotha*; Calvary is the Latin for the Place of a Skull. It must have been outside the city walls, for it was not lawful to crucify a man within the boundaries of the city. Where it was we do not certainly know. More than one reason has been put forward for the strange, grim name, the Place of a Skull. There was a legend that it was so called because the skull of Adam was buried there. There is a suggestion that it was so called because it was littered with the skulls of crucified criminals. That is not likely. By Roman law a criminal must hang upon his cross until he died from hunger and thirst and exposure, a torture which sometimes lasted for days. But by Jewish law the bodies must be taken down and buried by nightfall. In Roman law the criminal's body was not buried, but was simply thrown away for the vultures and the crows and the pariah dogs to dispose of; but that would have been quite illegal under Jewish law, and no Jewish place would be littered with skulls. It is much more likely that the place received its name because it was on a hill which was shaped like a skull. It was a grim name for a place where grim things were done.

So Jesus went out, bruised and bleeding, and with His flesh torn to ribbons by the scourging, carrying His own Cross, to the place where He was to die.

THE WAY TO THE CROSS

John 19: 17-22 *(continued)*

IN this passage there are two further things which we must note. The inscription on Jesus' Cross was in Hebrew, in Latin and in Greek. These were the three great languages of the ancient world, and they stood for three great nations. In the economy of God every nation has something to teach the world; and these three great nations stood for three great contributions to the world and to world history. Greece taught the world beauty of form and beauty of thought; Rome taught the world law and good government; the Hebrew nation taught the world religion and the worship of the true God. The consummation of all these things is seen in Jesus. In Him was the supreme beauty and the highest thought of God. In Him was the law of God and the Kingdom of God. In Him was the very picture and image of God. All the world's seekings and strivings found their consummation in Him. It was symbolic that in the three great languages of the world, men called Him King.

There is no doubt that Pilate put this inscription on the Cross of Jesus to irritate and to annoy the Jews. They had just said that they had no king but Caesar; they had just utterly and absolutely refused to have Jesus as their king. And Pilate, by way of a grim jest, put this inscription on the Cross of Jesus. The Jewish leaders repeatedly asked him to remove it; and Pilate refused. " What I have written," he said, " I have written." Here is Pilate the adamant, Pilate the inflexible, Pilate the man who will not yield an inch to the appeals of the Jews. So very short a time before, this same Pilate had been weakly vacillating as to whether to crucify Jesus or to let Him go. In the end this very Pilate had allowed himself to be bullied, coerced and blackmailed into giving the Jews their will. He was adamant enough about the inscription; he was weak enough about the decision of the Cross.

It is one of the curious paradoxical things in life that we can be stubborn enough about things which do not matter, and weak enough about things which are of supreme importance. We can dig our heels in and refuse to budge an inch about some trifle which is of no importance, and we can weakly give way on some issue which involves the greatest principles in life. If Pilate had only withstood the blackmailing tactics of the Jews, and if he had refused to be coerced into giving them their will with Jesus, he might have gone down to history as one of the great, strong men. But because he yielded on the great thing, and stood firm on the unimportant thing, his name is the name of shame. Pilate was the man who took a stand— on the wrong things and too late.

THE GAMBLERS AT THE CROSS

John 19: 23, 24

> When the soldiers had crucified Jesus, they took His clothes, and they divided them into four parts, a part for each soldier; and they took His tunic.

It was a tunic which had no seam, woven throughout in one piece from the top. They said to each other: " Don't let's cut it up, but let us cast lots for it, and settle that way who will have it." This happened that the passage of scripture which says, " They divided my clothes among themselves, and they cast lots for my raiment," might be fulfilled. So, then, that is what the soldiers did.

WE have already seen that a criminal was escorted to the place of execution by a quaternion of four soldiers. One of the perquisites of these soldiers, who were on duty at an execution, was the clothes of the victim. Every Jew wore five articles of apparel. There were his shoes, his turban, his girdle, his tunic, and his outer robe. There were four soldiers, and there were five articles of apparel. They diced for them, and each had his pick and the inner tunic was left. It was a seamless robe, woven all in one piece. To have cut it into four pieces would have been to render it useless, and so they diced again to see who would possess it. So the soldiers gambled at the foot of the Cross. There are many things in this vivid picture.

(i) Studdert Kennedy has a poem based on this scene. The soldiers were gamblers; and so in a sense was Jesus. Jesus staked everything on His utter fidelity to God; He staked everything on the Cross. The Cross was His last and greatest appeal to men, and His last and His greatest act of obedience towards God.

> " And, sitting down, they watched Him there,
> The soldiers did;
> There, while they played with dice,
> He made His sacrifice,
> And died upon the Cross to rid
> God's world of sin.
> He was a gambler too, my Christ,
> He took His life and threw
> It for a world redeemed.
> And ere His agony was done,
> Before the westering sun went down,
> Crowning that day with its crimson crown,
> He knew that He had won."

There is a sense in which every Christian is a gambler for every Christian must venture for His name.

(ii) There is no picture which so shows the indifference of the world to Christ. There, on the Cross, Jesus was dying in agony; and there at the foot of the Cross the soldiers threw their dice as if it did not matter. An artist painted a picture. He shows Christ standing with hands outstretched, nail-pierced hands, in a modern city, while the crowds surge by. Not one of them is even sparing Him a look, except only one young hospital nurse; and beneath the picture there is the question: " Is it nothing to you all ye that pass by? " (*Lamentations* I: 12). The tragedy is not the hostility of the world to Christ; the tragedy is the world's indifference, that indifference which treats the love of God as if it did not matter.

(iii) There are two further points which we must note in this picture. There is a legend that Mary herself had woven the seamless tunic, and had given it as a last gift to her Son when He went out into the world. If that be true—and it may well be true, for it was a custom of Jewish mothers to do just that—there is a double pathos and a double poignancy in the picture of these insensitive, un-understanding soldiers gambling for the robe of Jesus which was His mother's gift.

(iv) But there is something half-hidden here. Jesus' tunic is described as being without seam, and woven in one piece from top to bottom. That is the precise description of the linen tunic which the High Priest wore. Let us remember the function of the priest. The function of the priest was to be the liaison between God and man. The Latin for priest is *pontifex*, which means *bridge-builder*. The function of the priest was to build a bridge between God and man. No one ever did that as Jesus did. He was the perfect High Priest through whom men come to God. Again and again we have seen that there are two meanings in so many of John's statements, a meaning which lies on the surface, and a richer and a deeper inner meaning. When John tells us of the seamless tunic of Jesus it is not just a description of the kind of clothes that Jesus wore; it is something which tells us that Jesus is the perfect priest, opening the perfect way for all men to the presence of God.

(v) Lastly we may note that in this incident John finds a fulfilment of Old Testament prophecy. He reads back into it the saying of the Psalmist: " They part my garments among them, and cast lots upon my vesture " (*Psalm* 22: 18).

A SON'S LOVE

John 19: 25-27

> But His mother, and His mother's sister, and Mary the wife of Clopas, and Mary from Magdala, stood near the Cross of Jesus. So Jesus saw His mother, and He saw the disciple whom He loved standing by, and He said to His mother: " Woman! See! Your Son." Then He said to the disciple: " See! Your mother! " And from that hour the disciple took her into his own home.

IN the end Jesus was not absolutely alone. At His Cross there were these four women who loved Him. There are some commentators who explain their presence there by saying that in those days women were so unimportant and so despised that no one ever took any notice of women disciples, and that therefore these women were running no risk at all by being near the Cross of Jesus. That surely is a poor and an unworthy explanation. It was always a dangerous thing to be an associate of a man whom the Roman government believed to be so dangerous a criminal that he deserved a Cross. It is always a dangerous thing to demonstrate one's love for someone whom the orthodox regard as a sinner and a heretic. The presence of these women at the Cross was not due to the fact that they were so unimportant that no one would notice them; their presence was due to the immortal fact that perfect love casteth out fear.

When we look at them they are a strange company. There is one, Mary the wife of Clopas, of whom we know nothing. But we do know something of the other three.

(i) There was Mary, Jesus' mother. Maybe Mary could not understand, but Mary could love. Her presence there was the most natural thing in the world for a mother. Jesus might be a criminal in the eyes of the law, but He was her son. As Kipling had it:

> " If I were hanged on the highest hill,
> *Mother o' mine, O mother o' mine!*
> I know whose love would follow me still,
> *Mother o' mine, O mother o' mine!*
>
> If I were drowned in the deepest sea,
> *Mother o' mine, O mother o' mine!*
> I know whose tears would come down to me,
> *Mother o' mine, O mother o' mine!*
>
> If I were damned of body and soul,
> I know whose prayers would make me whole,
> *Mother o' mine, O mother o' mine!* "

The eternal love of the heart of motherhood is in Mary at the Cross.

(ii) There was Jesus' mother's sister. In John she is not named, but a study of the parallel passages (*Mark* 15: 40; *Matthew* 27: 56) makes it quite clear that she was Salome, the mother of Zebedee's children, that is, the mother of James and John. Now the strange thing about Salome is that she received from Jesus a very definite and a very stern rebuff. Once she had come to Jesus to ask Him to give her sons the chief place in His Kingdom (*Matthew* 20: 20), and Jesus had taught her how wrong such thoughts of ambition were, and how His way was the way of the bitter cup. Salome was the woman Christ rebuked—and yet she was there—at the Cross. Salome's presence says much for her, and much for Jesus. It shows that she had the loving humility to accept rebuke and to love on with undiminished devotion; it shows that Jesus could rebuke a person in such a way that His love shone through the rebuke. Salome's presence is a lesson to us on how to give, and how to receive, a warning and a rebuke.

(iii) There was Mary from Magdala. All that we know about her is that out of her Jesus cast seven devils (*Mark* 16: 9; *Luke* 8: 2). Mary from Magdala could never forget what Jesus had done for her. His love had rescued her, and her love was such that it could never die. It was Mary's motto, written on her heart: " I will not forget what He has done for me."

But here in this passage there is something which is surely one of the loveliest things in all the gospel story. When Jesus saw Mary, His mother, there, He could not but think of the days ahead. He could not commit her to the care of His brothers, for His brothers did not believe in Him yet (*John* 7: 5). And, after all, John had a double qualification for the service Jesus entrusted to him—he was Jesus' cousin, because he was Salome's son, and he was the disciple whom Jesus loved. So Jesus committed Mary to the care of John, and John to the care of Mary, that these two should comfort each other's loneliness when He was gone.

There is something infinitely moving in the fact that Jesus in the agony of the Cross, in the moment when the salvation of the world hung in the balance, thought of the loneliness of His mother in the days when He was taken away. Jesus never forgot the duties that lay to His hand. He was Mary's eldest son, and even in the moment of His cosmic battle, He never forgot the simple things that lay near home. To the end of the day, even on the Cross, Jesus was thinking more of the sorrows of others than of His own.

299

THE TRIUMPHANT ENDING

John 19: 28-30

> After that, when Jesus knew that everything was completed, He said, in order that the scripture might be fulfilled: " I thirst." There was a vessel standing there full of vinegar. So they put a sponge soaked in vinegar on a hyssop reed, and put it to His mouth. When He had received the vinegar, Jesus said: " It is finished." And He leaned His head back, and gave up His spirit.

HERE in this passage John brings us face to face with two things about Jesus.

(i) He brings us face to face with the human suffering of Jesus. When Jesus was on the Cross, He knew the agony of thirst. When John was writing his gospel round about A.D. 100 a certain tendency had arisen in religious and philosophical thought. It is called by the name of Gnosticism. One of the great tenets of gnosticism was that spirit is altogether good and matter is altogether evil. Since the gnostics believed that, they drew certain conclusions from it. One of their conclusions was that God, who is pure spirit, could never take upon Himself a body, because a body is matter, and matter is evil. They therefore taught that Jesus never had a real body. They said that Jesus was only a phantom in human form in which the Spirit of God took shape. They said, for instance, that when Jesus walked, His feet left no footprints on the ground, because He was pure spirit in a phantom body. They went on to argue that God cannot really ever suffer, and that therefore Jesus never really suffered; that He went through the whole experience of the Cross without any real pain. When the Gnostics thought like that, they believed that they were honouring God and honouring Jesus; but what they were doing was that they were destroying Jesus. If Jesus was ever to redeem man, He must become man. He had to become what we are in order to make us what He is. That is why John stresses the fact that Jesus felt thirst; he wished to show that Jesus was really a human being, and really underwent the pain and the agony of the Cross. John goes out of his way to stress the real humanity, the real manhood, and the real suffering of Jesus.

(ii) But, equally, John brings us face to face with the triumph of Jesus. When we compare the four gospels we find a most illuminating thing. The other three gospels do not tell us that Jesus said, " It is finished." But they do tell us that Jesus died with a great shout upon His lips (*Matthew* 27: 50; *Mark* 15: 37; *Luke* 23: 46). On the other hand, John does not speak of the great cry, but he does say that Jesus' last words were, " It is finished." The explanation of this difference is that the great shout, and the words, " It is finished," are one and the same thing. " It is finished " is one word in Greek—*tetelestai*—and Jesus died with a shout of triumph on His lips. He did not say, " It is finished," in weary defeat; He said it as one who shouts for joy because the victory is won. Jesus seemed to be broken on a Cross, but He knew that His victory was won.

The last sentence of this passage makes the thing even clearer. John says that Jesus leaned back His head and gave up His spirit. The word that John uses is the word which might be used for settling back upon a pillow. For Jesus the strife was over and the battle was won, and even on the Cross He knew the joy of victory, and the rest of the man who has completed his task and who can lean back, content and at peace.

Two further things we must notice in this passage. John traces back Jesus' cry, " I thirst," to the fulfilment of a verse in the Old Testament. He was thinking of *Psalm* 69: 21. " They gave me also gall for my meat; and in my thirst they gave me vinegar to drink."

The second thing we must notice is another of John's hidden things. John tells us that it was on a hyssop reed that they put the sponge in which the vinegar was. Now a hyssop reed is an unlikely thing to use for such a purpose, for it was only a stalk, like strong grass, at the most two feet long. So unlikely is it that some scholars have thought that it is a mistake for a very similar word which means a *lance* or a *spear*. But it was *hyssop* which John wrote and *hyssop* which John meant. When we go away centuries back to the first Passover on that night when the children of Israel left their slavery in Egypt, we remember how the angel of death was to walk abroad that night and how he was to slay every first born son of the Egyptians. We remember how the Israelites were to slay the Passover lamb and how they were to smear the doorposts of their houses with the blood of that lamb, so that the avenging angel of death would *pass over* their houses. And the ancient instruction was: " And ye shall take a *bunch of hyssop* and dip it in the blood that is in the bason, and strike the lintel and the two side posts with the blood that is in the bason " (*Exodus* 12: 22). It was the blood of the Passover lamb which saved the people of God; it was the blood of Jesus which was to save the world from sin. The very mention of *hyssop* would take the thoughts of any Jew back to the saving blood of the Passover lamb; and this is John's way of saying that Jesus was the great Passover Lamb of God whose death was to save the whole world from sin.

THE WATER AND THE BLOOD

John 19: 31-37

> Since it was the day of preparation, so that the bodies should not remain on the cross on the Sabbath (for that Sabbath was a very important day) the Jews asked Pilate to break their limbs, and to have the bodies removed. So the soldiers came, and they broke the limbs of the first criminal, and of the other who had been crucified with him. When they came to Jesus, and when they saw that He was already dead, they did not break His limbs. But one of the soldiers pierced

His side with a spear, and immediately water and blood came forth. And he who saw it is a witness to this, and his word is true. And he knows that he is speaking the truth, that you also may believe. These things happened that the passage of scripture which says: " His bone shall not be broken," should be fulfilled. And again another passage says: " They shall see Him whom they have pierced."

IN one thing the Jews were more merciful than the Romans. When the Romans carried out crucifixion under their own customs, the victim was left to die on the cross, even if it took days for him to die. He might hang for days in the heat of the midday sun and the cold of the night, tortured by thirst, tortured by the gnats and the flies in the weals on his torn back after the scourging. Often men died raving mad on their crosses. Neither did the Romans bury the bodies of crucified criminals. They simply took them down and threw them away and let the vultures and the crows and the dogs feed upon them. But the Jewish law was different. It laid it down: " If a man have committed a sin worthy of death, and he be put to death, and thou hang him upon a tree, his body shall not remain all night upon the tree, but thou shalt in any wise bury him that day " (Deuteronomy 21: 22, 23). The Mishnah, the Jewish scribal law, lays it down: " Everyone who allows the dead to remain overnight transgresses a positive command." And the Sanhedrin actually was charged to have two burying places ready for those who had suffered the death penalty if they were not to be buried in the burying place of their fathers. On this occasion it was even more important that the bodies should not be allowed to hang on the crosses overnight, because the next day was the Sabbath, and a very special Sabbath, for it was the Passover Sabbath.

A grim method was used to despatch criminals who lingered on. Their limbs were smashed with a mallet until they died. That was what was done to the criminals who were crucified with Jesus, but mercifully Jesus was spared that, for Jesus was already dead. John sees that sparing of Jesus as a symbol of another Old Testament passage. It was laid down of the Passover Lamb that not a bone of it should be broken (*Numbers* 9: 12). Once again John is seeing Jesus as the Passover Lamb who delivers His people from death.

Finally there follows a strange incident. When the soldiers saw that Jesus was already dead they did not break His limbs with the mallet; but one of them—it must have been to make doubly sure that Jesus was dead—thrust a spear into His side. And there flowed out water and blood. Now John attaches special importance to that. He sees in it a fulfilment of the prophecy in *Zechariah* 12: 10: " They shall look on me whom they have pierced." And he goes out of his way to say that this is an eye-witness account of what actually happened, and that he personally guarantees that it is true.

First of all, let us ask what actually happened. It is something of which we cannot be sure, but it may well be true that Jesus died literally of a broken heart. Normally of course the body of a dead man will not bleed. It is suggested that what happened was that Jesus' experiences, physical and emotional, were so terrible that His heart was ruptured. When that happened the blood of the heart mingled with the fluid of the pericardium which surrounds the heart. The spear of the soldier pierced the pericardium and the mingled fluid and blood came forth. It would be a poignant thing to believe that Jesus died in the literal sense of the term of a broken heart.

But, even so, why does John stress it so much? He stresses it for two reasons.

(i) To John it was the final, unanswerable proof that Jesus was a real man with a real body. Here was the answer to the gnostics with their ideas of phantoms and spirits and an unreal manhood. Here was the proof that Jesus was bone of our bone and flesh of our flesh.

(ii) But to John this was more than a proof of the manhood of Jesus. It was a symbol of the two great sacraments of the Church. There is one sacrament which is based on water—the sacrament of baptism; and there is one sacrament which is based on blood—the sacrament of the Lord's Supper with its cup of scarlet, blood-red wine. The water of baptism is the sign of the cleansing grace of God in Jesus Christ. The wine of the Lord's Supper is the symbol of the blood which was shed to save men from their sins. The water and the blood which flowed from the side of Christ were to John the sign of the cleansing water of baptism and the cleansing blood, which is commemorated and experienced in the Lord's Supper. John saw in that grim incident a sign and a symbol, and a forecast of the cleansing grace, and the forgiving power which flow from Jesus Christ and from His Cross. As Toplady wrote:

> " Rock of ages, cleft for me,
> Let me hide myself in Thee;
> Let the water and the blood,
> From Thy riven side which flowed,
> Be of sin the double cure,
> Cleanse me from its guilt and power."

THE LAST GIFTS TO JESUS

John 19: 38-42

After that, Joseph from Arimathaea, who because of fear of the Jews was a secret disciple of Jesus, asked Pilate to be allowed to take away Jesus' body, and Pilate gave him permission to do so. So he came and took His body away. Nicodemus, who first came to Jesus by night, came too, bringing a mixture of myrrh and aloes, about a hundred pounds in weight. So they took Jesus' body and they wrapped it in linen clothes with spices, as it is the Jewish custom to lay a body in the tomb. There was a garden in the place where He was crucified; and in the garden there was a new tomb in which no one had ever been laid. So they laid Jesus there, because it was the day of preparation for the Sabbath, because the tomb was near at hand.

So Jesus died, and what had to be done must be done quickly, for the Sabbath was almost on them, and on the Sabbath no work could be done. The friends of Jesus were poor, and they could not have given Him a fitting burial; but it was then that two people came forward.

Joseph of Arimathaea came forward; he had always been a disciple of Jesus; he was a great man and a member of the Sanhedrin, and up to now he had kept his discipleship secret for he was afraid to make it known. Nicodemus came forward. It was the Jewish custom to wrap the bodies of the dead in linen clothes, and to put sweet spices between the folds of the linen. Nicodemus brought enough spices for the burial of a king. So Joseph gave to Jesus a tomb; and Nicodemus gave Him the clothes to wear within the tomb.

There is both tragedy and glory here.

(i) There is tragedy. Both Nicodemus and Joseph were members of the Sanhedrin, but they were secret disciples. Either they had absented themselves from the meeting of the Sanhedrin which examined Jesus and which formulated the charge against Him, or they had sat silent through it all. What a difference it would have made to Jesus, if, among these condemning, hectoring voices, one voice had been raised in His support. What a difference it would have made to see loyalty on one face amidst that sea of bleak, envenomed faces. But Nicodemus and Joseph were afraid. We so often leave our tributes until people are dead. How much greater would loyalty in life have been than a new tomb and a shroud fit for a king in death! One flower in life is worth all the wreaths in the world in death; one word of love and praise and thanks in life is worth all the panegyrics in the world when life is gone.

(ii) But there is glory here too. The death of Jesus had done for Joseph and Nicodemus what not even the life of Jesus could do. No sooner had Jesus died on the Cross than Joseph forgot his fear and bearded the Roman governor with the request for the body of Jesus. No sooner had Jesus died on the Cross than Nicodemus was there to bring a tribute that all men could see. The cowardice, the fear, the hesitation, the prudent concealment were gone. Those who had been afraid when Jesus was alive declared for Him in a way that everyone could see as soon as He was dead. Jesus had not been dead on the Cross for an hour when His own prophecy came true: " I if I be lifted up from the earth will draw all men unto me " (*John* 12: 32). It may be that the silence or the absence of Nicodemus from the Sanhedrin brought sorrow to Jesus; but it is certain that He knew of the way in which they cast their fear aside after the Cross, and it is certain that already His heart was glad, for already the power of the Cross had begun to operate, and already the Cross was drawing all men unto Him. The magnet of the Cross even then had begun to act; the power of the Cross was even then turning the coward into the hero, and the waverer into the man who had taken his irrevocable decision for Christ.

BEWILDERED LOVE

John 20: 1-10

On the first day of the week, very early in the morning, while it was still dark, Mary from Magdala came to the tomb; and she saw the stone taken away from the tomb. So she ran and came to Simon Peter, and to the other disciple whom Jesus loved, and she said to them: " They have taken the Lord away from the tomb, and we do not know where they have laid Him." So Peter went out with the other disciple, and they set out for the tomb. The two were running together. The other disciple ran on ahead faster than Peter, and he was the first to come to the tomb. He stooped down and he saw the linen clothes lying there, and he saw the napkin, which had been upon Jesus' head, not lying with the rest of the linen clothes, but lying apart from them, still in its folds, by itself. So then, the other disciple, who had arrived first at the tomb, went in too, and he saw, and believed. For as yet they did not realize the meaning of scripture, that Jesus should rise from the dead. So the disciples went back to their lodgings

No one ever loved Jesus so much as Mary Magdalene. Luke tells us that out of her there had gone seven devils. Jesus had done something for Mary that no one else could ever do, and Mary could never forget. Tradition has always had it that Mary was a scarlet sinner, whom Jesus reclaimed and forgave and purified. Henry Kingsley has a lovely poem about Mary Magdalene.

> " Magdalen at Michael's gate
>   Tirled at the pin;
> On Joseph's thorn sang the blackbird,
>   ' Let her in!   Let her in!'
>
> ' Hast thou seen the wounds?' said Michael,
>   ' Knowest thou thy sin?'
> ' It is evening, evening,' sang the blackbird,
>   ' Let her in!   Let her in!'
>
> ' Yes, I have seen the wounds,
>   And I know my sin.'
> ' She knows it well, well, well,' sang the blackbird.
>   ' Let her in!   Let her in!'
>
> ' Thou bringest no offerings,' said Michael,
>   ' Nought save sin.'
> And the blackbird sang, ' She is sorry, sorry, sorry.
>   ' Let her in!   Let her in!'
>
> When he had sung himself to sleep,
>   And night did begin,
> One came and opened Michael's gate,
>   And Magdalen went in."

Mary had sinned much and Mary loved much, and love was all she had to bring.

It was always the custom in Palestine to visit the tomb of a loved one for three days after the body had been laid in the tomb. They believed that for three days the spirit of the dead person hovered and waited round the tomb; and that only after that did the spirit depart, for the body had by then become unrecognizable through decay. Jesus' friends could not come to the tomb on the Sabbath, because to make the journey on the Sabbath day would have been to break the law. Sabbath is our Saturday, so it was on Sunday morning that Mary came first to the tomb. She came very early. The word that is used for *early* is *prōi*. That word was the technical word for the last of the four watches into which the night was divided, the watch which ran from 3 a.m. to 6 a.m. It was still grey dark when Mary came, because she could no longer stay away.

When she came to the tomb she was shocked and amazed. Tombs in ancient times were not commonly closed by doors. In front of the opening there ran a groove in the ground; and in the groove there ran a stone, circular like a cartwheel; and the stone was wheeled into position to form a door. Further, Matthew tells us that the authorities had actually sealed the stone to make sure that no one would move it (*Matthew* 27: 66). Mary was astonished to find the stone removed. Two things must have entered her mind. She may have thought that the Jews had taken away Jesus' body; that, not satisfied with killing Him on a cross, they were inflicting further indignities on His dead body. But also one of the grimmest features of ancient crime was that there were ghoulish creatures who made it their business to rob tombs. And Mary may have thought that the tomb had been broken into and the body of Jesus desecrated.

This was a situation that Mary felt that she could not face herself; so she returned to the city to seek out Peter and John. Mary is the great example of bewildered love; Mary is the supreme instance of one who went on loving and believing even when she could not understand; and that indeed is the love and the belief which in the end finds its glory.

THE GREAT DISCOVERY

John 20: 1-10 (*continued*)

ONE of the illuminating things in this story is that Peter
was still the acknowledged leader of the apostolic band.
It was to him that Mary went. In spite of his denial—and
a story like that would not be long in being published or
broadcast—Peter was still the leader. We often talk of
the weakness and the instability of Peter, but there must
have been something outstanding about the man who could
face his fellow men after that disastrous crash into cowardice; there must have been something about the man
whom men were prepared to accept as leader even after
that. His moment's weakness must never blind us to the
moral strength and stature of Peter, and to the fact that
he was a born leader of men.

So, then, it was to Peter and John that Mary went; and
they immediately set out for the tomb. They went at a
run; and John must have been a younger man than Peter
for John lived on until the end of the century, and he
outstripped Peter in this breathless race. When they came
to the tomb, John looked in, but went no farther. Peter
with typical impulsiveness not only looked in, but went in.
For the moment Peter was only amazed at the empty
tomb; but then things began to happen in John's mind.
If someone had removed Jesus' body, if tomb-robbers
had been at work, why should they leave the grave clothes?
And then something else struck John—the grave clothes
were not dishevelled and disarranged; they were lying
there *still in their folds*—that is what the Greek means—
the clothes for the body where the body had been; the
napkin where the head had lain. The whole point of the
description is that the grave clothes did not look as if they
had been put off or taken off; they were lying there in
their regular folds as if the body of Jesus had simply
evaporated out of them and left them lying. The sight
suddenly penetrated to John's mind; he realized what had

happened—and he believed. It was not what John had read in scripture which convinced him that Jesus had risen; it was what with his own eyes he saw.

The part that love plays in this story is extraordinary. It was Mary, who loved Jesus so much, who was first at the tomb. It was John, the disciple whom Jesus loved, and who loved Jesus, who was first to believe in the Resurrection. That must always be John's great glory. He was the first man to understand and to believe. Love gave him eyes to read the signs, and a mind to understand.

Here we have the great law of life. In any kind of work it is true that we cannot really interpret the thought of another person, unless between us and him there is a bond of sympathy. No one can lecture or write effectively on the life and work of a man with whom he is out of sympathy. It is at once clear when the conductor of an orchestra is in sympathy with the music of the composer whose work he is conducting. Love is the great interpreter. Love can grasp the truth when intellect is left groping and uncertain. Love can realize the meaning of a thing when research is blind. It is told that once a young artist brought a picture of Jesus, which he had painted, to Dorè for his verdict upon it. Dorè was slow to give it; but at last he gave it in one sentence: " You don't love Him, or you would paint Him better." We can neither understand Jesus or help others to understand Him, unless we take our hearts to Him as well as our minds.

THE GREAT RECOGNITION

John 20: 11-18

> But Mary stood weeping outside at the tomb. As she wept she stooped down, and looked into the tomb, and she saw two angels sitting there in white robes, one at the head, and the other at the feet of the place where Jesus' body had been lying. They said to her: " Woman, why are you crying? " She said to them:

" Because they have taken my Lord away, and I do not know where they have laid Him." When she had said this, she turned round, and saw Jesus standing there, and did not know that it was Jesus. Jesus said to her: " Women, why are you crying? Who are you looking for? " She, thinking that He was the gardener, said to Him: " Sir, if you are the man who has removed Him, tell me where you have laid Him, and I will take Him away." Jesus said to her: " Mary! " She turned, and said to Him in Hebrew, " Rabbouni! " which means, " Master! " Jesus said to her: " Do not touch me! For I have not yet ascended to the Father. But go to my brethren, and say to them that I am going to ascend to my Father and your Father, to my God and your God." Mary of Magdala came to the disciples, telling them: " I have seen the Lord," and telling them what He had said to her.

SOMEONE has called this story the greatest recognition scene in all literature. To Mary belongs the glory of being the first person to see the Risen Christ. The whole story is scattered with indications of Mary's love. She had come back to the tomb; she had taken her message to Peter and John, and then she must have been left behind in their race to the tomb, and, by the time she got there, they were gone. So she stood there weeping. There is no need to seek for elaborate reasons why Mary did not know Jesus. The simple and the poignant fact is that she could not see Him through her tears. Her whole conversation with the person she thought to be the gardener shows her love. " If you are the man who has removed Him, tell me where you have laid Him." She never mentioned the name of Jesus; she thought everyone must know of whom she was thinking; her mind was so full of Jesus that there was not anyone else for her in all the world. " I will take Him away." How was her woman's strength to do that? Where was she going to take Him? She had not even thought of these questions and these problems. Her one desire was to weep her love over Jesus' dead body. As soon as she had answered the person she took to be the gardener, she must have turned again to the tomb, because she could not take her eyes off it, and so turned her back on Jesus. Then came Jesus' single word, " Mary! " and her single answer, " Master! " (*Rabbouni* is simply an Aramaic form of *Rabbi*; there is no difference between the words).

So we see there were two very simple and yet very profound reasons why Mary did not recognize Jesus.

(i) She could not recognize Him because of her tears. Her tears blinded her eyes so that she could not see. When we lose a dear one, one whom we loved, there is always sorrow in our hearts, and tears shed or unshed in our eyes. But there is one thing that we must always remember—at such a time our sorrow is in essence a selfish sorrow. It is of our loneliness, our sorrow, our loss, our desolation, that we are thinking. We cannot be weeping for one who has gone to be the guest of God; we cannot be weeping for one who, after life's fitful fever, sleeps well. It is for ourselves we weep. That is natural and inevitable. But, at the same time, we must never allow our tears to blind us to the glory of heaven and of eternal life. Tears there must be, but through the tears we must glimpse the glory.

(ii) She could not recognize Jesus because she insisted on facing in the wrong direction. She could not take her eyes off the tomb, and she had her back to Jesus. Again it is so often so with us. At such a time our eyes are upon the cold earth of the grave. But we must wrench our eyes away from that; that is not where our loved ones are; their worn-out bodies are there; but the body is not the person; the real person is in the heavenly places in the fellowship of Jesus face to face, and in the glory of God.

When sorrow comes to us, we must never let tears blind our eyes to glory; and we must never fasten our eyes upon the grave and forget the heavens. Alan Walker in *Everybody's Calvary* tells of officiating at a funeral for people to whom the funeral service was only a form, and who had neither Christian faith nor Christian connection. " When the service was over a young woman looked into the grave, and said brokenly: ' Good-bye, father.' It is the end for those who have no Christian hope." But for us at such a time, it is literally " Adieu! To God! " and it is literally, " Until we meet again."

SHARING THE GOOD NEWS

John 20: 11-18 (*continued*)

THERE is one very real difficulty in this passage. When the recognition scene is complete, at first sight, at all events, Jesus said to Mary: " Touch me not, for I have not yet ascended to the Father." Just a few verses later we find Him *inviting* Thomas to touch Him (*John* 20: 27). In Luke we read of Jesus inviting the terrified disciples: " Behold my hands and feet, that it is I myself; handle and see; for a spirit hath not flesh and bones, as ye see me have " (*Luke* 24: 39). In Matthew's story we read that " they came and held Him by the feet and worshipped Him " (*Matthew* 28: 9). Even the form of John's statement is difficult. He makes Jesus say: " Touch me not, for I have not yet ascended to my Father," as if to say that He could be touched after He had ascended. No explanation of this is fully satisfying.

(i) The whole matter has been given a spiritual significance. It has been argued that the only real contact with Jesus does in fact come after His Ascension; that it is not the physical touch of hand to hand that is important, but the contact which comes through faith with the Risen and Ever-living Lord; that the important thing is not that a body can be touched, but that spirit with spirit can meet. That is certainly true, and certainly precious, but it does not seem to be the meaning of the passage here.

(ii) It is suggested that the Greek is really a mistranslation of an Aramaic original. Jesus of course would speak in Aramaic, and not in Greek; and what John gives us is a

translation into Greek of what Jesus said. It is suggested
that what Jesus really said was: " Touch me not; but
before I ascend to my Father go to my brethren and say
to them . . . " It would be as if Jesus said: " Do not
spend so long in worshipping me in the joy of your new
discovery. Go and tell the good news to the rest of the
disciples." It may well be that here we have the explanation. The imperative in the Greek is a *present* imperative,
and strictly speaking it ought to mean: " Stop touching
me." It may be that Jesus was saying to Mary: " Don't
go on clutching me selfishly to yourself. In a short time
I am going back to my Father. I want to meet my disciples
as often as possible before then. Go and tell them the good
news that none of the time that we and they should have
together may be wasted." This may be a commandment
to Mary to leave go of Jesus, not to clutch Him to herself,
but to go and tell the blessed news to others. That would
make excellent sense, and that in fact is what Mary did.

(iii) There is one further possibility. In the other three
gospels, the *fear* of those who suddenly recognized Jesus
is always stressed. In *Matthew* 28: 10 Jesus' words are:
" Be not *afraid*." In *Mark* 16: 8 the story finishes: " For
they were *afraid*." In *Luke* 24: 5 it is said that they were
" sore *afraid*." In John's story as it stands there is no
mention of this awe-stricken fear. Now, sometimes the
eyes of the scribes who copied the manuscripts made
mistakes, for the manuscripts are not easy to read. Some
scholars think that what John originally wrote was not
MĒ APTOU, Do not touch me, but, MĒ PTOOU, Do
not be afraid. The verb PTOEIN means *to flutter with fear*.
In that case Jesus would have said to Mary: " Don't be
afraid; I haven't gone to my Father yet; I am still here
with you."

No explanation of this saying of Jesus is altogether
satisfying, but perhaps the second is the best of the three
which we have considered.

Whatever happened, Jesus sent Mary back to the disciples with the message that what He had so often told them was now about to happen—He was on His way to His father; and Mary came with the news, " I have seen the Lord."

In that message of Mary there is the very essence of Christianity. A Christian is essentially one who can say: " I have seen the Lord." Christianity does not mean knowing about Jesus; it means knowing Jesus. It does not mean arguing about Jesus; it means meeting Jesus. It means the certainty of experience that Jesus is alive.

THE COMMISSION OF CHRIST

John 20: 19-23

> Late on that day, the first day of the week, when for fear of the Jews the doors had been locked in the place where the disciples were, Jesus came and stood in the midst of them, and said: " Peace be to you." And when He had said this He showed them His hands and His side. So the disciples rejoiced because they had seen the Lord. Jesus again said to them: " Peace to you. Even as the Father sent me, so I send you." When He had said this, He breathed on them and said to them: " Receive the Holy Spirit. If you remit the sins of any, they are remitted; if you retain them they are retained."

IT is most likely that the disciples continued to meet in the upper room where the Last Supper had been held. But they met in something very like terror. They were afraid; they knew the envenomed bitterness of the Jews; the Jews had compassed the death of Jesus, and the disciples were afraid that their turn might come next. So they were meeting in terror, listening fearfully for every step on the stair and for every knock at the door, lest the emissaries of the Sanhedrin should come to arrest them too. As they sat there, Jesus was suddenly in the midst of them. He gave them the normal everyday eastern greeting:

" Peace be to you." It means far more than: " May you be saved from trouble." It means: " May God give you every good thing." Then Jesus gave the disciples the commission which the Church must never forget.

(i) He said that as God had sent Him forth, so He sent them forth. Here is what Westcott called " The Charter of the Church." It means three things. (*a*) It means that Jesus Christ needs the Church. This means exactly the same thing as Paul later meant when he called the Church " the body of Christ " (*Ephesians* I: 23; I *Corinthians* I2: I2). Jesus had come with a message for all men; now He was going back to His Father; that message could never be taken out to all men, unless the Church took it. The Church was to be a mouth to speak for Jesus, feet to run upon His errands, hands to do His work. The message of Christ was delivered into the hands of the Church. Jesus could never become the possession and the Saviour of the world unless the Church took His story out to all the world. Therefore, the first thing that this means is that *Jesus is dependent on His Church.* (*b*) It means that the Church needs Jesus. A person who is to be sent out needs someone to send him; he needs a message to take; he needs a power and an authority to back his message; he needs someone to whom he may turn when he is in doubt and in difficulty. The Church needs Jesus. Without Him she has no message, without Him she has no power; without Him she has no one to turn to when she is up against it; without Him she has nothing to enlighten her mind, to strengthen her arm, and to encourage her heart. So, then, this means that *the Church is dependent on Jesus.* (*c*) But there remains still another thing here. The sending out of the Church by Jesus is parallel to the sending out of Jesus by God. But no one can read the story of the Fourth Gospel without seeing that the relationship between Jesus and God was continually dependent on Jesus' perfect obedience, perfect submission and perfect love. Jesus could only be God's messenger because He rendered to

317

God that perfect obedience and that perfect love. Therefore, it follows that the Church is only fit to be the messenger and the instrument of Christ when she perfectly loves Him and perfectly obeys Him. The Church must never be out to propagate her message; she must be out to propagate the message of Christ. She must never be out to follow her own man-made policies; she must be out to follow the will of Christ. The Church fails whenever she tries to solve some problem in her own wisdom and strength, and whenever she fails to seek the will and the guidance of Jesus Christ.

(ii) Jesus breathed on His disciples and gave them the Holy Spirit. There is no doubt that when John spoke in this way, he was thinking back to the old story of the creation of man. There the old writer says: "And the Lord God formed man of the dust of the ground, and breathed into his nostrils the breath of life; and man became a living soul" (*Genesis* 2: 7). This was the same picture as Ezekiel saw when he saw the valley of dead, dry bones, and when he heard God say to the wind: "Come from the four winds, O breath, and breathe upon these slain that they may live" (*Ezekiel* 37: 9). The coming of the Holy Spirit is like a new creation; it is like the wakening of life from the dead. When the Holy Spirit comes upon the Church she is reawakened and recreated for her task.

(iii) Jesus said to the disciples: "If you remit the sins of anyone, they are remitted; if you retain them, they are retained." This is a saying whose true meaning we must be careful to understand. One thing is quite certain—no man can forgive any other man's sins. But another thing is equally certain—it is the great privilege of the Church to convey the message and the announcement and the fact of God's forgiveness to men. Now, suppose someone brings us a message from someone else, our assessment of the value of that message will depend on how well the bringer of the message knows the person who sent the message. If someone proposes to interpret someone else's thought to us, we know that the value of his interpretation depends entirely on his closeness to the other person. The apostles had the best of all rights to bring Jesus' message to men, because they knew Jesus best. If they knew that a person was really penitent, then they could with absolute certainty proclaim to him the forgiveness of Christ. But equally, if they knew that there was no penitence in a man's heart, or that he was trading on the love and the mercy of God, they could tell him that until his heart was altered there was no forgiveness for him. This sentence does not mean that the power to forgive sins was ever entrusted to any man or to any men; it means that the power to proclaim that forgiveness was so entrusted; and it means that the power to warn that that forgiveness is not open to the impenitent was also entrusted to them. This sentence lays down the duty of the Church to convey forgiveness to the penitent in heart, and to warn the impenitent that they are forfeiting the mercy of God.

THE DOUBTER CONVINCED

John 20: 24-29

> But Thomas, who is called Didymus, one of the Twelve, was not with them when Jesus came. The other disciples told him: "We have seen the Lord." He said to them: "Unless I see the print of the nails in His hands, and put my finger in the print of the nails, and unless I put my hand into His side, I will not believe." Eight days later the disciples were again in the room, and Thomas was with them. When the doors were locked, Jesus came and stood in the midst of them, and said: "Peace be to you." Then He said to Thomas: "Stretch out your finger here, and look at my hands; stretch our your hand and put it into my side; and show yourself not faithless but believing." Thomas answered: "My Lord and my God!" Jesus said to him: "You have believed because you have seen me. Blessed are those who have not seen and who have believed."

To Thomas the Cross was only what he had expected. When Jesus had proposed going to Bethany, when the news of the illness of Lazarus had come, Thomas's reaction had been: " Let us also go, that we may die with Him " (*John* II: 16). Thomas never lacked courage, but Thomas was the natural pessimist. There can never be any doubt that Thomas loved Jesus. He loved Him enough to go to Jerusalem to die with Him when the other disciples had been hesitant and afraid. What Thomas had expected had happened, and when it came, for all that he had expected it, Thomas was broken-hearted. So broken-hearted was he that he could not meet the eyes of men; all that Thomas wanted was to be alone with his grief. King George the Fifth used to say that one of his rules of life was: " If I have to suffer, let me be like a well-bred animal, and let me go and suffer alone." Thomas had to face his suffering and his sorrow alone. So it happened that, when Jesus came back again, Thomas was not there; and the news that Jesus had come back seemed to him far too good to be true, and he refused to believe it. Belligerent in his pessimism, he said that he would never believe that Jesus had risen from the dead until he had seen and handled the print of the nails in Jesus' hands and thrust his hand into the wound the spear had made in Jesus' side. (There is no mention of any wound-print in Jesus' feet because in crucifixion the feet were not nailed, but only loosely bound to the cross.)

So another week elapsed and Jesus came back again; and this time Thomas was there. And Jesus knew Thomas's heart. He repeated Thomas's own words, and invited Thomas to make the test that he had demanded. And Thomas's heart ran out in love and devotion, and all he could say was: " My Lord and my God! " So Jesus said to him: " Thomas, you needed the eyes of sight to make you believe; but the days will come when men will see with the eye of faith, and will believe."

In this story the character of Thomas stands out clear before us.

(i) Thomas made one mistake. He withdrew from the Christian fellowship. He sought loneliness rather than togetherness. And because he was not there with his fellow Christians he missed the first coming of Jesus. We miss a great deal when we separate ourselves from the Christian fellowship, and when we try to be alone. Things can happen to us within the fellowship of Christ's Church which will not happen to us when we are alone. When sorrow comes to us, and when sadness envelops us, we often tend to shut ourselves up and to refuse to meet people. That is the very time when, in spite of our sorrow, we should seek the fellowship of Christ's people, for it is there that we are likeliest of all to meet Him face to face.

(ii) But Thomas had two great virtues. Thomas absolutely refused to say that he believed when he did not believe. Thomas would never say that he understood what he did not understand, or that he believed what he did not believe. There is an uncompromising honesty about Thomas. Thomas would never still his doubts by pretending that they did not exist. Thomas was not the kind of man who would rattle off a creed without understanding what it was all about. Thomas had to be sure—and Thomas was quite right. Tennyson wrote:

> " There lives more faith in honest doubt,
>   Believe me than in half the creeds."

There is more ultimate faith in the man who insists on being sure than in the man who glibly repeats things which he has never thought out, and which he does not really believe. It is a doubt like that which in the end arrives at certainty.

(iii) Thomas's other great virtue was that when he was sure, he went the whole way. " My Lord and my God! " said Thomas. There was no halfway house about Thomas. Thomas was not airing his doubts just for the sake of mental acrobatics; Thomas doubted in order to become sure; and when he did become sure his surrender to certainty was complete. If a man fights his way through his doubts to the conviction that Jesus Christ is Lord, he has attained to a certainty that the man who unthinkingly accepts things can never reach.

THOMAS IN THE AFTER DAYS

John 20: 24-29

WE do not know for sure what happened to Thomas in the after days; but there is an apocryphal book called *The Acts of Thomas* which purports to give his history. It is of course only legend, but there may well be some history beneath the legend; and certainly in it Thomas is still true to character. Here is part of the story which it tells.

After the death of Jesus the disciples divided up the world among them, so that each might go out to some country to preach the gospel. India fell by lot to Thomas. This much is certain that the Thomist Church in South India does trace its origin to Thomas. At first Thomas refused to go. He said that he was not strong enough for the long journey. He said: " I am an Hebrew man; how can I go amongst the Indians and preach the truth? " Jesus appeared to him by night and said: " Fear not, Thomas, go thou unto India and preach the word there, for my grace is with thee." But Thomas still stubbornly refused. " Whither thou wouldest send me, send me," he said, " but elsewhere, for unto the Indians I will not go."

Now it so happened that there had come a certain merchant from India to Jerusalem called Abbanes. He had been sent by King Gundaphorus to find a skilled carpenter and to bring him back to India, and Thomas was a carpenter. Jesus came up to Abbanes in the market place and said to him: " Wouldest thou buy a carpenter? " Abbanes said: " Yes." Jesus said: " I have a slave that is a carpenter, and I desire to sell him," and he pointed at Thomas in the distance. So they agreed on a price and Thomas was sold, and the agreement ran: " I, Jesus, the son of Joseph the carpenter, acknowledge that I have sold my slave, Thomas by name, unto thee Abbanes, a merchant of Gundaphorus, king of the Indians." When the deed was drawn up Jesus found Thomas and took him to Abbanes. Abbanes said: " Is this your master? " Thomas said: " Indeed he is." Abbanes said: " I have bought thee from him." And Thomas said nothing. But in the morning Thomas rose early and prayed, and after his prayer he said to Jesus: " I will go whither thou wilt Lord Jesus; thy will be done." It is the same old Thomas, slow to be sure, slow to surrender; but once his surrender is made, it is complete.

The story goes on to tell how Gundaphorus commanded Thomas to build a palace, and Thomas said that he was well able to do so. The king gave Thomas money in plenty to buy materials and to hire workmen, but Thomas gave it all away to the poor. Always he told the king that the palace was rising steadily. The king was suspicious. In the end he sent for Thomas: " Hast thou built me the palace? " he demanded. Thomas answered: " Yes." " When, then, shall we go and see it? " asked the king. Thomas answered: " Thou canst not see it now, but when thou departest this life, then thou shalt see it." At first the king was very angry and Thomas was in danger of his life; but in the end the king too was won for Christ, and so Thomas brought Christianity to India.

There is something very lovable and very admirable about Thomas. Faith was never an easy thing for Thomas; obedience never came readily to him. Thomas was the man who had to be sure. Thomas was the man who had to count the cost. But once he was sure, and once he had counted the cost, Thomas was the man who went to the ultimate limit of faith and of obedience. A faith like Thomas's faith is better than any glib profession; and an obedience like Thomas's obedience is better than an easy acquiescence which agrees to do a thing without counting the cost, and which then goes back upon its word.

THE AIM OF THE GOSPEL

John 20: 30, 31.

> Jesus did many other signs in the presence of His disciples which have not been written in this book. These have been written that you may believe that Jesus is the Anointed One, the Son of God, and that believing you may have life in His name.

IT is quite clear that as the gospel was originally planned, it comes to an end with this verse. Here we have the natural end, and Chapter 21, which follows, is to be regarded as an appendix and an afterthought.

There is no passage in the gospels which better sums up the aim of the writers of all the gospels than this passage does.

(i) It is quite clear that the gospels never set out to give, or claimed to give, a full account of the life of Jesus. They do not follow Him from day to day from hour to hour. The gospels are selective. They give us, not an exhaustive account of everything that Jesus said or did, but a selection of typical incidents which show what He was like and the kind of things He was always doing.

(ii) Further, it is quite clear that the gospels were not meant to be biographies of Jesus; they are meant to be appeals to take Jesus as Saviour, Master and Lord. Their aim was, not to give information, but to give life. Their aim is to paint such a picture of Jesus that the reader will be bound to see that the person who could speak and teach, and act and heal like this can be none other than the Messiah and the Son of God; and that in that belief he might find the secret of real life.

When we approach the gospels as history and biography, we approach them in the wrong spirit altogether. We must

read them, not primarily as historians seeking historical ⟩
information, but as men and women seeking God.

John 21

ON any view the twenty-first chapter of John is a strange
chapter. The gospel comes to an end at the end of chapter
twenty; and then it seems to begin again in chapter
twenty-one. Unless there had been certain very special
things that he wanted to say, the man who put the gospel
into its final form would never have added this chapter.
We know that in John's gospel there are often two meanings,
a meaning which lies on the surface, and a deeper meaning
which lies beneath. So, then, as we study this chapter, it
will be our effort to find out the reasons why it is so
strangely added after the gospel seemed to have come to an
end.

THE RISEN LORD

John 21: 1-14

After these things Jesus again showed Himself to the
disciples by the Sea of Tiberias. This was the way in
which He showed Himself. Simon Peter, and Thomas,
who is called Didymus, and Nathanael, who came from
Cana in Galilee, and the sons of Zebedee, and two
other disciples, were together. Simon Peter said to
them: " I am going to fish." They said to him: " We,
too, are coming with you." They went out, and went
on board the boat, and that night they caught nothing.
When early morning had come, Jesus stood on the
seashore. But the disciples did not know that it was
Jesus. So Jesus said to them: " Lads, have you got
any fish? " They answered: " No." He said to them:
" Cast your net on the right hand side of the ship, and
you will find a catch." So they cast the net, and now
they could not haul it in for the great number of the
fishes. The disciple whom Jesus loved said to Peter:
" It is the Lord." So, when Simon Peter heard that it
was the Lord, he put on his tunic (for he was stripped
for work) and jumped into the sea. The other disciples
came to shore in the boat (for they were not far from

the land, only about a hundred yards) dragging the net full of fishes. When they had disembarked on land, they saw a charcoal fire set there, and fish on it, and bread. Jesus said to them: " Bring some of the fish you have just caught." So Simon Peter went on board and hauled the net to land, full of large fishes, one hundred and fifty-three of them; and although there were so many of them the net was not broken. Jesus said to them: " Come and have breakfast." None of the disciples dared to ask Him: " Who are you? " because they knew that it was the Lord. Jesus came and took bread and gave it to them, and He gave them the fish in the same way. This was the third time Jesus showed Himself to the disciples after He had been raised from among the dead.

It was certainly someone who knew the fishermen of the Sea of Galilee who wrote this story. The night-time was the best time for fishing. W. M. Thomson in *The Land and the Book* describes night fishing. He writes: " There are certain kinds of fishing always carried on at night. It is a beautiful sight. With blazing torch, the boat glides over the flashing sea, and the men stand gazing keenly into it until their prey is sighted, when, quick as lightning, they fling their net or fly their spear; and often you see the tired fishermen come sullenly into harbour in the morning, having toiled all night in vain."

The catch here is not described as a miracle, and it is not meant to be. The description here is the description of something which still frequently happens on the lake. Remember that the boat was only about a hundred yards from land. H. V. Morton describes how he saw two men fishing on the shores of the lake. The one man had waded out from the shore and he was casting a bell net into the water. " But time after time the net came up empty. It was a beautiful sight to see him casting. Each time the neatly folded net belled out in the air and fell so precisely on the water that the small lead weights hit the lake at the same moment making a thin circular splash. While he was waiting for another cast, Abdul shouted to him from the bank to fling to the left, which he instantly did. This time he was successful. . . . Then he drew up the net and we could see the fish struggling in it. . . . It happens very often that the man with the hand-net must rely on the advice of someone on shore, who tells him to cast either to the left or the right. because in the clear water he can often see a shoal of fish invisible to the man in the water." Jesus was acting as guide to His fishermen friends, just as people still do to-day.

It may be that it was because it was the grey dark that they did not recognize Jesus. But the eyes of the disciple whom Jesus loved were sharp. He knew it was the Lord; and when Peter realized who it was he leaped into the water. Peter was not actually naked. He was girt with a loin cloth as the fisher always was when he plied his trade. Now it was the Jewish law that to offer greeting was a religious act, and to carry out a religious act a man must be clothed; so Peter, before he set out to come to Jesus, put on his fisherman's tunic, for he wished to be the first to greet His Lord.

THE REALITY OF THE RESURRECTION

John 21: 1-14 (continued)

Now we come to the first great reason why this strange chapter was added to the already finished gospel. It was added to demonstrate once and for all *the reality of the Resurrection*. There were many who said that the appearances of the Risen Christ were nothing more than visions which the disciples had. Many would admit the reality of the visions but would insist that they were still only visions. Some would go further and would say that they were not visions but hallucinations. Now, the gospels go far out of their way to insist that the Risen Christ was not a vision, not an hallucination, not even a spirit, but a real person. The gospels insist that the tomb was empty. The gospels insist that the Risen Christ had a real body which still bore the marks of the nails and the sword thrust in his side.

But this story goes a step further. A vision or a spirit would not be likely to point out a shoal of fish to a party of fishermen. A vision or a spirit would not be likely to kindle a charcoal fire on the seashore. A vision or a spirit would not be likely to cook a meal and to share it out. And yet, as this story has it, the Risen Christ did all these things. When John tells how Jesus came back to His disciples when the doors were shut, he says: " He showed them His hands and His side." (*John* 20: 20). Ignatius. when he was writing to the Church at Smyrna, relates an even more definite tradition about that. He says: " I know and believe that He was in the flesh even after the Resurrection, and when He came to Peter and his company, He said to them: ' Take, handle me, and see that I am not a bodiless demon.' And straightway they touched Him, and they believed, for they were firmly convinced of His flesh and blood. . . . And after His Resurrection He ate and drank with them as one in the flesh."

The first and the simplest aim of this story is to make quite clear the reality of the Resurrection. The Resurrection was not a vision; it was not the figment of someone's excited imagination; it was not the appearance of a spirit or a ghost; it was Jesus who had conquered death and who had come back.

THE UNIVERSALITY OF THE CHURCH

John 21: 1-14 (*continued*)

BUT there is a second great truth symbolized here. In the Fourth Gospel everything is meaningful, and it is therefore hardly possible that John gives the definite number one hundred and fifty-three for the number of the fishes without meaning something by it. It has indeed been suggested that the fishes were counted simply because the catch had to be shared out between the various partners and the crew of the boat, and that the number was recorded simply because it was so exceptionally large. But when we remember John's way of putting hidden meanings for those who have eyes to see, in his gospel we must think that the number has more meaning than that.

Many ingenious suggestions about the meaning of the hundred and fifty-three have been made.

(i) Cyril of Alexandria said that the number 153 is made up of three things. First, there is 100; that represents " the fullness of the Gentiles." 100, he says, is the fullest number. The shepherd's full flock is 100 (*Matthew* 18: 12). The seed's full fertility is 100-fold. So the 100 stands for the fullness of the Gentiles who will be gathered in to Christ. Second, there is the 50. The 50 stands for the remnant of Israel who will be gathered in. Third, there is the 3; and the 3 stands for the Trinity to whose glory all things are done. That is at least an ingenious and an interesting explanation.

(ii) Augustine has another ingenious explanation. He says that 10 is the number of the Law, for there are ten commandments; 7 is the number of grace, for the gifts of the Spirit are sevenfold.

> " Thou the anointing Spirit art,
> Who dost Thy sevenfold gifts impart."

Now $7+10$ makes 17; and 153 is the sum of all the figures, $1+2+3+4 \ldots$, up to 17. Thus 153 stands for all those who either by Law or by grace have been moved to come to Jesus Christ.

(iii) The simplest of the explanations is that given by Jerome. Jerome said that in the sea there are 153 different kinds of fishes; and that the catch stands for a catch which included every kind of fish; and that therefore the number symbolizes the fact that some day all men of all nations will be gathered together to Jesus Christ.

But we may note a still further point. This great catch of fishes was gathered into the net, and the net held them all, and the net was not broken. The net stands for the Church. There is room in the Church for all men of all nations. Even if they all come in, the Church is big enough to hold them all.

Here John is telling us in his own vivid yet subtle way that the Church is wide enough to grasp within her embrace all men of all nations. He is telling us of the universality of the Church. There is no kind of exclusiveness in the Church; there is no kind of colour bar or selectiveness. The embrace of the Church is as universal as the love of God in Jesus Christ. It will lead us on to the next great reason why this chapter was added to the gospel if we note that it was Peter who drew the net to land (*John* 20: 11).

THE SHEPHERD OF CHRIST'S SHEEP

John 20: 15-19

> When they had breakfasted, Jesus said to Simon Peter: " Simon, son of Jonas, do you love me more than these? " He said to Him: " Yes, Lord; you know that I love you." He said to him: " Be a shepherd to my lambs." Again He said to him a second time: " Simon, son of Jonas, do you love me? " He said to Him: " Yes, Lord. You know that I love you." He said to him: " Be a shepherd to my sheep." He said to him the third time: " Simon, son of Jonas, do you love me? " Peter was vexed when He said to him the third time: " Do you love me? " So he said to Him: " Lord, you know all things. You know that I love you." Jesus said to him: " Feed my sheep. This is the truth I tell you—when you were young, you fastened your girdle around you and you went where you wished. But when you grow old, you will stretch out your arms, and another will gird you, and will carry you to a place not of your own choosing." He said this to show by what kind of death Peter was going to glorify God. When He had said this, He said to Peter: " Follow me! "

HERE is a scene which must have been printed for ever on the mind of Peter.

(i) First we must note the question which Jesus asked Peter: " Simon, son of Jonas, do you love me more than these? " As far as the language goes that can mean two things equally well. (*a*) It may be that Jesus swept His hand round the boat and its nets and its equipment and the catch of fishes, and said to Peter: " Simon, do you love me more than these things? Are you prepared to give them all up, to abandon all hope of a successful career, to give up a steady job and a reasonable comfort, in order to give yourself for ever to my people and to my work? " This may have been a challenge to Peter to take the final decision to give all his life to the preaching of the gospel and the caring for Christ's folk. (*b*) It may be that Jesus looked at the rest of the little group of the disciples, and said to Peter: " Simon, do you love me more than your fellow-disciples do? " It may be that Jesus was gently looking back to a night when Peter said: " Though all man shall be offended because of Thee, yet will I never be offended. It doesn't matter what the others do, I love you enough to be for ever true." (*Matthew* 26: 33). It may be that Jesus was gently reminding Peter how once he had thought that he alone could be true, and how his courage had failed his heart. It is more likely that the second meaning is right, because in his answer Peter does not make comparisons any more; he is content simply to say: " You know that I love you."

(ii) We must note how often Jesus asked this question. He asked it three times; and there was a reason for that. It was three times that Peter denied his Lord, and it was three times that his Lord gave him the chance to affirm his love. Jesus, in His gracious forgiveness, gave Peter the chance to wipe out the memory of the threefold denial by a threefold declaration of love.

(iii) We must note what love brought Peter. (*a*) Love brought him a task. " If you love me," Jesus said, " then give your life to shepherding the sheep and the lambs of my flock." We can only prove that we love Jesus by loving others. Love is the greatest privilege in the world, but love brings the greatest responsibility in the world. (*b*) Love brought Peter a cross. Jesus said to Peter: " When you are young you can choose where you will go; but the day will come when they will stretch out your hands on a cross, and you will be taken on a way you did not choose." The day came when, in Rome, Peter did die for his Lord; Peter, too, went to the Cross, and when he was being nailed to it, he asked to be nailed to it head downwards, for he said that he was not worthy to die as his Lord had died. Love brought Peter a task, and love brought Peter a cross. Love always involves responsibility, and love always involves sacrifice. And we do not really love Christ unless we are prepared to face His task and to take up His Cross.

It was not for nothing that John recorded this incident. He recorded it to show Peter as the great shepherd of Christ's people. It may be, indeed it was inevitable, that people would draw comparisons in the early Church. Some would say that John was the great one, for his flights of thought went higher than those of any other man. Some would say that Paul was the great one for he fared to the ends of the earth for Christ. But this chapter says that Peter, too, had his place. He might not write and think like John; he might not voyage and adventure like Paul; but he had the great honour, and the lovely task, of being the shepherd of the sheep of Christ. And here is where we can follow in the steps of Peter. We may not be able to think like John; we may not be able to go out to the ends of the earth like Paul; but each one of us can guard some one from going astray, and each one of us can feed the lambs of Christ with the food of the word of God.

THE WITNESS TO CHRIST

John 21: 20-24

> Peter turned and saw the disciple whom Jesus loved following, the disciple who at their meal reclined on Jesus' breast and said: " Lord, who is it who is to betray you?" When Peter saw this disciple, he said to Jesus: " Lord, what is going to happen to this man?" Jesus said to him: " If I wish him to remain

> till I come, what has that got to do with you? Your job is to follow me." So this report went out to the brethren, that this disciple would not die. But Jesus did not say to him that he would not die. What He did say was: " If I wish him to remain till I come, what has that got to do with you?" This is the disciple who bears witness to these things, and who has written these things, and we know that his witness is true.

THIS passage makes it quite clear that John must have lived to a very old age; he must have lived on until the report went round that he was going to go on living until Jesus came again. Now, just as the previous passage assigned to Peter his place in the scheme of things, this passage assigns to John his place. It was John's function to be pre-eminently the witness to Christ. Again, people in the early Church must have made their comparisons. They must have pointed out how Paul went away to the ends of the earth. They must have pointed out how Peter went here and there shepherding his people. And then they must have wondered what was the function of John who had lived on in Ephesus until he was so old that he was past all activity. And here is the answer: Paul might be the pioneer of Christ, Peter might be the shepherd of Christ, but John was the witness of Christ. John was the man who was able to say: " I saw these things, and I know that they are true."

To this day the final argument for Christianity is Christian experience. To this day the Christian is the man who can say: " I know Jesus Christ, and I know that these things are true." So, at the end, this gospel takes two of the great figures of the Church, Peter and John. To each Jesus had given his function. It was Peter's function to shepherd the sheep of Christ, and in the end to die for Christ. It was John's function to witness to the story of Christ, and to live to a great old age and to come to the end in peace. That did not make them rivals and competitors in honour and prestige; that did not make the one greater or less than the other; it made them both servants of Christ. Let a man serve Christ where Christ has set him. As Jesus said to

Peter: " Never mind the task that is given to someone else. Your job is to follow me." And that is what He still says to each one of us. Our glory is never in comparison with men; our glory is the service of Christ in whatever capacity has been allotted to us.

THE LIMITLESS CHRIST

John 21: 25

> There are many other things that Jesus did, and if they were written down one by one, I think that not even the world itself would be big enough to hold the written volumes.

IN this last chapter the writer of the Fourth Gospel has set before the Church for whom he wrote certain great truths. He has reminded them of the reality of the Resurrection; he has reminded them of the universality of the Church; he has reminded them that Peter and John are not competitors in honour, but that Peter is the great shepherd and John the great witness. And now he comes to the end; and he comes to the end thinking once again of the splendour of Jesus Christ. Whatever we know of Christ, we have only grasped a fragment of Him. Whatever the wonders we have experienced, they are as nothing to the wonders which we will yet experience. Human categories are powerless to describe Christ, and human books are inadequate to hold Him. And so John ends with the innumerable triumphs, the inexhaustible power, and the limitless grace of Jesus Christ.

NOTE ON THE STORY OF THE WOMAN TAKEN IN ADULTERY

John 8: 2-11

To many this is one of the loveliest and the most precious stories in the gospels; and yet it is a story which has great difficulties attaching to it.

It is obvious that the older the manuscripts of the New Testament are the more valuable they are. They were all copied by hand, and obviously the nearer they are to the original writings the more likely they are to be correct. We call these very early manuscripts the Uncial manuscripts, because they are written in capital letters; and we base the text of the New Testament on the earliest ones which date from the fourth to the sixth century. Now the fact is that out of all these early manuscripts this story only occurs in one, and that one is not one of the very best. Six of them omit it completely with no mention whatever. Two of them leave a blank space where it should come, but do not have it. It is not till we come to the late Greek manuscripts and the mediaeval manuscripts that we find this story, and even then it is often marked with a mark to show that it is doubtful.

Another source of our knowledge of the text of the New Testament is what is called the versions; that is, the translations into other languages than Greek. This story is not included in the early Syriac version, nor in the Coptic or Egyptian versions, nor in some of the early Latin versions.

Again, none of the early fathers, in the very early days, seem to know anything about it. Certainly they never mention it or comment on it. Origen, Chrysostom, Theodore of Mopsuestia, Cyril of Alexandria on the Greek side know nothing of it, or do not mention it. The first Greek commentator to comment on it is Euthymius Zigabenus whose date is A.D. 1118, and even he says that it is not in the best manuscripts.

Where, then, did it come from? We know for certain that Jerome knew it in the fourth century, for he included it in the Vulgate. We know that Augustine and Ambrose both knew it, for they comment on it. We know that it is in all the later manuscripts. It is to be noted that its position varies a great deal. In some manuscripts it is put at the end of the Fourth Gospel; and in some it is inserted after *Luke* 21: 38.

But we can trace it even further back than that. It is quoted in a third century book called *The Aqostolic Constitutions*, where it is given as a warning to bishops who are too strict. Eusebius, the Church historian, says that Papias tells a story " of a woman who was accused of many sins before the Lord," and Papias lived not very long after A.D. 100.

Here, then, we have the facts. This story can be traced as far back as very early in the second century. When Jerome produced the Vulgate he, without question, included it. The later manuscripts and the mediaeval manuscripts all have it. And yet none of the great manuscripts include it. None of the great Greek fathers of the Church ever mention it or comment on it or preach on it. But some of the great Latin fathers did know it, and speak of it.

What is the explanation? We need not be afraid that we shall have to let this lovely story go; for it is guarantee enough of its genuineness that we can trace it back to almost A.D. 100. But we do need some explanation of the fact that none of the great manuscripts include it. Moffatt, Weymouth and Rieu print it in brackets; and the American Revised Standard Version prints it in small type at the foot of the page.

Augustine gives us a hint. He says that this story was removed from the text of the gospel because " some were of slight faith," and " to avoid scandal." We cannot tell for certain, but it would seem that in the very early days the people who edited the text of the New Testament thought that this was a dangerous story, a justification for a light view of adultery, and therefore omitted it. After all, the Christian Church was a little island in a sea of paganism. Its members were so apt to relapse into a way of life where chastity was unknown; and they were for ever open to pagan infection. But as time went on the danger grew less, or then perhaps the danger was less feared, and the story, which had always circulated by word of mouth, and which one manuscript retained, came back.

It is not likely that it is now in the place in which it ought to be. It was probably inserted here to illustrate Jesus saying in *John* 8: 15: " I judge no man." In spite of the doubt that the modern translations cast on it, and in spite of the fact that the early manuscripts do not include it, we need not doubt that this is a real story about Jesus, although it was a story so gracious that for long men were afraid to tell it.

NOTE ON THE DATE OF THE CRUCIFIXION

THERE is one great problem in the Fourth Gospel which we did not notice at all when we were studying it. Here we can only note it very briefly, for it is really an unsolved problem on which the literature is immense.

It is quite certain that the Fourth Gospel and the other three gospels give different dates for the Crucifixion, and take a different view of what the last meal together was.

In the Synoptic gospels it is quite clear that the Last Supper was the Passover and that Jesus was crucified on Passover Day. It must be remembered that the Jewish day began at 6 p.m. on what to us is the day before. The Passover fell in 15th Nisan; but 15th Nisan began on what to us is 14th Nisan at 6 p.m. Therefore the Passover day ran from 6 p.m. on the one day to 6 p.m. on the next. Mark seems to be quite clear; he says: " And the first day of unleavened bread, when they killed the Passover, His disciples said unto Him, Where wilt thou that we go and prepare that Thou mayest eat the Passover? " Jesus gives them instructions. And then Mark goes on: " And they made ready the Passover, and in the evening, He cometh with the twelve." (*Mark* 14: 12-17). Undoubtedly Mark wished to show the Last Supper as a Passover Meal and to show that Jesus was crucified on Passover day; and of course Matthew and Luke follow Mark.

On the other hand John is quite clear that Jesus was crucified on the day *before* the Passover. He begins his story of the last meal: " Now before the Passover . . ." (*John* 13: 1). When Judas left the upper room they thought he had gone to *prepare* for the Passover (*John* 13: 29). The Jews would not enter the judgment hall lest they should become unclean and be prevented from eating the Passover (*John* 18: 28). The judgment is during the *preparation* for the Passover (*John* 19: 14).

There is here a contradiction for which there is no compromise solution. Either the Synoptic Gospels or John is correct. Scholars are much divided. But it seems most likely that the Synoptic gospels are correct. John was always looking for hidden meanings. In his story Jesus is crucified at somewhere near the *sixth hour* (*John* 19: 14). What was happening then? *It was just then that in the Temple the Passover lambs were being killed.* By far the likeliest thing is that John dated things so that Jesus would be crucified at exactly the same time as the Passover lambs were being killed, so that Jesus might be seen as the great Passover Lamb who saved His people and who took away the sins of the world. It seems that the Synoptic gospels are right in *fact*, while John is right in *truth*; and John was always more interested in eternal truth than in mere historic fact.

There is no full explanation of this obvious discrepancy; but this seems to us the best.